Action Words

Verbs

Anita Ganeri

Heinemann Library
Chicago, Illinois

www.capstonepub.com
Visit our website to find out more information about Heinemann-Raintree books.

To order:
☎ Phone 888-454-2279
🖳 Visit www.capstonepub.com to browse our catalog and order online.

© 2012 Heinemann Library
an imprint of Capstone Global Library, LLC
Chicago, Illinois

Edited by Daniel Nunn, Rebecca Rissman, and Sian Smith
Designed by Joanna Hinton-Malivoire
Picture research by Tracy Cummins
Original illustrations © Capstone Global Library
Illustrated by Joanna Hinton-Malivoire
Production by Eirian Griffiths
Originated by Capstone Global Library Ltd
Printed and bound in China by South China Printing Company Ltd

15 14 13 12 11
10 9 8 7 6 5 4 3 2 1

Library of Congress Cataloging-in-Publication Data
Ganeri, Anita, 1961-
  Action words : verbs / Anita Ganeri.
     p. cm.—(Getting to grips with grammar)
  Includes bibliographical references and index.
  ISBN 978-1-4329-5810-7 (hbk) ISBN 978-1-4329-5817-6 (pbk)
  1. English language—Verb—Juvenile literature. 2. English language—Grammar—Juvenile literature. I. Title.
  PE1271.G36 2011
  428.1—dc22   2011014971

Acknowledgments
We would like to thank the following for permission to reproduce photographs and artworks: istockphoto pp.14 (© iofoto), 24 (© Thomas M Perkins), 27 (© devi); Shutterstock p5 (© Leah-Anne Thompson), 6 (© Kitch Bain), 8 (© Roca), 9 (© Angelika Smile), 10 (© Guido Vrola), 11 (© Blend Images), 17 (© Julien Tromeur), 18 (© naluwan), 19 (© luchschen), 20 (© Amanda Perkins), 21 (© Uryadnikov Sergey), 25 (© Galina Barskaya), 26 (© neff), 28, 29 (© Elena Elisseeva), 30a (© AYAKOVLEV.COM), 30b (© Nate A.), 30c (© hektoR).

Every effort has been made to contact copyright holders of any material reproduced in this book. Any omissions will be rectified in subsequent printings if notice is given to the publisher.

Disclaimer
All the Internet addresses (URLs) given in this book were valid at the time of going to press. However, due to the dynamic nature of the Internet, some addresses may have changed, or sites may have changed or ceased to exist since publication. While the author and Publishers regret any inconvenience this may cause readers, no responsibility for any such changes can be accepted by either the author or the Publishers.

Contents

Some words are shown in bold, **like this**.
You can find them in the glossary on page 31.

What Is Grammar?

Grammar is a set of rules that helps you to write and speak a language. Grammar is important because it helps people to understand each other.

in school I to morning. walk the

Without grammar, this **sentence** doesn't make sense.

In grammar, words are divided up into different types. They are called parts of speech. They show how words are used. This book is about the parts of speech called **verbs**.

Grammar turns the jumbled-up words into a sentence.

I walk to school in the morning.

What Is a Verb?

A **verb** is a doing or action word. It tells us what a person or thing is doing.

Winston bakes a cake.

"Bakes" is a verb. It tells you what Winston is doing.

Birds fly in the sky.

This is a sentence.
It has a verb ("fly").

Birds in the sky.

This is not
a sentence.
It does not
have a verb.

Every **sentence** needs to have a verb
in it. Otherwise, it doesn't make sense.
Look at the two examples above.

Spot the Verb

Look at this list of words. Can you see all the **verbs** in the list? Remember that a verb is a doing word.

jump

climb

castle

eat

smelly

sing

"Jump," "climb," "eat," and "sing" are verbs. "Castle" and "smelly" are *not* verbs.

Look at the two **sentences** below. How many verbs can you spot? There is one verb in the first sentence and there are two in the second sentence.

I play the piano.

Dogs bark and chase cats.

In the first sentence, the verb is "play." In the second sentence, the verbs are "bark" and "chase."

Subjects and Objects

In a **sentence**, a **verb** has to have a subject. The subject is the person or thing doing the action. The subject comes before the verb.

The rocket flew through space.

"The rocket" is the subject. "Flew" is the verb.

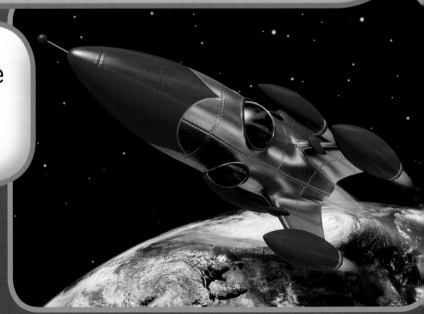

Ben builds a sandcastle.

"Ben" is the subject, "builds" is the verb, "a sandcastle" is the object.

In some sentences, the verb has an object as well. The object is the person or thing the verb is being done to. The object comes after the verb.

I, You, He/She/It

"I," "you," and "he/she/it" are called the first, second, and third person. You often have to change how you use a **verb** depending on whether your **sentence** is using the first, second, or third person.

(First person) I am **happy.**

(Second person) You are **happy.**

(Third person) He/she/it is **happy.**

This shows how the verb "to be" is used in the first, second, and third person.

The first, second, and third person can be **singular** or **plural**. "I," "you," "he," "she," and "it" are all singular. Singular means one person or thing.

I am flying a kite.

"I" is the first person singular.

"She" is the third person singular.

She is reading a book.

13

We, You, They

"We," "you," and "they" are the **plural** of the first, second, and third person. Plural means more than one person or thing.

(First person) We are happy.

(Second person) You are happy.

(Third person) They are happy.

These sentences are using the first, second, and third person plural.

I am picking some flowers.

This is written in the first person. The plural is "We are picking some flowers."

This is written in the third person. The plural is "They are playing soccer."

She is playing soccer.

Look at the two **sentences** above. They are **singular**. Can you rewrite them in the plural? Can you also say which person they are written in?

What Is a Tense?

Verbs also change when they describe things happening at different times. These changes are called **tenses**. The main tenses are the **present**, **past**, and **future**.

I ride **a horse.**

I rode **a horse.**

I will ride **a horse.**

The first sentence is in the present tense.
The second sentence is in the past tense.
The third sentence is in the future tense.

The tense of a verb tells you the time something happened. Look at these three **sentences**. Can you tell the tense?

We watched **television.**

Lucy smiles.

I will catch **a fish.**

The first sentence is in the past tense.
The second sentence is in the present tense.
The third sentence is in the future tense.

Present Tense

The **present tense** means that something is happening now. The two **sentences** below use the present tense. Can you think of any other examples?

I sing **a song.**

I drink **some juice.**

Both of these sentences are in the present tense.

There is also the present **continuous** tense. This is used to show that the action is going on for a while.

> **I** am singing **a song.**
>
> **I** am drinking **some juice.**

Both of these sentences are in the present continuous tense.

Past Tense

The **past tense** means that something has already happened. The **sentences** below use the past tense. Can you think of any more examples?

The giraffe munched **some leaves.**

The boat sank**.**

Both of these sentences are in the past tense.

The giraffe was munching some leaves.

The boat was sinking.

Both of these sentences are in the past continuous tense.

There is also the past **continuous** tense. This is used to show that the action went on for a while.

Changing Verbs

To make the **past tense**, you often add "ed" to **verbs**. For example, "clean" becomes "cleaned." But some verbs make the "ed" ending in a different way.

Present tense	Past tense
bat	batted
fit	fitted
cry	cried
bury	buried

With these verbs, you have to add or change some letters before you can add "ed" to make the past tense.

Some verbs completely change in the past tense. They are often verbs that you use a lot.

Present tense	Past tense
buy	bought
grow	grew
keep	kept
hide	hid
swim	swam
run	ran

You just have to learn the past tenses of these verbs. There is no easy rule to help you work out what they should be.

23

Future Tense

The **future tense** means that something will happen in the future. The **sentences** below use the future tense. Can you think of any more examples?

Both of these sentences are in the future tense.

I will do some shopping.

You will play tennis.

I will be doing **some shopping.**

You will be playing **tennis.**

Both of these sentences are in the future continuous tense.

There is also the future **continuous** tense. This is used to show that the action will go on for a while.

Helping Verbs

The **verb** "to have" is called a helping verb. It is used with other words to help make the different **tenses**.

The words "have" and "will have" come from the verb "to have."

They have worked hard.

He will have missed his train.

The verb "to be" is another helping verb. It is also used with other words to help make the different tenses.

The dog was **barking.**

A spider is **hiding in the tub.**

The words "was" and "is" come from the verb "to be."

Active and Passive

You can use a **verb** in two different ways. One way is to use it as an **active** verb. Using an active verb is a strong, direct way of saying something.

Here, the subject "Dad" did the verb "watered." The verb is active.

Dad watered the plants.

The plants were watered by Dad.

Here, the subject "plants" were having the verb done to them. The verb is passive.

The other way of using a verb is to use it as a **passive** verb. Using a passive verb is a gentler, less direct way of saying something.

Find the Verbs

Look carefully at the pictures below. Can you think of a **verb** to go with each one?

Answers
a: dance
b: eat or smile
c: climb

Glossary

active a way of using a verb in a strong, direct way

continuous something that goes on for a while

future something that may or will happen

grammar a set of rules that helps you to speak or write clearly

passive a way of using a verb in a gentler, less direct way

past something that has already happened

plural meaning more than one person or thing

present something that is happening now

sentence a group of words that makes sense on its own

singular meaning one person or one thing

tense different form of a verb that tells you when something happened

verb doing or action word

Find Out More

Books

Cleary, Brian P. *Slide and Slurp, Scratch and Burp: More About Verbs.* Minneapolis, MN: Lerner, 2010.

Dahl, Michael. *If You Were a Verb.* Mankato, MN: Picture Window Books, 2007.

Websites

http://media.arcademicskillbuilders.com/games/viper/viper.swf?0
This entertaining Website helps readers identify the correct tense to use with a fun, exciting game.

www.bradleys-english-school.com/online/jigword/jigpast1.html
This site challenges readers to complete a puzzle filling in the correct past tense words.

Index

Philip:
HAPPY BIRTHDAY
and much
ADMIRATION
and friendship

Ken & Rebecca
Sundance
2007

HISTORY OF THE
JEWS
IN UTAH AND IDAHO

Myrtle Friedman

HISTORY OF THE
JEWS
IN UTAH AND IDAHO

By

JUANITA BROOKS

Western Epics

Salt Lake City, Utah

1973

LITHOGRAPHED IN U.S.A.

PUBLISHERS PRESS
SALT LAKE CITY, UTAH

DEDICATION

It is a great privilege to sponsor and publish this history of the pioneer Jews of Northern Utah and Southern Idaho who, living in peace and harmony with pioneers of other faiths, helped to settle and develop one of the most beautiful and productive areas of our wonderful country.

This book was made possible at the suggestion of Ben Roe and through the efforts of Juanita Brooks, well-known author and historian, and is dedicated in loving memory of these parents, grandparents and all Jewish people who pioneered this territory.

Myrtle H. Friedman

FOREWORD

AUTHOR'S STATEMENT AND EXPLANATION

On January 1, 1966, I met with Mr. Ben Roe, Dr. Louis Zucker, and Dr. Sterling McMurrin in Mr. Roe's downtown office, to discuss the possibility of my writing a History of the Jews of Utah and Southern Idaho. It should cover the span of one hundred years, 1864 to 1964. I was to complete the work in two years.

At the end of eighteen months I had finished eight of the twelve chapters projected, so I brought these in to submit for scrutiny by Dr. Zucker, himself a writer of some skill.

He was not pleased with the work because it lacked the proper "Jewish Flavor." I returned and made a second attempt, and the suggestion was that I go ahead and finish, after which he would *rewrite* it. Perhaps too impulsively, I dropped the project entirely and turned my attention to subjects with which I was more familiar.

Without recrimination or bitterness, I finally came back in 1970 to pick up the unfinished manuscript to rework and bring it to a conclusion. At this time I found an entirely different climate in the relationship of the two Jewish Communities toward each other. Now there was cooperation at the Community Center, and in the Sabbath School as well, until by the end of 1972 there were plans in the making for a more complete merger. This seems an excellent tone upon which to close the book.

Juanita Brooks

ACKNOWLEDGMENTS

I acknowledge with gratitude the assistance of many people in the preparation of this manuscript:

First of all, MYRTLE FRIEDMAN, whose generosity made the whole project possible. She has been most cooperative and patient with me.

2—*Mr. Ben Roe* and his wife have been of great assistance in helping me to get acquainted with people in both congregations. Ben has been a constant source of strength to me.

3—*Mr. Alexander Simons* of Pocatello, Idaho, who met my plane and took me to visit the Temple, the Cemetery, and the town in general. He also gave me access to the Minute Book of Congregation Beth Israel, as well as an excellent biography of Governor Moses Alexander, the first Jew to be elected Governor of a state.

4—*Mr. Martin Heuman,* also of Boise, gave me information on Congregation Aharath Israel; *Sam Emrich* gave me material on the Jews of Weiser, Idaho.

5—*Mr. Edward Eisen* gave much valuable help by giving me access to the early records of Congregation Montefiore. He also introduced me to the grand Old Man, *Mr. Herman Finkelstein,* who told of the early activities of that congregation.

6—*Dan M. Eastman* of Evans & Early Mortuary, who secured the names, dates of death, and congregation of every Jew buried in Salt Lake City for the past twenty years.

7—*Mr. Ralph Tannenbaum,* who secured the names of every Jewish boy of Utah who served in World War II.

8—*Mrs. Esther Landa,* who read my manuscript and made many pertinent suggestions. She also loaned much historic information in the form of programs, booklets, and pamphlets.

9—*Mrs. Janet O'Dea,* who also read the manuscript, made many suggestions, and wrote a very comprehensive paper on early Jewish activities. I appreciated this very much.

10—*Dr. Billie Hollingshead,* of Hawaii, who presented me the book, *Jewish Concepts,* and clarified many things for me.

11—All the fine young men who came to lunch at Mr. Roe's invitation, and helped me to understand better the change that has taken place between the Congregations in Salt Lake City.

Juanita Brooks

CONTENTS

Page

Chapter One

INTRODUCTION

BEFORE BEGINNING OUR study of the Jews in Utah, we should perhaps take a brief overview of the history of the Jews in the United States, reminding ourselves that this people had some thirty-five hundred years of history behind it before America was discovered.

Textbooks in American history rarely tell that:

> Jewish history in America begins with the expulsion of the Jews from Spain in the same year and month that Columbus set sail on his first voyage in search of a trade route to India. Jews served on board his small flotilla as able-bodied seamen, map-readers, interpreters, and surgeons . . . The Indians on the caribbean island where the flotilla first landed were greeted in Hebrew and Arabic by one Luis de Torres, a Jewish interpreter on board the flag ship . . . It was Torres, incidentally, who discovered maize and brought it to Europe, where, with the potato, it enriched the diet of western man . . .

> Jewish history in the United States is usually dated from September 1654, when twenty-three of the fleeing Jews arrived in . . . New Amsterdam, and asked its choleric governor, Peter Stuyvesant, for permission to stay. . . .[1]

The Governor would have expelled them, but since they had helped the Dutch in Brazil as loyal citizens, they were permitted to stay. Within a few years the British ousted the Dutch from New Amsterdam, but permitted the Jews to remain, now as British colonials.

Jews were among the colonists in other towns along the seacoast, coming as individuals or small groups, not as entire communities such as came later. They dispersed through the

---

[1]Max L. Dimont, *Jews, God and History* (New York, 1962), p. 265.

cities and towns to be absorbed into the American social
system. An estimate of their numbers is to the effect that:

> . . . up to the eve of the American Revolution they numbered no
> more than 3,000 souls. And these 3,000 in a total population of
> more than 3 million were, in turn, scattered throughout the thirteen
> colonies: about one-half in the north, the other half below the
> Mason-Dixon line . . .[2]

Historians have generally agreed that Jewish immigration
to the United States has come in three periods, each representing a different land of origin. Thus from 1654 to about 1815
the largest number came from Portugal or were of Portuguese
origin; from 1815 to about 1880 they came largely from
Germany and Poland; from 1880 to 1924 they came from
Russia and the Near East. All historians admit that there
was some overlapping in all these dates, but accept this as a
convenient means of classification, sociologically sound.[3]

Without going into detail, we note that there were Jewish
organizations in the United States early — in Philadelphia,
Pennsylvania, in 1782; in Richmond, Virginia, in 1791; in
Cincinnati, Ohio, in 1819.[4] Records of many organizations
throughout all the larger cities are probably extant, each congregation adapting its own ritual to its need, all drawing
from the age-old Torah.

The story of the beginning of the Mormon Church is in
sharp contrast. Here is the claim of the restored Church of
Jesus Christ as given to the youthful prophet, Joseph Smith.
The formal organization was effected in Fayette, New York,
on April 6, 1830, with the required six members. It was one
of the many churches which sprang up in Western New York
during a period of religious excitement and revival.[5]

---

[2]Stuart E. Rosenberg, *The Search for Jewish Identity in America* (New York, 1964), p. 48.
[3]Marshall Sklare, *The Jews, Social Patterns of an American Group* (New York, 1957), p. 5.
[4]Benjamin II, *Three Years in America, I,* pp. 206, 209.
[5]For an extended discussion of the backgrounds see Whitney R. Cross, *The Burnt-Over District: The Social and Intellectual History of Enthusiastic Religion in Western New York, 1800-1850* (Ithaca: Cornell University Press, 1950.)

Their numbers grew rapidly, and soon, in line with the general westward movement, they set up headquarters at Kirtland, Ohio. Intensely interested in the Old Testament prophets, Joseph Smith in 1836 secured the services of Professor Joshua Seixas to teach classes in Hebrew, at least two sections daily. More than thirty adult men, among them the Mormon leaders, attended, but since the school lasted hardly three months, their knowledge of Hebrew would be very limited. All references to the teacher were highly laudatory.[6]

Another evidence of the importance of the Old Testament in Mormon theology is shown by the fact that they identify their members as descendants of Abraham, Isaac, and Jacob, through Joseph who was sold into Egypt. Indeed, every faithful Mormon who receives his patriarchal blessing is assured that he is of the lineage of either Ephraim or Manasseh, sons of Joseph. That they accept the Jews as God's chosen people is shown by their tenth Article of Faith, which begins: "We believe in the literal gathering of Israel, and in the restoration of the Ten Tribes. . . ."

Thus Mormon leaders have always been interested in the Jews and in their return to Jerusalem since, according to Mormon belief, this must be brought about before the Second Advent of Jesus Christ. In the hope that they might expedite this happy event, the Mormons have sent at least two missions to Palestine to dedicate the land for that purpose.[7]

The first Jew to write about the Mormons was Abraham Jonas, Grand Master of Masons in Illinois, who came to install a lodge at Nauvoo. Of this momentous event, Joseph Smith wrote on March 15, 1842, "I officiated as Grand Chaplain at the installation of the Nauvoo Lodge of Free Masons at the Grove near the Temple. Grand Master Jonas, of Columbus, being present, a large number of people assembled for the occasion."[8]

---

[6]*History of the Church of Jesus Christ of Latter-day Saints, Period I. History of Joseph Smith, the Prophet, by Himself,* ed, B. H. Roberts (Salt Lake City, 1904, II, pp. 285-286, *passim.* (Hereafter cited as *Doc. Hist.*)

[7]In 1841 Orson Hyde was sent to Palestine to dedicate the land preparatory to the return of the Jews. In October of 1872 George A. Smith, Lorenzo Snow, and Albert Carrington with a party of five others visited the area again for the same purpose. B. H. Roberts, *A Comprehensive History of the Church,* V, p. 474.

[8]*Doc. Hist.,* IV, p. 550.

At this time Mr. Jonas was editor of the *Columbus Advocate,* and later ran for a seat in the legislature. Upon his return from Nauvoo, he wrote an article describing his experience there. This was signed AN OBSERVER, and appeared in *The Advocate* on March 22, 1842, was reprinted in the Nauvoo *Times and Seasons* on April 1st, in the *Millennial Star* in England, and copied into the *Documentary History of the Church.*[9] The Mormons took great pride in quoting it, for it pictured just such a society as they wished to maintain. Better still, it described their Prophet as "a sensible, intelligent, companionable, and gentlemanly man."

Needless to say, at the next election Grand Master Jonas had an overwhelming Mormon vote. The relations between him and the Mormon leaders continued warm and cordial, so that after the death of Joseph Smith, Governor Thomas Ford selected Mr. Jonas to persuade the Mormons not to retaliate. Mr. Jonas' appeal was so effective that the Mormon audience responded with a hearty "Amen."[10]

Though they shared their respect for the Old Testament and other ancient writings, Mormon and Jew differed most sharply in their attitude toward converting new members. The Mormons from the first carried on a vigorous proselyting program, sending their missionaries to all the settled regions of the United States and Canada and, as early as 1837, to England. Here social conditions were such that they made many converts. Additional men were sent to open missions in Wales, Scotland, Scandinavia, and Germany, so that by 1845 thirty-two companies of converts with a total of approximately five thousand people were added to the population of Nauvoo.[11]

The Jews, on the other hand, had abandoned any concerted attempt to convert gentiles. Yet they insisted that born a Jew, a man continued to be a Jew as long as he lived. In the words of Charles E. Schulman, "All wings of Judaism

---

[9]*Times and Seasons,* III, pp. 749-750; *Millennial Star,* III, p. 25 (hereafter cited as *Mil. Star.*) ; *Doc. His.,* IV, p. 565.

[10]*Doc. Hist.,* VII, pp. 149-150.

[11]Gustive O. Larson, *Prelude to the Kingdom* (Francestown, New Hampshire, 1947), p. 50.

agree that a person born a Jew remains a Jew even though he be indifferent to the religious theories and practices of his religion. Only when he removes himself completely from his people does he cease to be a Jew."[12]

Coming to America as they did, singly, in family groups, or by villages, the Jews brought with them their prayer books and their *mezuzah* to carry privately until such time as they could place it upon the doorpost of a home. This scripture — Deuteronomy 6:4-9 and 11:13-21 — begins with the command: "Hear, O Israel; The Lord our God is one Lord: and thou shalt love the Lord thy God with all thine heart, and with all thy soul, and with all thy might. . . ." and closes with the admonition: "And thou shalt write them upon the door posts of thine house, and upon thy gates." Rolled up and inserted in a wooden or metal case and nailed in a slanting position to the right-hand doorpost, the *mezuzah* declares that in this home lives a family of faithful Jews. Carried privately it is a constant reminder of a Jew's obligations and of God's promises to him if he complies.

Many also carried small leather boxes called *phylacteries* or *Tefillin,* which contained sections from the Pentateuch, reminding the owner of the unconditional love of one God, and of the importance of worshipping Him only. Attached to the boxes were tapes so that they might be supported on the brow or wound about the left hand in accordance with the admonition: "And thou shalt bind them for a sign upon thy hand, and they shall be for frontlets between thine eyes."

The Jewish ritual of prayer three times a day and of observance of the Holy Days would be carried on privately until such time as ten or more male Jews over the age of thirteen had gathered, when they might form a *minyan,* or quorum necessary to carry on public worship.

Their creed demands freedom to think one's own thoughts and worship as one chooses, and the right to be different.

---

[12]Charles E. Schulman, *What It Means to be a Jew* (New York, 1959), p. 223.

The scholar, not the warrior, is their ideal; their second commandment is to love and care for the unfortunate.

Judaism is not a religion of salvation by faith, but of cooperation with God to improve the world. Most Jews look upon God as a personal influence in their lives, arguing for His existence that as a coat implies a weaver or a chair a a carpenter, so the universe declares a Creator. They do not attempt to describe Him, and feel it a sacrilege when others presume to paint pictures of Him. Among their basic tenets are:

1. Unity. God is the source of all life. Man is a partner with God in running the universe. The quest of the Unknown God constitutes man's greatest adventure on earth.

2. Sanctity. Life is sacred. No man is good enough to rule another. Life is to be carefully guarded. "Thou shalt not kill," but "Thou shalt love thy neighbor as thyself."

3. Sanity. Life is sane, balanced, reasonable, sensitive. Ignorance and selfishness are the twin evils of this world . . . Knowledge is the handmaiden of sensitiveness in human life. Education may not solve all the problems of existence, but it clears out the jungle of fear and ignorance which breeds social evil, and it paves the road to a better tomorrow.

The daily struggle for bread has meaning because it is related to man's upward and onward climb to partnership with God in making a decent place upon this earth.[13]

It is not likely that during their stay in Nauvoo or earlier, Mormons and Jews took much time to compare basic principles and beliefs, as, indeed, they did not do later, and still do not do today. That early Mormon leaders respected and admired those Jews with whom they came in contact is evident. That they saw in their own persecutions and drivings a parallel in Jewish experiences is also evident. As their wagons worried through the spring mud on the Iowa plains after they had abandoned Nauvoo, the recorder opened each day's account with the heading: CAMP OF ISRAEL. They

---

[13]*Ibid.*

thought of themselves as a modern Israel on their way to build a new Zion in the tops of the mountains, according to prophecy.[14]

They were indeed going to a relatively unknown land, to a place that no one else wanted, barren, forbidding, and sterile, the last area of the United States to be explored and settled. Around the region still hung tales of the mythical seven golden cities and of a great river opening to the sea. Not until the 1844 exploration of John C. Fremont were these legends dispelled. . . .[15]

Names of some explorers still cling to the land: Provost, Weber, Ogden, Bonneville, Ashley, and others. Two companies of emigrants had preceded the Mormons into the valley of the Great Salt Lake: the Bidwell-Bartleson Party and the Donner Trains of 1846. These two passed on, the one to its destination and the other to tragedy. Within the region which would later become Utah was only one permanent settler, Miles Goodyear, who had built a stockade around his cabin, corrals, and garden plot on the Weber River, and had plowed some land outside. His holdings were on the present site of Ogden.

The Mormon pioneer group, consisting of 143 men, two women, and three children arrived in the valley of the Great Salt Lake on July 24, 1847. Immediately they sent out scouts to assess the area as to its resources of timber, feed, and arable land. Then they surveyed and plotted their city, which like Jerusalem of old as described in Nehemiah 7:2 ". . . was large and great, but the people were few therein and the houses not builded."

Close upon the heels of the pioneer group came a contingent of the Mormon Battalion and some nineteen families from Mississippi who had all wintered in Pueblo, Colorado. And returning to Winter Quarters, Brigham Young met five

---

[14]Isaiah 2:2-3. "And it shall come to pass in the last days, that the mountain of the Lord's house shall be established in the tops of the mountains, and shall be exalted above the hills; and all nations shall flow unto it."

[15]Gloria Griffen Cline, *Exploring the Great Basin* (University of Oklahoma Press, 1963), pp. 18-27.

additional companies of his own people, which brought the total in the valley for the winter of 1847 to 2,095 souls, all short of supplies.[16] The emigration of 1848 brought an additional 5,315. . . .[17]

Then in 1849, unexpectedly, came the gold rush, and the Mormons found themselves in the midst of the nation's busiest thoroughfare. For three months emigrants came in a perfect swarm, all needing food, provender, and fresh animals, and all willing to trade goods for them.[18]

For several years the pattern was the same. Mormons came by ship and then by wagon train, with each person accounted for, so that they have been called "the most systematic, organized, disciplined, and successful pioneers in our history. . . ."[19]

On August 24, 1849, Captain Howard Stansbury, in charge of a government survey, arrived in Salt Lake City, his supply trains having preceded him. His description of this two-year-old city seems worthy of inclusion here because it was the pattern by which every town and village in Mormondom was built. Each must have wide, straight streets, uniform blocks, and a public square reserved in the center for church, school, and other community activities. Many included a bandstand and recreational areas.

Of Salt Lake City in the fall of 1849, Captain Stansbury wrote:

> A city has been laid out upon a magnificent scale, being nearly four miles in length and three in breadth; the streets at right angles with each other, eight rods or one hundred and thirty-two feet wide, with sidewalks of twenty feet; the blocks forty rods square, divided into eight lots, each of which contains an acre and a quarter of ground. By an ordinance of the city, each house is to

---

[16]Kate B. Carter, "They Came in '47," *Heart Throbs of the West,* VIII, pp. 401-448.

[17]*Ibid.,* IX, pp. 467-521.

[18]Every diarist tells of the profits of this summer's trade in Salt Lake City. See John D. Lee, Hosea Stout, Lorenzo Brown, as well as B. H. Roberts, *Comprehensive History of the Church,* III, pp. 339-353.

[19]Wallace Stegner, *The Gathering of Zion, The Story of the Mormon Trail* (McGraw-Hill, 1964), p. 6.

be placed twenty feet back from the line of the lot, the intervening space being designed for shrubbery and trees.

Through the city itself flows an unfailing stream of pure sweet water, which by an ingenious mode of irrigation, is made to traverse each side of every street, whence it is led into every garden spot, spreading life, verdure and beauty over what was heretofore a barren waste. . . .

The city was estimated to contain about eight thousand inhabitants, and was divided into numerous wards, each, at the time of our visit, enclosed by a substantial fence for the protection of the young crops. . . . The houses are built principally of adobe or sundried brick, which when well covered with a tight, projecting roof, made warm comfortable dwellings. Buildings of a better description are being introduced, although slowly, owing to the difficulty of procuring the necessary lumber, which must always be dear in a country so destitute of timber.

Upon a square appropriated to the public buildings, an immense shed had been erected upon posts, which was capable of containing three thousand persons. It was called "the Bowery" and served as a temporary place of worship until the construction of the great Temple. . . .

A mint was already in operation, from which were issued gold coins of the Federal denominations, stamped without assay, from the dust brought from California.[20]

From the time they left Nauvoo, the Mormons had carried out a cooperative program in which individual desires were made second to the good of the group. Brigham Young had promised that all who wished to go should be taken, but they could not all be taken at once. So they worked on a relay plan with some left at way stations to clear land and plant crops while their teams were taken to bring up others who had been left behind.

In 1849 Brigham Young reminded the people in Salt Lake City that many of their friends were still at Kanesville, Iowa, unable to come to Zion, and made a plea for outfits to go for them. This grew into a Perpetual Emigration program by which not only the saints in Kanesville but those from

---

[20]Captain Howard Stansbury, *An Expedition to the Valley of the Great Salt Lake of Utah* (Philadelphia, 1855), pp. 218-219.

Europe might be brought to Utah, each paying a little in advance and signing a promise to pay in cash or labor on public works after he arrived. By the time this program was dissolved in 1887, it had been the means of bringing more than 85,000 people to Utah.[21]

As they arrived in organized groups, so they were moved to the different settlements in planned and organized groups. Towns and cities were colonized by people especially selected because of their skills. One man could not fight the desert alone. It took many to build a dam in the river, to dig the canals and ditches for the water, to clear and plant enough land to support a village. On November 26, 1848, President Young announced the method of procedure:

> The new order of things meant that men might be called at any time for any purpose, that it was equally a mission whether a man went to preach the gospel in South Africa or to colonize a desert outpost. A man's life belonged to the Church; when he was "called," his standing in the priesthood was at stake, and his hope of salvation. He might have lived ten years in one place, broken the earth and made it blossom, but if he was "called" for a mission of colonization, he must sell out and go. It was not enough that he leave his property and go; where a man's wealth was, there his heart was also, and a man must serve God with a whole heart.[22]

Hosea Stout, listening to the speech that day made a more brief report: "went to meeting . . . President Young said that they were about raising a company to explore this country under the direction of Amasa Lyman. That when men were wanted they would be called on and they would be expected to obey and that it was not the way for men to volunteer, &c."[23]

This whole colonization plan was exactly opposite to the traditional idea of American "free enterprise."

Thus when a settlement was to be created, men of different skills would be called so that there would be farmers

---

[21]Larson, *op. cit.*, p. 234.
[22]Dale L. Morgan, *The Great Salt Lake of Utah* (New York, 1947), pp. 218-219.
[23]Hosea Stout, *On the Mormon Frontier, the Diaries of Hosea Stout,* ed. Juanita Brooks (Salt Lake City, 1964), p. 335.

and tradesmen, builders, teachers, and artisans enough to supply the need. Along with this went the idea that the land was not to be sold, but that every colonist should receive as his inheritance a lot in town and acreage in a field — all he could put to profitable use. After the site for the village had been surveyed according to the plan, the lots were numbered, corresponding numbers put into a hat, and each adult male drew out the number of the site which would be his. He might barter or trade it or do with it as he saw fit, but he was expected to build a home, gather around himself the necessary animals and equipment to carry on his work, provide for his family, and raise them as faithful members of the church.[24]

Conversely, "Outsiders" would not have an inheritance in Zion. They were welcome to the rich farm lands of the east or the gold fields or orchards of California, but this land belonged to the Mormons by reason of their being first upon it. Those who had left valuable holdings in Missouri and Illinois considered the purchase price dear. Thus for the first years in Utah, "outsiders" were strongly discouraged from trying to get land. Several folk tales of these incidents persist, but one at least is recorded by George Laub, eloquent despite his spelling. From the name, this man might well have been a Jew.

> Friday 27 [March 1857] . . . In the Evening I went to prayer Sircle to tenth ward Schoolhouse. This Quorum met at 7 pm. Letter red from Moris Snediler from Texas concerning the treatment he receaved from Ten men who took him out of bed &

---

[24]St. George, Utah, was typical of the transported town. In the fall of 1861, three hundred families were called to raise cotton and other semi-tropical plants. Of those who listed their occupations, there were:

In the general building trades: 37 farmers, 14 blacksmiths, 10 coopers, 6 carpenters, 4 cabinet makers and 1 chair maker; 3 wheelwrights & machinists, 6 millers & millwrights, 5 masons, 1 adobe maker, 1 plasterer, 1 painter, 3 miners & mineralogists.

In the clothing trades: 2 wool-carders, 1 weaver, 1 tailor, 1 hatter, 1 brush maker, 1 tanner, and 5 shoemakers.

Professional men were: 4 musicians & 1 fiddler, 3 schoolteachers, 4 clerks, 1 lawyer, 1 baker, 1 printer, 1 castor-oil maker, 1 drum major and 1 sailor.

The point to be made here is just that none of these came to Dixie because they wished to come. They came because they were Called. (Material assembled from James G. Bleak, *Annals of the Southern Mission*, Book A. Typescript, pp. 59-64.)

gave him noe time to put on Shoes or hat. But draged him over prickly Pares and gravil & Kicked him & pulled his hair & beat him with clubs all Night runing him toe & froe over the Prairie till the brake of day then set him on his horse & told him to Leave that country for he was a god damned heretick & he made his Escape not knowin his doom.[25]

Mormon organization made it possible for the leaders to know every person in every settlement. Larger cities were divided into "Wards" of approximately 500 to 600 people; each village constituted a ward, or nearby small villages were consolidated to form one. Each ward was presided over by a bishop and two counselors, who, in turn, appointed all other officers. Such a close-knit theocracy left no place for the nonmember or "outsider" or gentile, especially any known to be past enemies.

As the Jews had found life in other parts of the United States different from what they had left in the Old World, so they early found that in Utah it was different again. Here they were held in esteem, often called "Brother Jew," and considered important in the over-all plans of God for the last days. Nor was there pressure to convert them to Mormonism, since their destiny was so clearly spelled out in scripture. So long as they did not actively align themselves with the militant anti-Mormons, they might live in peace, and order their lives as they wished.

---

[25]Entries found by date. Photographs of the George Laub Diaries are at Henry E. Huntington Library, San Marino, California. Typescripts at Brigham Young University.

Chapter Two

JEWS IN UTAH TO 1857

No Jews ARRIVED in Utah in the 1847 immigration; so far as we can learn, none came in 1848, either. But the rush of 1849 to the California gold fields certainly must have carried some Jews, as well as people of every other faith. We can only surmise, though an occasional mention is made. One such was by Lorenzo Brown, whose diary entry for March 1, 1851 read:

> Called to see some Hungarian Jews living in the ward. They are emigrants bound for the mines were forced to leave their native land on account of the revolution. One of them is a painter. Saw some window blinds painted in the best of style. He makes about six dollars a day.[1]

The 1850 Census is an excellent source of information on the inhabitants of the territory, giving as it does not only the names of the heads of families, but the age, place of birth, occupation, and property owned. Whether or not there had been a marriage within the current year, whether or not a child attended school during the previous winter, whether or not an adult could read and write, are also indicated. Every family is listed in a numbered "abode," whether that be a house, a tent, or a wagon.

In the Weber County Census we note that most of the foreign-born are in abodes numbered from 193 to 210, evidently an emigrant camp which has wintered there, since no one owns any real estate, no children attended school here during the previous winter, and the parents were born in Germany, Poland, Prussia, or France. Every man has a trade,

---

[1]Lorenzo Brown, "Diaries." Typescript at Brigham Young University, Provo, Utah under "Journals of Lorenzo Brown," p. 66.

there being a bookbinder, a tailor, a blacksmith, a cooper, a baker, a farmer, a chairmaker, two merchants, and two carpenters among them. Several names seem to be Jewish.[2]

The first Jewish couple to set up a business in Salt Lake City,

JULIUS GERSON BROOKS AND FANNY BROOKS arrived in July, 1853. They had come from Galena, Illinois, in a prairie schooner with a company of fourteen other wagons. By this time the road west was a well-marked highway, with guidebooks to show almost every mile. The wagons also were built to specifications, sturdy and well constructed, with tool box, grub box, and strong box — this last for carrying money and valuables of every kind. There was also ample space for storage without overloading the team, so they had traveled without dangerous incident.

But at its best this was an arduous journey, with much walking, some pushing on the steep places, with billows of dust and hours of boredom. It is possible that, as they emerged from the canyon and paused to get their first view of the valley, they felt something of the same emotion that Sir Richard Burton expressed:

> The valley presently lay full before our sight. At this place the pilgrim emigrants . . . give vent to the emotions long pent up within their bosoms by sobs and tears, laughter and congratulations, psalms and hysterics. It is indeed no wonder that children dance, that strong men cheer and shout, and that nervous women, broken with fatigue and hope deferred, scream and faint; that the ignorant should fondly believe that the "Spirit of God pervades the very atmosphere," and that Zion on the tops of the mountains is nearer heaven than other parts of the earth. In good sooth . . . even I could not, after nineteen days in a mail-wagon, gaze upon the scene without emotion.[3]

Most newcomers were impressed with the city, partly, perhaps, because it was a relief to find people settled and

---

[2]Rudolph Glanz, *Jew and Mormon* (New York, 1963), p. 169, designates the family of Michael Meller, bookbinder born in Poland, as Jews. Several others of the group might have been also.

[3]Richard F. Burton, *The City of the Saints and Across the Rocky Mountains to California*, ed. Fawn M. Brodie (New York, 1963), p. 213.

about their business. Almost without exception they wrote about the wide streets shaded with trees, the water running along the curb, the quiet, simple, neighborly life of the citizens. Always they noted the home of Brigham Young, for it dominated the landscape. The wife of a Federal Judge, arriving in 1852, exclaimed, "What a singular Spectacle! We beheld what seemed a thickly settled neighborhood, about a mile distant from us, composed of low, lead-colored dwellings, with a single white building occupying a prominent position. . . ."[4]

At this time Salt Lake City was scarcely six years old. Most of the inhabitants were middle-class or poor people, who found it difficult to provide the bare necessities. Their homes were small, temporary ones, to be enlarged or replaced later.

Only four public buildings were completed: 1 — The Council House on the corner of South Temple and Main; 2 — The Tithing Office with the *Deseret News* publication rooms attached; 3 — The Old Tabernacle, a long, barn-like structure built of adobes; 4 — The Social Hall, where theaters, dances, lectures, lyceums, and all social parties were held. It was dedicated on New Year's Day, 1853.

The *Deseret News* began publication in 1850, and from its advertisements one may gain a good indication of the business activities of the city. All kinds of goods and services were offered: "Fashionable Tailoring," "Saddelry," "Blacksmithing," "Brandy, Whiskey, and Wine for sale by the gallon or barrel." Nowhere in its pages can be found the name of the Brookses. Of their adjustments, we know only that they secured a place on the west side of Main Street, just below Third South. Here they promptly opened a millinery shop and, within the year, a bakery also.

Although the *Deseret News* did not mention the Brookses, the Assessor, I. Y. Hutchinson, accounted for them. His roll, made in the summer of 1853, is a mine of information on Salt Lake City and its people. The title page is done in

---

[4] *Fifteen Years' Residence with the Mormons . . . by a Sister of One of the High Priests* (Chicago, 1876), pp. 146-147.

heavily shaded script with many flourishes, and the double
pages of this very large book are ruled off to record the following items taxed: Wagons & Carriages, Horses, Mules,
Oxen, Cows, Watches & Clocks, Sheep, Pigs, Farmers &
Mechanics Tools, Money loaned or on Hand, Household Furniture, Other Personal Property, Improvements on Real Estate, Total Amount of Tax. Additional lines divide the tax
into its various uses: Territorial tax at 1 percent, County tax
at ½ percent, Road tax at ¼ percent. Between are spaces
to show payment, for "Amount paid in cash," and "Amount
paid otherwise."

Names are listed alphabetically by surname, and are
subdivided by location, beginning with the First Ward and
running through all the numbered ones, then adding the outlying areas: Mill Creek Ward, Big Cottonwood, Little Cottonwood, Willow Creek, Western Sands Settlement, West Jordan
Settlement. Even faraway Green River Settlement was included, though there were only four families there.

Sixty-one double pages are numbered, and at the end
is an unnumbered one labeled MERCHANT'S ASSESS-
MENTS. Here are thirteen firms, the highest with a stock
of goods valued at $53,726.00, the lowest with merchandise
worth only $1,500.00. Eighth on the list is Isabell Brooks
with Millinery Stock, $2,200.00, and a total tax of $5.50.
She is one of the very few who had paid her tax in full.[5]

That Mrs. Isabell Brooks on the records of the tax
collector should be Mrs. Fanny Brooks in her home and
among her friends, should give us no concern, for to have a
nickname was an established custom in many Jewish homes.
We can be certain that she had a millinery shop in operation
in 1853, and by the next year had opened a bakery. Though
she did not herself advertise her shop, others did in such
entries as: "GEORGE GODDARD'S FANCY STORE, Between Reeses' and The Bakery." This appears many times.
The only other bakery advertised is the one operated by
Mr. H. L. Southworth on East Temple and later moved to
South Temple.

---

[5]Assessment Rolls, Utah State Archives, State Capitol. Microfilm in the
hands of the author.

The Brookses had been in Salt Lake City a year before Alexander Neibaur entered in his diary the note: "July 9, 1854, Mr. Julius Brooks from Schweidnitz, in Silesia, informed me that he had seen my father."[6] With all his interest in his own people, he had missed this couple.

Another evidence of the activities of the Brookses is found in the *Millennial Star*. A letter from Salt Lake City, dated August 29, 1854, listed twenty-two companies in business there, all of which were prospering. Last on the list is "Mrs. Brooks, Millinery Store and Bakery."[7] Though two competitors advertised in the *Deseret News,* they did not do enough business to be entered on the list.

This year Utah was visited by the most important Jew yet to come,

SOLOMON NUNES CARVALHO.

Born in South Carolina 27 April 1815, of Portuguese descent, he was well educated. His home background was such that his religion was a vital force in his life. Wherever he went, he was conscious of his duty, both to God and to his neighbors.[8]

He left his business as portrait painter in Baltimore to join Colonel John C. Fremont's last exploring expedition to the Rocky Mountains, as the artist to photograph and make daguerreotype pictures of the scenery en route. Overtaken by winter in the high mountains, the company came near perishing from cold and hunger. They staggered into the village of Parowan, in southern Utah, on 7 February 1854.[9]

---

[6]"Diary of Alexander Neibaur," Archives of the L.D.S. Church, 47 East South Temple, Salt Lake City. Entries under date.

[7]"Letter from George A. Smith," August 29, 1854, *Millennial Star,* XVI, pp. 732-733.

[8]For an excellent short biography of Solomon Nunes Carvalho, see Harry Simonhoff, *Jewish Notables in America, 1776-1865; Links of an Endless Chain* (New York: Greenburg, 1956), pp. 335-339.

[9]John C. L. Smith, who was in charge of the settlement at Parowan, wrote an account of the arrival of Fremont and his party. The letter, dated March 16, 1854, was published in the *Deseret News,* V. 2-4, p. 245.

Regarding the death of Mr. Fuller of the party, Joseph Fish wrote: ". . . After Fremont got into Parowan Simeon F. Howd and Mr. Davis went out and buried Fuller at a point 22 miles from Parowan, about a mile and a half above what is known as Mule Point." John M. Krenkel (ed.), *The Life and Times of Joseph Fish, Mormon Pioneer* (Dansville, Illinois, 1970), pp. 48-49.

Unable to continue with Fremont to California, Carvalho
and his Jewish companion, Egloffstein, convalesced in a Mormon home for a few weeks, and then went in to Salt Lake
City with a local wagon train going to conference. They
arrived on March 1st. Learning that Lieutenant Beckwith
and Captain Morris of the Gunnison Party were in the city,
Carvalho contacted them and accepted their invitation to
board with them at the home of E. T. Benson. Here they
learned of the massacre by Indians of Captain J. W. Gunnison
and six of his men. Since Egloffstein was a topographical
engineer, he accepted employment with Lieutenant Beckwith
to take the place of one of the men who had been killed.

Carvalho decided to set up in business as a portrait
painter in order to earn enough money to take him home.
He painted two portraits of Brigham Young and one each of
Lieutenant General Daniel H. Wells, General James Ferguson,
Attorney General Seth Blair, Apostle Wilford Woodruff,
Bishop A. O. Smoot, Colonel Feramorz Little and wife.[10]
Thus he became acquainted with many of the elite of the city.

Brigham Young evidently was impressed with the young
Jew, for he permitted him to attend a baptismal ceremony
on March 30, at which three persons were immersed in the
icy water, one after the other. The first was a girl of eighteen,
the second a woman of seventy-eight who came to the water
side on a crutch, the third a young man of about twenty.
Of him Carvalho wrote, "His face was the impersonation of
faith and purity. I should like to have painted him as a
study for a 'Saint John'."[11]

Toward the end of April Carvalho was invited to a ball
sponsored by Brigham Young. By dint of some scheming,
borrowing, and renting, Carvalho was finally decked out in
a striped cassimere, a black frock coat, and white vest, so

---

[10]None of the portraits done by Carvalho in Salt Lake City has been found.
The Indian sketches made as he was leaving the state, and of "A Utah Boy"
were reproduced, without a credit line, in Fremont's *Memoirs of My Life* (Chicago
and New York, 1887). The explanation is given in the Introduction, p. xvi. The
Indian pictures appear on pages 186, 196, 224, 240, and 386; the "Utah Boy" on
p. 212.
[11]Solomon Nunes Carvalho, *Incidents of Travel and Adventure in the Far
West* (New York, 1857), p. 147.

that he remarked that, "I was as fashionably attired as anyone whom I met during the evening. . . .

"A larger collection of fairer and more beautiful women I never saw in one room. All of them were dressed in white muslin; some with pink, others with blue sashes. Flowers were the only ornaments in the hair. . . . I returned to my quarters at twelve o'clock, most favorably impressed with the exhibition of public society among the Mormons."[12]

In the meantime, he was eating his way back to health. If he knew of the Jewish couple who were operating a bakery in the city, he made no mention of it. Instead he evidently patronized the shop of H. L. Southworth on South Temple, though he did not name him directly:

> There resided in Great Salt Lake City, in the year 1854, a jolly old Scotchman, who rejoiced in the cognomen of "Golightly," he was a baker by trade, a musician by nature, and a good Mormon by practice. He made first-rate bread, biscuits, and cakes, and cooked to order splendid beefsteaks and mutton chops, as my fellow traveller Egloffstein and myself can fully testify, for we patronized him daily in all the branches of gastronomy, for which he was famous.
>
> His bakehouse was attached to his shop; a small house about a rod on one side, was his dwelling, and immediately back of the oven, in the open yard, was a covered wagon, which was used as the parlor and bedchamber of his old wife, and three daughters, aged respectively thirteen, fifteen, and seventeen. . . . He was an active member of a musical association and performed well on the Kent bugle.[13]

Carvalho evidently visited the places his host wished him to see, so he wrote quite honestly:

> During a residence of ten weeks in Salt Lake City . . . it is worthy of record, that I never heard any obscene or improper language; never saw a man drunk; never had my attention called to the exhibition of vice of any sort. There are no gambling houses, grog shops, or buildings of ill fame, in all their settlements.[14]

---

[12]*Ibid.*, pp. 156-157.
[13]*Ibid.*, p. 160.
[14]*Ibid.*, p. 143.

Remy and Brenchley, the French scientists who visited Salt Lake City five months later, made a similar comment:

> Neither grog shops, gaming houses, nor brothels are to be met with. There are no such resorts among the Mormons. The only places of public assembly are the Temple, the schools, the drill ground, and from time to time the social hall, where they have dancing and singing, where theatrical representations are given, and scientific and historical lectures are delivered.[15]

Yet on Sunday, September 12, 1852, Hosea Stout returned from the Sunday service to record:

> . . . J. M. Grant and others spoke against the distillerys and grog shops tipling shops &c also against some paper money now in the city being put into circulation, &c &c.[16]

While he found much to admire, Carvalho found also much to criticize. Of these things he wrote with equal vigor. He loathed polygamy, and told of several instances of broken-hearted women. Of the land policy he was very frank and exactly right:

> . . . all the real estate in the valley is the property of the church, for proprietors have only an interest in property so long as they are members of the Mormon Church, and reside in the valley. The moment they leave or apostatize, they are obliged to abandon their property, and are precluded from selling it, or if they do give the bill of sale it is not valid — it is not tenable by the purchaser. This arrangement was proposed by the governor and council, at the conference which took place during my residence among them in 1854, and thousands of property holders subsequently deeded their houses and lands to the church, in perpetuity.
>
> Under the operation of this law, nobody but Mormons can hold property in Great Salt Lake City. There are numbers of citizens who are not Mormons, who rent properties; but there is no property for sale. . . .[17]

The mail which arrived from California on April 16 brought word of the murder of one Mr. Lamphere who was traveling with it. The carriers, Atwood and Murray, reported

---

[15] Jules Remy and Julius Brenchley, M.A., *A Journey to Salt Lake City* (London, 1861), I, p. 198.
[16] Hosea Stout, *Diaries, op. cit.,* p. 451.
[17] Carvalho, *Incidents,* pp. 142-143.

that this happened on the Santa Clara in the extreme southern part of the state. Carvalho was much shaken by this report, feeling that a man traveling alone would probably not survive the trip. Brigham Young reassured him, saying that he himself would be going south in early May. Carvalho would be welcome to travel with the company.

Carvalho was not ready when the group pulled out on May 4, but followed two days later. He had a riding horse for himself and a large pack mule to carry bedding, supplies, and equipment, the whole representing an investment of some $350.00. Fully recovered in health, his weight back to normal, he faced this trip confidently, though he must travel alone for the first three days.

As he had written about Salt Lake City, so he decided to describe the towns through which he passed. If his figures are sometimes exaggerated, they are the ones given him by his hosts. Of Provo he said:

> Provost City is a large settlement, containing about eight hundred and sixty families, equal to five thousand inhabitants, two thousand head of cattle, three thousand sheep, five hundred horses, several woollen manufactures and carding machines, shingle machines, two saw mills, a seminary and several schools, pottery, tannery, Etc. Here are five hundred men capable of bearing arms.

> Provost City is built on Provost River, which abounds in salmon trout of delicious flavor and large size. Evan M. Green is mayor; Elias Blackburn bishop. There are four bishops to this city.[18]

Carvalho overtook the company as they arrived at Payson, earlier called Peteetneet. Brigham Young's group consisted of 82 men, 14 women, and five children traveling in 34 carriages or wagons, with 95 animals — a long and imposing train.[19]

---

[18]*Ibid.,* p. 184.

[19]Thomas Bullock was official recorder. He wrote in detail of each day's activities: distance traveled, nature of the terrain, towns visited, meetings held, speakers and subject. These are recorded in the "Journal History" under date. On May 10 the camp was officially organized, with a Commander-in-Chief, Captain of the Guard, Historians, Chaplains, Interpreters, Bishops, a Patriarch, and a Doctor. Each wagon was numbered, and traveled in its proper order, the whole train in motion being more than a mile long.

Carvalho arrived after the evening camp had been made. Brigham Young greeted him warmly and sent him to lodge at the home of Ezra Parrish, who the next morning would not accept pay for the bed, food, or care of his animals. At the evening meeting Carvalho was much entertained by the fact that "Apostle Benson also preached a sermon on the restoration of Israel to Jerusalem, which would have done honor to a speaker of the Hebrew persuasion. . . . These Mormons are certainly the most earnest religionists I have ever been among."

He described the town as containing "one thousand inhabitants, five thousand head of cattle, one hundred and fifty horses, five hundred sheep, two saw mills, a flour mill, etc. It is organized as a city, enclosed in a high wall; the houses are generally built of logs and 'adobes', one story high."

By five o'clock the next afternoon they had reached Nephi, where one hundred and fifty men were capable of bearing arms, but the town was without a surrounding wall. Chief Walker's camp was near this settlement, and it was an important part of the trip that President Young hold a peace council with him. Carvalho described the day-long meeting and the purchase of two Indian children who were being transported to Mexico to be traded there for horses.

"I never saw a more piteous sight than those two *naked infants,* in bitter cold weather on the open snow, reduced by starvation to the verge of the grave — no, not the grave; for if they had died, they would have been thrown on the common for the wolves to devour!"[20]

The next morning through his conversation with Chief Walker, Carvalho learned that Colonel Fremont had given Jose, the Mexican, a mule and several Indians to go back and recover the cache of photographic materials and other goods which had been left behind at that tragic, desperate camp in the mountains about a hundred miles from Parowan. Though Jose and his men had been gone for about one moon

---

[20]Carvalho, *Incidents,* p. 194.

— twenty-eight days — Walker had heard nothing of their success or failure.[21]

Carvalho persuaded Walker to sit for a portrait, and after it was done, he made sketches of Squash-head, Baptiste, Grosepine, Petetnit, and Kanosh. It was with this last named, the chief of the Pauvan Indians, that he probably did his best work. Of it he wrote:

> I found him well armed with a rifle and pistols, and mounted on a noble horse. He has a Roman nose, with fine, intelligent cast of countenance, and his thick black hair brushed off his forehead, contrary to the usual custom of his tribe. He immediately consented to my request that he would sit for his portrait; and on the spot, after an hour's labor, I produced a strong likeness of him. . . .[22]

Carvalho identified many places along the route. He examined the sulphur springs near Beaver and described some remarkable hieroglyphics in Red Canyon. He sketched the Little Creek Canyon Pass.

As they passed along, he did not always get information on towns other than population figures, and to note as he did at Fillmore that ". . . A wall of adobes is built all around the city, protecting the inhabitants from Indians aggressions." He did not know that this site was to be the seat of the State Capitol, where for one year the government functions would be carried out.

So far as Mormon historians are concerned, perhaps the most important item that he recorded was to the effect that

[21]Nowhere in Carvalho's writings do we learn anything about the goods Fremont cached in the mountains. We are indebted to the *Autobiography of George Washington Bean* (Salt Lake City, 1945) for the account. He met Chief Walker (Wakara) at Beaver. "He had with him a Mexican named Vincente Chavez, who had dropped out of Captain John C. Fremont's exploring party at Parowan a month or so previous." (p. 93)

"About this time Walker sent his half-brother Ammon with the Mexican Chavez with ten pack animals to raise the Cache made by Fremont a few months before in Rabbit Valley, near where the town of Fremont now stands. They succeeded in getting everything, consisting of tents, blankets, camp vette (kettles, guns, ammunition, tools of various kinds), even including Odometer, irons and the Daguerreotype apparatus of Senor Carvajo [Carvalho], the Italian artist of the company; and on the return through Willow Creek canyon, Chavez was waylaid and shot, as reported, by the wild Shiverets Indians, but more likely by some of their own party, as by that affair the whole booty fell into Walker's [Wakara's] hands." (p. 95)

[22]Carvalho, *Incidents, op. cit.,* pp. 196-197.

Chief Kanosh gave him the details of the Gunnison massacre and made it very clear that it was truly an Indian affair with no Mormons involved.[23]

At Parowan the citizens all came out to meet the train and hoisted the flag on the liberty pole as they entered the town, in honor of Brigham Young. Of their attitude toward him, Carvalho wrote:

> I could never have imagined the deep idolatry with which he is almost worshipped. There is no aristocracy . . . about the Governor; he is emphatically one of the people; the boys call him Brother Brigham and the elders call him Brother Brigham. They place implicit confidence in him, and if he were to say he wanted a mountain cut through, instantly every man capable of bearing a pick-ax would commence the work, without asking any questions, or entertaining expectation of payment for services.[24]

The friends Carvalho had made at Parowan earlier could hardly recognize in this healthy man the emaciated skeleton they had taken into their home a few months before.

Carvalho's description of Cedar City is significant in that it represents the yeasty, hopeful spirit of the people. The converts from England and Wales felt that the Kingdom would soon be prosperous so that each would own a home and land and live in comfort.

The picture drawn here is representative of what happened in so many small communities begun with high hope, maintained through desperate labor, and finally abandoned.

> With twenty-two men he (Henry Lunt) arrived at the present site of the city, two and a half years ago, to form a settlement.

> Cedar City contains one thousand inhabitants, who possess fifteen hundred head of cattle, besides a large number of horses, mules, and sheep. The city is a half a mile square, and completely surrounded by an adobe wall twelve feet high, six feet at base and two and a half at the top; the building of the wall was attended by a great deal of labor; the persevering industry of the people is unsurpassed. A temple block is in the center of the city, covering

---

[23]*Ibid.,* pp. 197-198.
[24]*Ibid.,* pp. 207-208.

twenty acres of ground, the building lots are twenty rods by four rods. . . .

Immediately in the vicinity of the city is an extensive bituminous coal mine.

Iron ore of superior quality, eighty percent pure iron, is found in great quantities; four miles from the city are two mountains of solid ore.

Iron works are in successful operation, all the railroad iron necessary to complete a road from there to San Bernardino, can be procured here.

The city is destined to become a great place of business, and, in case the Pacific Railroad does not come through or near Great Salt Lake City, it will be the channel through which all importations for the Territory of Utah will come.[25]

On the strength of such hopes, some of the settlers had even taken the tires off their wagon wheels to melt and cast into the needed machinery, certain that with the great production they could soon be replaced. But unforeseen problems arose. The "pure" iron ore contained chemicals which they did not know how to extract. The smelter was primitive; the coal not so good as they had thought. After living on hope and hard labor for another year, many of those who had tires on their wagons moved on to California. When a disastrous cloudburst cut a swath through the workings and damaged them beyond repair, the project was abandoned. This, combined with the tragedy at the Mountain Meadows in the fall of 1857, caused so many people to leave that there were hardly three hundred left, and within a few years the city as described by Carvalho was only a memory.

On May 22, Carvalho took leave of Brigham Young and set out with Parley P. Pratt's group of missionaries traveling in six wagons. They crossed the desert to Las Vegas and on to San Bernardino, where they arrived June 9. After a brief rest, Carvalho went on to Los Angeles where, happy to find some of his own people, he helped to organize a Benevolent Society and to secure a burial ground. He put so much

[25]*Ibid.,* pp. 210-211.

enthusiasm into the projects that he received a citation of thanks from the group, dated July 2, 1854.[26]

Of the four Jews in the Territory of Utah during 1854, Carvalho's stay was shortest, his contribution greatest. Besides the portraits already mentioned and his pencil sketches of Utah Indians, there is still his book. This may be criticized for its lack of specific dates and places, its failure anywhere to give names other than an occasional last name, and its too evident attempts to idealize Mr. Fremont. Yet for students of the early history of Utah he gives the clearest summary of every village on the route south toward San Bernardino that has yet been written.

His description of spring on the desert after he left the last Mormon settlement contrasts with the present barren aspect, and points up the fact that for more than a hundred years the area has grown hotter and drier.

> The meadow formed a perfect carpet of various colored flowers, among which were larkspurs, lupins and many varieties of wild flowers which I have never seen before. . . . I observed a rose tree in full bearing, also cottonwood, ash, besides shrubs of different kinds, all in bloom. The air was filled with fragrance, and the scene presented a harmonious and refreshing landscape. This paradise is without a solitary living inhabitant. These plants and flowers were literally "Wasting their sweetness on the desert air. . . ."[27]

It was the same for days. He delighted in the scenery, the birds, of which there were many varieties, the trees. One covered with white flowers hanging in tassels he pronounced "certainly the most beautiful ornamental tree I ever saw. . . . Thousands of party-colored flowers cover the dry, sandy bottoms. It is a marvel to me how the loose dry sand can yield nourishment sufficient to enable them to grow so luxuriantly." A beautiful pen picture of an area so changed!

From the day he entered Parowan until he left the Territory Carvalho had received every consideration from his

---

[26]For some details of Carvalho's activities here, see Max Vorspan and Lloyd P. Gartner, *History of the Jews in Los Angeles* (San Marino, Calif.: Huntington Library, 1970), pp. 12-14, 19, 21.
[27]Carvalho, *Incidents*, p. 217.

Mormon hosts. His clear descriptions of life in Utah more than repaid his debt and as if in part a tribute to him, the editorial page of the *Deseret News* carried an article to gladden the heart of every Israelite who saw it.

POSITION AND INFLUENCE OF THE JEWS

The existence of the Jews is the living miracle of the world. They are scattered and down-trodden, and yet, according to the most accurate statistics, are as numerous as they were when they left the land of Egypt — the returns of Bonaparte giving about three millions. Expatriated, they become citizens of the world: and wherever tolerated they commence traffic, and become thrifty. Everywhere they are at home. They may be banished, but cannot be expelled; be trodden down, yet cannot be crushed. Only in the United States, France, Holland, and Prussia are they fully citizens; but in spite of British statutes, the Russian ukase and the Turkish curse, they prosper still.

The great nations of antiquity, the Egyptians and Assyrians, the Romans and Saracens, have attempted to destroy them, but in vain; while penal laws and cruel tortures have only served to increase their number and reinforce their obstinacy.

But the Jews exist not only as a monument and a miracle; the Jewish mind has exerted a powerful influence in the world. Favored by Napoleon, the Hebrew race at once developed power which had never been suspected. Soult, Ney, and Massena, who thus altered his name from Mannassah, to escape the odium of being an Israelite, were all Marshals of France under the eye of the greatest warrior of his age. In politics, the Jews have Metternich in Austria; D'Israeli in England, a convert to the Christian faith, while the Autocrat of Russia has had a Jew for his confidential counsellor, and Spain a Prime Minister of Finance. In the United States, Jews begin to figure in our national councils; Mr. Julse, late member of the Senate from Louisiana being of Hebrew stock. Mr. Cremieux, one of the most eminent lawyers of France, was what we should call the Attorney-General upon the flight of Louis Phillippe.

In money power the Jews hold in their hands the destiny of kingdoms and empires, whose governments become bankrupt, and their sovereigns turn beggars at a Hebrew's nod. Half a dozen Jews can do more to preserve the peace of Europe by sitting behind their desk, and persistently saying "No!" to the royal applicants for money, than all the Peace Congresses and Conventions in Christendom. The Rothschilds, the Barings and Sir John [Sic!] Montefiore, are all Jews, and with their banking establishments scattered over Europe and Asia, wield a Sceptre more powerful than monarchs can hold.

Coming to the literary profession, and inquiring into the lineage of many of the most distinguished scholars and men of science, we find the Jews prominent here as well as in active life. The most renouned in astronomy have been Jews, as the Herschells in England, Arago in France, the astronomer under Louis Phillippe, who has filled the world with fame. Those German works which are deluging the world are the productions of Christianized Jews, as those of Henstenburg, Tholuch, Schliermacher, Gresenus, Neander, Hievuhr, and others, whose learned treatises, Biblical criticisms, didactic theology, and general sacred literature, are found in the library of every theological student. Spinosa, the famous infidel, was a Jew, and so are Ronge and Czerski, who took the lead of a new religious reformation in Germany in our day.

Such have been and are the Jews! Mysterious nation! A living, perpetual, omnipresent miracle! A race so indomitable, so unperishable, must have been raised up and preserved for some grand purpose.[28]

Since 1854 marked the bi-centennial anniversary of the Jews in America, this article was appropriate, and Editor Albert Carrington evidently found it appealing. It was intended to interest his Mormon readers, for Julius and Fanny Brooks were the only Jews in Utah at that time.

If Mormon writers could boast of prosperity in Utah during 1854, they would have to admit a decline in trade during 1855. The advertisements in the *Deseret News* give evidence of this, for all notices are much smaller than they were the year before. Livingston, Kinkead & Sons, who had carried full-length, large-print ads, have theirs now only four inches long. J. M. Horner & Company are selling horses and mules and "wagons suitable for the California trade" at public auction. On February 8, 1855, George Goddard is also selling his goods at auction; later he serves as auctioneer for William Mac. The Reese Brothers, Enoch and John, are advertising their Post in Carson Valley.

---

[28]*The Deseret News,* Editorial Page, August 31, 1854, quoting *The Congregational Journal* (no date cited).

An interesting visitor to Utah in the fall of 1855 was William Chandless, of England. He caught his first glimpse of the Valley of the Great Salt Lake on November 6. "I do not know what may be the feeling of emigrants who have left all to come here and look, for the first time, on their Sion and Promised Land. I recollect my own well: instinctively I rushed up a small eminence to my right, and then turned and gazed. I said nothing, but in my heart shouted 'Hosanna! Hosanna!' "[29]

With the city itself, he was not impressed:

> Architecturally, the city is nothing; few houses are over two stories, and many are one only: style there is none; it should be added that there are no "follies." Brigham Young's house alone is pretentious, and looks well enough because it is large, and its walls are newly painted white, and the green venetians refreshed continually. . . . The social hall, a place that may be used for any kind of public amusements, balls, theatre, &c., and the tabernacle and council house are mere useful conventicles.[30]

Chandless discussed some points of Mormon theology, he talked about plural families he knew, but his greatest interest seemed to be in the economy of the area. The business of making a living where there was no money in circulation was considered at some length. In his immediate neighborhood there lived a cabinetmaker, a carpenter, a tinman, a Nottingham stocking-weaver, a Cornish miner, and a Yorkshire tailor. He became friendly with each of these, and learned something of their problems in marketing their wares or exchanging them for necessities.

He noted that men in the building trades were all busy, especially masons, carpenters, and plasterers. He found much exchange of labor among these, so that, even without money, houses were being built everywhere. The stores had placed set prices on some articles such as butter, eggs, flour, wheat, corn, lumber, and lard. They also accepted livestock. The owner would bring the animal in; an appraisal of its value

[29]William Chandless, *A Visit to Salt Lake . . . and a Residence in the Mormon Settlements in Utah* (London, 1857), p. 131.
[30]*Ibid.*, p. 152.

would be agreed upon and entered on the books. Then the family could get goods up to that amount.[31]

At the time of his visit the population of Salt Lake City was considered to be about 15,000. Of these, he said that the greater part were of American or British stock, with a few Germans and Italians, one Irishman, one Jew, and one Negro.[32]

By 1855 only two Jewish families had been converted to Mormonism. The first was Frederick Levi and his wife, who were baptized 25 September 1837, in Essex County, Canada. They moved with their three children to Hancock County, Illinois, the next spring, where two additional children were born. Their eldest son, David, came to Salt Lake Valley in 1848 as a teamster. The family followed in 1850 and settled in Ogden, where they lived the remainder of their lives, their three daughters all marrying there. The two sons, David and Joseph Hyrum, moved south to Beaver County, where they became prominent ranchers.[33]

The best known Jew to become a Mormon was Alexander Neibaur, mentioned earlier. Born in Prussia, he was given the training in languages to become a rabbi, but he chose instead to study dentistry in England. He married a Christian girl and later was baptized a Mormon on 9 April 1838. On his arrival in Nauvoo he set up his dental office in Brigham Young's front room. He also taught German to Joseph Smith. Most important of all, he kept a diary from the day he set sail for America, which has become an important source of information on events of all those early years.[34]

One other Jew, Levi Abrams, was in Utah as early as 1853, perhaps earlier. He was commonly called "Abraham

[31]*Ibid.*, pp. 215-219.

[32]*Ibid.*, p. 154.

[33]L. D. S. Genealogical Library, 107 South Main, Salt Lake City. Genealogical Sheets, alphabetically arranged; information supplied by Ada Oakden, 760 North 5 East, Price, Utah.

[34]Eliza R. Snow's "Biography of Alexander Neibaur," *Utah Genealogical Magazine* (Salt Lake City, 1914), V, p. 53-63, was excerpted by Kate B. Carter in *Treasures of Pioneer History* (Salt Lake City), I, pp. 336-342. For his place in Utah's medicine, see *Utah Historical Quarterly,* X, pp. 32-33. His original "Diaries" are in the L.D.S. Archives, 47 East South Temple.

the Jew"; letters under that name were advertised at the post office. Although no date of his baptism has been found, it is quite evident that he was a Mormon.

On June 17, 1854, Thomas D. Brown, recorder for the Southern Indian Mission, wrote that Colonel Reese's train of goods en route to Salt Lake City from San Bernardino was camped on the Santa Clara. "Abraham the Jew, with a stock of goods, hauled by Father Sherwood, was in camp, and they were much annoyed with each other, weak teams the cause."[35]

Evidently their differences compounded, for after they arrived at Salt Lake City they took their case into court, where it occupied all of July 25-26, and then was given to the High Council for settlement. Their decision was that Abrams should pay to Sherwood one hundred and ninety-seven dollars ($197.00), but that Sherwood must stand the cost of court, an arrangement which left both men the poorer.[36]

That they made peace with each other is shown by the fact that the following year on July 1, 1855, Brown again noted, as his party was camped on the lower Virgin River, "Father Sherwood was in the Company, bringing along some merchandise for Abraham, a Jew, also in the Co'y."[37]

The name of Abraham the Jew appears several times in the records of Hosea Stout, but never with another judgment against him. During the winter of 1855-56 the government functions were moved to the new state capitol at Fillmore, six long days' travel from Salt Lake City, and Abraham the Jew was taken along as a prisoner to answer a charge of the murder of an Indian. He was quickly acquitted of the charge, went back to Salt Lake City for a supply of goods, and returned to set up a small store and gaming place in Fillmore. After all, for the next two or three months most of the money in the Territory would be circulating here where all the fed-

---

[35]Thomas D. Brown, *Journal of the Southern Indian Mission,* ed. Juanita Brooks, (Utah State University Press, Logan, Utah, 1972) pp. 62.

[36]Hosea Stout, *On the Mormon Frontier, Diaries of Hosea Stout,* ed. Juanita Brooks, 2 vols. (Salt Lake City, 1964), pp. 523-524.

[37]Brown, *op. cit.,* p. 133.

eral appointees as well as the legislature and the people
attending upon the officers lived.

At this time Judge Drummond was presiding over the
Court. On November 1, 1855, the two French scientists, Jules
Remy and Julius Brenchley, arrived in Fillmore. They re-
ported that:

> There we found Judge Drummond, whom we had known at
> Great Salt Lake City, and who had come with the lovely Ada, his
> concubine, and big Cato, his negro, to preside over the district
> court. . . . We passed the evening listening to the anti-Mormon
> dissertations of Judge Drummond, in which his fair companion took
> part, who seemed as if she could not say often enough how tired
> she was of her long stay in Utah. . . .

> It will be remembered it was Mr. Drummond's malice which
> more than anything else, gave rise to the military expedition against
> the Mormons. Those who desire to ascertain the earliest causes
> of this costly campaign, must search for them in the illicit union
> of this magistrate with his charming Ada. The contempt with
> which he was overwhelmed by all within his jurisdiction when the
> fact got the wind, the spite he felt and the vengeance he chose to
> take by such means as shame and hatred dictate to ignoble minds,
> — all this it was, insignificant as it seems, that brought about the
> crisis by which a nation was led to throw millions to the winds.
> History, alas! is full of wars which were not a particle wiser. . . .[38]

The story of how the Judge lost his money to the Jew
in a card game and then sent his colored man to get revenge
has been told many times, with as many different versions.
All agree that the judge sent his colored man to whip the
Jew; the Jew swore out a warrant charging assault with an
intent to kill; the Judge was arrested and brought a prisoner
in his own court, where he was subjected to ridicule and
embarrassment. One account said that the Negro only pulled
the Jew over the counter, but refrained from attacking him
further, because the Jew had a knife.[39]

The official account, made from the report of Judge
Appleby, said that:

---

[38]Remy and Brenchley, *op. cit.*, II, pp. 341-343.
[39]"Millard County, 1851-1875. The Diary of Volney King, Part 2," *Western
Humanities Review* (Salt Lake City, 1947), I, pp. 160-171.

A remark made by one Levi Abrahams, a Jew convert to "Mormonism," and a shop keeper at Fillmore, led Judge Drummond to send his negro body servant to horsewhip the Jew. This was done and both the Judge and Cato, the negro servant, were arrested. . . .[40]

William Chandless had left Salt Lake City on January 1, and arrived in Fillmore on Sunday afternoon, January 6, following the difficulties of the Friday night and the arrest of the Judge on Saturday. According to him:

The Judge fell to playing at cards with Abraham, the one Jew of Utah; a quarrel arose; the judge restrained his own hands, but next morning his servant Cato, the one negro in Utah, spat in Abraham's face and pulled his nose. The Jew appealed to the laws of the country; for he was a Mormon and an American citizen. Here was a grievous offence: it was not simply an assault, but the assailant was one of the accursed race, 'the descendants of Cain and Canaan,' and he attacked one of the chosen race, and the solitary one whom Mormonism had a claim to. The Judge and Cato were summoned before the very probate judge whose jurisdiction Judge Drummond denied: in fact, he ought himself to have heard the case. . . .[41]

Hosea Stout gave the legal story, with the names of the lawyers on each side. Most surprising of all, he told how a posse of armed horsemen would not permit the Judge to go to his own court, but forced him instead into a private home, where they held their session.[42] It was such tactics as this that gave justification to Judge Drummond's bitterness and desire for revenge.

There is no evidence that the Jew participated in any of this after he had signed his name to the complaint. So far as we can learn he went about his business as usual, without even being called to appear.[43]

But the forces that were set into motion by his altercation with the colored man in his little shop grew into such power

[40]Brigham H. Roberts, *A Comprehensive History of the Church of Jesus Christ of Latter-day Saints, Century I* (Provo, Utah, 1965), IV, p 202.

[41]Chandless, *op. cit.*, p. 278.

[42]Hosea Stout, *Diaries*, pp. 583-584.

[43]"Abraham the Jew" is listed in the 1874 *Directory* of Salt Lake City as "Abrahams L., saloon-keeper, 14 Ward, South Temple, south side between West Temple and 1st West, p. 185.

that they affected the lives of twenty-five hundred soldiers
and most of the people in Utah.

Conflicts had grown out of many conditions, as we have
noted earlier: first, the feeling that the land belonged to the
Mormons because they were on it first; and second, their complete allegiance to Brigham Young, which made all federal
officers totally ineffective among them.

One by one the public appointees left Utah in disgust or
fear, the tenor of their complaints being that they had no
support from either the public or the Church leaders. On
October 3, 1856, W. M. F. Magraw wrote a letter of complaint to President Pierce. This was not acted upon at the
time, but was later given some consideration by President
Buchanan. Judge W. W. Drummond wrote of his experiences
in Utah in his letter of resignation to Hon. Jeremiah S.
Black, Attorney-General of the United States. This was dated
March 30, 1857. This, with a letter of April 2, enclosing sub-
stantiating witnesses to his charges, caused the President to
pay attention. In addition to Judge Drummond's personal
indignities, he complained that the public records had been
stolen and burned.

In the spring of 1857, with Congress adjourned, President
Buchanan and John B. Floyd, Secretary of War, decided to
name new officials for Utah and to send a military escort to
support their authority. This resulted from Drummond's suggestion:

> I do believe that if there was a man put in office as Governor
> of that Territory, who is not a member of the church (Mormon),
> and he supported with a *sufficient* military aid, much good would
> result from such a course.[44]

General orders were issued May 28, 1857, for the assem-
blage of 2,500 troops at Fort Leavenworth, Kansas, to be dispatched to Utah. Two thousand head of beef cattle were to
be procured and driven along the line of march. Equipment
and supplies for the troops were transported across the plains
by contracting freight companies.

---

[44]Norman F. Furniss, *The Mormon Conflict* (New Haven 1960), p. 57.

So the "Utah War" was on, and the Territory of Utah would never be the same again. As tensions mounted, Julius and Fanny Brooks, not wishing to become involved, gathered up their belongings, hitched up the team, and pulled out along the northern route to Marysville, California, to try their luck in a new environment. Ten years later they would return.

Chapter Three

ESTABLISHED AS A COMMUNITY

"IF OUR ENEMIES will give us ten years, we will ask no odds of them," Brigham Young had said when he arrived in the Valley of the Great Salt Lake on July 24, 1847. Strangely enough, word of the approaching army reached him on July 24, 1857, as he was celebrating the tenth anniversary of that day with a large group of his people in Cottonwood Canyon. His response was instant: "With God's help, they shall NOT come here!"

Since the Mormon War has been much written about,[1] we shall deal with it only briefly. Martial law was declared. Every man old enough to carry a gun was mustered into service, drilled, and trained. Groups of horsemen "scouted" the approaching army, driving off cattle and burning supply trains; infantry troops worked at fortifications in the narrow canyon; horsemen carried the word to the outlying settlements. One group nearly lost their lives in the Nevada deserts in the urgency to secure ammunition. San Bernardino, Fort Supply, and the Carson Valley settlements were all abandoned, and missionaries were all called home as Zion girded for battle.

---

[1]a) Norman Furniss, *The Mormon Conflict, 1850-1859* (Yale, 1966) is a scholarly study of the Mormon War.

b) LeRoy R. Hafen and Ann W. Hafen, *The Utah Expedition, 1857-1858, A Documentary account of the United States Military Movement under Colonel Albert Sidney Johnston and the Resistance by Brigham Young and the Mormon Nauvoo Legion.* (The West and Rockies Series No. VIII, Arthur H. Clark Co., Glendale, Calif., 1958) This includes official documents, newspaper accounts, and excerpts from soldiers in both camps.

c) Jesse A. Gove, *The Utah Expedition 1857-1858,* (Concord, N. H. 1928). This consists of the letters of Captain Gove, and summary articles chronologically arranged.

d) *The Utah War, Journal of Albert Tracy, 1858-1860.* (ed. J. Cecil Alter) *Utah Historical Quarterly* Vol. 13, 1945.

Armed conflict was prevented by the sudden descent of winter in a storm on October 19, which stopped the army in its tracks and held it until spring. That gave time for the official peace commissioners to arrive from President Buchanan and for that friend of the Mormons, Thomas L. Kane, to reach Salt Lake City and go on to army headquarters. After the grandiose gesture of moving his people out of the city that it might be burned if the enemy tried to occupy it, Brigham Young was persuaded to accept Governor Alfred A. Cumming as the official executive of the Territory. On June 6, 1858, the army marched through the deserted city and took up quarters some thirty-six miles southwest. They named their post Camp Floyd in honor of the Secretary of War. Later, when he joined the Confederate forces in the Civil War, they changed the name to Camp Crittenden.

As the soldiers built their quarters, the saints all returned to their homes and peace was restored. The whole procedure was effectively summarized by Captain Jesse A. Gove, who wrote: "Killed, none; wounded, none; fooled, everybody."[2]

But everybody was not fooled. From this time forth things were different in Utah, now part of the United States first and the citadel of Mormonism second. Twenty-five hundred soldiers, though stationed a day's long journey away from the city, made a great difference in the whole economy. Now there was a market for whatever the Mormons could supply: lumber, farm produce, and services. Long freight trains carried goods from the East across the great plains; other long trains came from San Diego via San Bernardino on the west, and money circulated more freely for all.

The army brought the pony express mail, better transcontinental stage service and other conditions which made it profitable for traders and merchants and craftsmen to come to Utah. Among these were some Jews, one of the first being Nicholas Siegfried Ransohoff. There is evidence that Ransohoff brought a load of freight to Camp Floyd in 1858, for his name is on the list of Masons there in April 1859. It was

---

[2]Jesse A. Gove, quoted by Furniss, *op. cit.*, p. 227.

reported that when the camp was abandoned, Ransohoff, not wishing to handle pork himself, since Jewish dietary law forbade the use of it, loaned Brigham Young $30,000.00 with which to purchase the entire lot.[3] In 1861 the *Deseret News* reported that he was erecting a stone building for a store on Main Street in Salt Lake City.

Samuel H. Auerbach, who had been in business in California, also furnished goods for Camp Floyd in 1859, when his diary notes that by that time two hundred fifty adobe buildings had been erected there.[4] Samuel Kahn joined a wagon train with a stock of merchandise in 1859, sold out, and went back, to return again the next year. He became temporarily affiliated with Ransohoff, but in 1863 joined with George Bodenberg under the firm name of Bodenberg & Kahn in groceries, distributing in Idaho and Montana. The firm continued until 1867, when it became Kahn Brothers.[5]

The Mormon leaders had insisted that the army be stationed far enough from any of their settlements that the soldiers could not have any association with their people, the implication being that soldiers generally are seducers. Actually there must have been many among the army men of high integrity and ideals. The first Masonic Lodge in Utah was organized at Camp Floyd, with a personnel of officers and soldiers. The first detachment had reached the site on July 8, 1858, and the Lodge was operating in April, 1859.

This group of forty men[6] built their own Masonic temple, an adobe structure thirty by sixty feet, with a dirt floor and

---

[3]John Hanson Beadle, *Life in Utah* (Philadelphia, 1870), pp. 199-200.

[4]*Journal of Captain Albert Tracy, op. cit., Utah Historical Quarterly,* V. 13, p. 52. Captain Tracy gives a remarkably clear picture of the general layout of Camp Floyd and of his own quarters there.

[5]Leon L. Watters, *Pioneer Jews of Utah,* (American Jewish Historical Society, New York, 1952), p. 128.

[6]FREEMASONRY IN UTAH, Rocky Mountain Lodge No. 205, F. & A.M. At Camp Floyd, April 1859 - July 1861. The complete roll:

Ackley, Richard Thomas	Brotherton, C. H.
Archer, Samuel	Crawford, R. (P.M.)
Bainbridge, E. C.	Dewkins, D. D.
Berry, Thomas J.	Dost, George W.
Bristol, H. B.	Gove, Jesse (P.M.)
Brooks, Edward J.	Halsey, W. L.

roof of planks covered with sod. The list of names clearly suggests that several Jews were among them, but only Ransohoff seems to have remained in Utah. He was not a soldier, but a freighter and merchant.

While the Mormons were allowed to trade with the army, the basic supplies were freighted annually by the firm of Russell, Majors, and Waddell, who occasionally held auction sales of worn-out animals and heavy wagons, oxen often being sold for $25.00 a yoke, and freight wagons for as little as $10.00 each. Some 3,500 wagons were sold at one time by the contractors, who preferred buying new outfits to driving the old ones back.

Dr. Rudolf Glanz names two early Jewish freighters and merchants, Mr. B. Bachman and the I. Calisher & Company, each bringing mule trains of goods into Utah in 1861.[7] They were operating between Denver and the Pacific coast, and their merchandise would be lightweight and easy-packing such as ribbons, lace, trimmings, buttons, etc., with perhaps some spices and groceries. Their business terminated at the end of one year.

Soon the reaction in the East to the "Utah Expedition" turned against the President, and there were cries of corruption and waste.[8] The number of soldiers was gradually de-

Hamilton, William (M.D.)
Hawes, J. M.
Heth, Henry (S.W.)
Hobbs, J. (M.D., P.M.)
Howe, F. J.
Howe, M. L. (P.M.)
Kearney, William
March, R. B.
McManus, T. P.
Mead, Raf (M. Secy)
Miller, ...
Montgomery, S. H.
O'Hara, Patrick
Ransohoff, Nicholas S.
Rosenwald, I. (P.M.)
Ruggles, Daniel
Selden, H. R. (P.M.)
Sharp, J. (P. M.)
Smith, M. J.
Sobert, A. A.
Stevenson, Carter L. (1st J.W.)
Strauss, P. L. (P.M.)
Thomas, B. M.
Tracy, Henry W. (1st S.W.)
Webb, W. A.
Wilson, Richard (Secy)
Wingate, Benjamin

Members of this group were divided in their loyalties. Six of them later fought in the Confederate Army as did their leader, General Albert Sidney Johnston.

[7]Dr. Rudolf Glanz, *Jew and Mormon, Historic Group Relations and Religious Outlook* (New York, 1963), pp. 172-174.

[8]William P. Mackinnon, "The Buchanan Spoils System: Careers of W. M. F. Magraw and John M. Hockaday," *Utah Historical Quarterly*, Vol. 31, No. 2, Spring 1963, pp. 127-151.

creased until by July 1861 only about 1,500 men were left, and with the beginning of the Civil War these were called east. On July 16, 1861, there began the largest sale of government goods ever held up to that time. The Army disposed of over four million dollars' worth of goods for approximately $100,000, about 40 percent of which was purchased by Hiram B. Clawson, agent for Brigham Young. But many individuals also benefited, among them Ransohoff, Auerbach, Kahn, and the Walker Brothers.[9]

Thus the Mormons felt that the coming of the army was a blessing to them. William Clayton wrote that the expedition had cost the government millions and accomplished nothing except making the saints comparatively rich and improving the circumstances of most of the people of Utah.[10] This was especially true in the contracts which Brigham Young secured to help with the Pony Express and the Overland Telegraph.[11] But Camp Crittenden, as Camp Floyd was now called, was a scene of desolation, with every building razed and the surplus ammunition detonated like a sham battle. Only the graves remained in mid-July 1861.

Within two weeks after the withdrawal of the troops, Salt Lake City was visited by one of the most interesting Jewish characters ever to come to Zion of the West. This was Israel Joseph Benjamin, later known as Benjamin II. Born in 1818 of Jewish parents who had fled Poland and Russia to what was later Romania, he grew up with the traditional training of a Jewish boy. In his youth he wished to emulate the great medieval traveler whose name he bore, Benjamin of Tudela, who had made a circuit of the known

[9]Edward W. Tullidge, *History of Salt Lake City,* (Salt Lake City, Star Printing Company 1886), pp. 248-249 gives a good account. Also, B. H. Roberts, *A Comprehensive History of the Church of Jesus Christ of Latter-day Saints, Century 1* (6 Volumes Salt Lake City, Deseret News Press, 1930), Vol. IV, p. 541 and Leonard J. Arrington, *Great Basin Kingdom, An Economic History of the Latter-Day Saints, 1830-1900* (Harvard Univ. Press 1958), pp. 196-199.

[10]Roberts, *Comp. Hist., op. cit.,* p. 542.

[11]Arrington, *op. cit.,* pp. 200-201.

world about 1170 to seek out and describe the scattered remnants of the tribes of Israel.[12]

At about the age of twenty-five, having suffered some financial reverses, he decided to travel through the East as a *maggid*, or itinerant preacher, collecting en route money enough to sustain him and to publish his story. After some time FIVE YEARS OF TRAVEL IN THE ORIENT, 1846-1851, was published under the signature of Benjamin II, Traveler and Author. This book met with fair success, so he determined to visit the western world in the same way. He left Hanover, sailing for New York in July, 1859.

He remained a year in the East, visiting Philadelphia, Baltimore, Washington, D.C., Richmond, Cincinnati, New Orleans, and Louisville. In each city he listed the number of Jewish congregations, giving the type of ritual, the date of founding, sometimes the number of families. His report adds up to a very valuable overview of the Jews in these areas both as to religious activity and as to economic status.

On January 1, 1861, he arrived in San Bernardino. Since the Mormons who moved there in 1852 had been recalled in 1857, there were only about 500 people left in the colony, but they still published a newspaper. He sought out the members of his faith and reported:

> On January 1, 1861, the Jews of San Bernardino met — in all only thirty persons — and felt themselves impelled to form a benevolent society, so as not to be behind fellow Jews in other communities of California. . . . It was also decided to buy a cemetery. I was very happy to have originated so worthy an enterprise in that wilderness and to have met with Jewish hearts everywhere among the Jewish residents.[13]

---

[12]The location and fate of the "Lost Ten Tribes" continues to be a topic of discussion, with much folk-lore and many tall tales attached. Perhaps even more than the Jews, the Mormons have their varying answers: that the tribes are in the far north; that they are within a hollow part of the globe; that they are on a distant star. But, wherever they are, they are to return in a body, marching with banners.

[13]Israel Joseph Benjamin II, *Three Years in America,* 1859-1862, 2 vols. Translated from the German by Charles Reznikoff, with an introduction by Oscar Handlin. (The Jewish Publication Society of America, 1956), p. 220.

In his introduction to the English edition of the works of Benjamin II, Oscar Handlin says that "He did not understand the fact that religion in America was voluntary, that people could change their allegiance at any time, that new sects could spring up anywhere. . . . The most dramatic example, in Benjamin's eyes, was the Mormon Church of Latter Day Saints. . . ."[14]

His travel account is challenging because often his spelling is phonetic, as with "American Port," [Fork] "Coton Wat," [Cottonwood] and "Big Coton Wat." Nevertheless, "on the fifteenth day of July, [1861] at half past two in the afternoon, we arrived in Salt Lake City. . . . The distance from the last station was twenty miles. There are forty-two stations from Carson City to Salt Lake City and the distance is 622 miles."[15]

Being very eager to meet Brigham Young, he sent his card in and was invited to call that very evening. Of his visit he wrote:

> His house is two stories high and is in a sort of courtyard since it is completely surrounded by a wall that is half the height of the house itself. . . . On the roof of the house is a bee-hive, the escutcheon of the Mormons, or as it is called in the speech of their revelation, a "deseret." There is a doorman before the house as watchman. . . .

Admitted inside, he was well impressed with the room and with Brigham Young himself:

> His behavior to strangers is on the whole very friendly and courteous, particularly to Hebrews who are called by the sect "Brother Jews." A few Jews have joined his church. According to the Mormons, they themselves are descendants of the ten tribes, particularly the tribe of Ephraim. I showed him how false this claim was. . . . He could only refer to what was for him divine revelation. . . .[16]

---

[14]*Ibid.*, V. I, p. 29.

[15]*Ibid.*, V. II, p. 222.

[16]*Ibid.*, V. II, p. 224.

His summary as he left the city was:

> Brigham Young is highly respected and esteemed by the Mormons and is regarded as the ruler and the source of all legislation in the Territory. His wishes are carried out as law — without hesitation. His enemies say that he has often instigated the Indians to numerous murders of immigrants, but that is a statement for which we will not assume any responsibility.

> The population of Salt Lake City amounts to from thirteen to fifteen thousand. Of these only a few, mostly Americans, are not Mormons. There are five Israelites here. Two of these have become Mormons. The other three are merchants and are doing very well. In general, there is little trading in the city, for most of the inhabitants are engaged in farming.[17]

> Finally, to sum up the impression the Mormons made on me, I must say that, although they are tainted with many faults, still, on the whole, they appear to be a quiet, industrious, peaceful people who claim tolerance for themselves and their supposed truth, but are willing enough to grant it to those of other faiths.[18]

Because of his detailed reporting on the numbers and activities of the Jewish people in every city he visited, we may accept his account here as valid. The two Israelites who had become Mormons could have been Alexander Neibaur and his son-in-law, Morris Rosenbaum, who had been baptized on April 27, 1858. Or since Neibaur had recorded just three months earlier, April 7, 1861, that his son-in-law Rosenbaum had moved to Brigham City, the other could well have been Levi Abrams, mentioned earlier as Abraham the Jew. The three merchants were no doubt N. S. Ransohoff, Samuel H. Auerbach, and Samuel Kahn.

For fifteen months Utah had been left to manage without any military supervision. Then on October 26, 1862, Colonel Patrick Edward Connor with 750 men marched to the music of the band into Salt Lake City. Silent people lined the streets as the soldiers passed and halted before the mansion of Governor Stephen H. Harding. He welcomed them in a brief speech in which he assured them that they

[17]*Ibid.*, V. II, p. 251.
[18]*Ibid.*, V. II, p. 255.

need not have trouble with the citizens if they themselves maintained proper decorum.[19]

It had been generally supposed that Colonel Connor would occupy the site of Camp Crittenden, but he chose instead the elevated bench land, now Fort Douglas, east of the city, with an unobstructed view of the home of Brigham Young. He was to guard the mail route and protect the emigration from the Indians, but he evidently wished also to keep an eye on the Mormons.

Colonel Connor and Brigham Young understood each other well; they were unequivocal enemies, neither asking nor giving quarter.

Colonel Connor has been called "the first Gentile in Utah," and indeed he was the first Gentile of power. He was the first to use an electric light; first to operate a steamboat on the lake; first to publish a daily paper; and, most important, first to encourage the development of the mineral resources of Utah. To fill their time and keep them out of the city, he directed his men to prospect for metals and advertised their findings through his paper, *The Daily Vedette,* later the *Daily Union Vedette.* This brought in prospectors and miners, and men with capital.[20]

In spite of his efforts, some of his men did find entertainment in the city. Transportation was provided by a double-decker bus drawn by four horses, making regular, scheduled trips. The camp record shows a total of thirty-nine marriages solemnized there, in which twenty-four of the girls were from Salt Lake City, two from Beaver, and six from the employees of the camp itself, a total of thirty, all probably Mormon girls.[21]

Through the influence of Colonel Connor, people of all classes came to Utah — lawyers and financiers and men of influence as well as businessmen and tradesmen, all having one thing in common: they were NOT Mormons.

[19]Fred B. Rogers, *Soldiers of the Overland,* . . . (San Francisco, 1938), p. 46.
[20]Irma Watson Hance and Irene Warr, *Johnston, Connor, and the Mormons, An Outline of Military History in Northern Utah* (Salt Lake City, 1962), pp. 30-31.
[21]*Ibid.* "Marriages Recorded in the Union Vedette," pp. 162-165.

Among the newcomers were many Jews, some of whom did not affiliate themselves with the Jewish community. For example, the *Deseret News* for April 20, 1864, p. 233 noted:

> Our friend, Nat. Stein Esq. who has been in charge of the Overland Stage affairs in this city for something over a year, is, we understand, to represent Ben. Holliday, contractor, at Virginia City, Idaho.* Aaron Stein, brother of Nat. is now a clerk in the Overland Mail office. We notice these gentlemen with satisfaction, as they do not fail to command the respect of all who have business relations with them.

There were four Siegel brothers in Utah in 1864. They opened their first store on the corner of East Temple and First South on July 12, 1864. On July 1, 1865, the Salt Lake *Telegraph* announced that, "The advance of Messrs Siegel's train of clothing and furnishings arrived last evening. This is the first mercantile arrival from the east this season." By 1866 the Siegel Brothers were operating two stores in Salt Lake City.

The Ellis Brothers, Nathan and James M., were also in business in 1864. The *Telegraph* for October 5, 1864, announced that: "Ellis Bros. expect to open on Thursday with a full and complete assortment of general merchandise which they intend to sell cheaper than the cheapest and to constantly replenish." Later they opened a store in Logan also.

Louis Kolitz ran a candy store on Main Street just above First South. One day Bishop Nibley called and offered to sell him a load of sugar for 1¢ a pound, which would barely cover the cost of freight. The reason for this price was that en route west the sugar had been tainted with kerosene.

Kolitz purchased the load, and a short time later asked Bishop Nibley if he had any more tainted sugar. He would like to buy another load on the same terms.

"What did you do with the first load?" the Bishop asked.

"I made it into candy, which I sold as cough drops. They went like hot cakes."

---

*During the earliest digging in the Idaho Gold belt, one claim seemed so promising that it was named "Virginia City." But the vein ran out and was closed before the name was put on any map.

Charles Popper, a loyal and active Jew who ran a butcher shop in Salt Lake City in 1864, opened also a soap and candle factory by which to utilize the excess fat, the first of such factories in all the intermountain area.[22]

The first non-Mormon meeting place in the Salt Lake City area was no doubt the "Chapel Tent" set up by Chaplain John A. Anderson of Colonel Connor's command. This had been fitted out and donated by the First Presbyterian Society of San Francisco and served all non-Mormon groups until Anderson was transferred in 1863.

On December 1, 1864, a Young Men's Literary Institute was organized at the Provost Marshal's office at Camp Douglas. This was a nondenominational group seeking self-improvement through reading, discussion, and speech. Several young Jews were charter members, and when the decision was made to erect a building in the city, they were generous with both money and labor. Among those most responsible were: William J. Appleby, Fred Auerbach, Nels Boukofsky, John Bowman, John Cunningham, Samuel Dean, Frank B. Gilbert, Charles H. Hempstead, Samuel Kahn, R. A. Keyes, John W. Kerr, Samuel J. Lees, Howard Livingston, J. Mechling, Elias Ransohoff, J. King Robinson, D. D. Stover, William Sloan, S. S. Walker, Horace Wheat, W. H. Whitehill, "and many others."

The building, called *Independence Hall,* was located on Third South just west of Main Street, and became the center of all non-Mormon activities — religious, social, and political. Unpretentious as this small adobe house was, its influence can hardly be overestimated. The first Christian (non-Mormon) services held in Salt Lake City were conducted by Reverend Norman McLeod, a Congregational Minister, on January 19, 1866. During the summer of that year Reverend McLeod had in his audience Schuyler Colfax, then Speaker of the House of Representatives. (Colfax would visit Utah again four years later as vice-president of the United States.)

---

[22]Edward W. Tullidge, *History of Utah,* . . . V. 2, pp. 535-536.

The *Daily Union Vedette* referred often to the Independence Hall during its construction, predicting its completion several times before it was actually finished. For example:

> November 3, 1865. NEARLY FINISHED. Rev. N. McLeod's new Congregational Church Hall is nearly completed. He intends to open it with religious services next Sunday a week. It will be a handsome hall, and a credit to the Gentile churchmen of this Mormon Metropolis. More anon.
>
> November 11. The new Independence Hall is not finished yet, so there will be no Christian Services held in it until a week from Sabbath next. Teachers and students of the Sabbath School . . . requested to meet and get books and paper.

The Young Men's Literary Association did meet in the yet unfinished hall for its semi-annual election. After another mention and announcement, the dedicatory dance was held, with the *Vedette* giving a glowing report on November 20, 1865.

> HIGH LIFE IN SALT LAKE CITY—
>
> The grand anniversary ball of the Young Men's Literary Association held at their fine new Independence Hall on Friday evening was a grand and glorious success.
>
> About one hundred couples were in attendance . . . the Hall brilliantly lighted . . . As stylish an assemblage as you dare drum up in Gotham or the "Hub" of Boston. . . ."

One hundred couples would find dancing in this small hall something of an experience unless, following the Mormon fashion, they should give each man a number and permit him to dance only when his number was called. Even so, the dance marked a continuation of a social life in Salt Lake City distinct from that of the Mormons and rivaling their best entertainment.

The erection of Independence Hall seemed to encourage non-Mormon activities, for on January 15, 1866 — four days before Reverend McLeod held his first service — a group gathered to organize the first Independent Order of Odd Fellows. At this meeting, which was held at the Daft Hall, Charles Popper was the leading spirit, and among the assembly were several other Jews. When the organization was effected, James M. Ellis, a Jew, was elected president. Fred and Theodore Auerbach and Ichel and Abraham Watters were among the first group, with Nelson Boukofsky, Simon Bamberger, Elias Siegel, Henry Cohn, Louis Humas, Samuel Levy, M. Meyers, and Moss Woolf. This group through the years cooperated in rendering help to the needy and in assisting with the burial, not only of their own members, but of indigents in the city.

Since the Masonic Lodge organized at Camp Floyd in 1859 had surrendered its charter and dissolved in 1861, a group gathered on November 11, 1865, at the Odd Fellow's Hall to plan for another organization. Among them were eight prominent Jews: J. M. Ellis, W. G. Higley, Louis Cohn, William L. Halsey, Theo. Auerbach, Oliver Durrant, Charles Popper, and James Thurmond. Their organization meeting followed on February 5, 1866, also in the Odd Fellow's Hall. The *Daily Union Vedette* of February 7 reported that "between 50 and 60 military citizens in full Masonic regalia marched through the principal streets." They followed the band to a meeting of stirring speech and music, all reflecting pride and optimism and a determination to carry out Masonic ideals.

As was true of all non-Mormon settlers, Connor's army was largely responsible for the arrival of the first Jews to remain in Utah. Some few, like Isadore Morris, came as soldiers and remained after being mustered out. Others came as traders to supply food or needed articles, while still others, encouraged by the atmosphere of confidence and optimism, decided to set up in business, so that by 1864 there were enough to form a congregation and hold a formal service. It is probable that family groups had met earlier to share observance of the Sabbath or of other Holy Days.

The first gathering to receive public notice was held October 9, 1864, and reported two days later in the Salt Lake *Telegraph*. The reporter was evidently ignorant of the service.

> The respectable portion of our Israelite citizens commenced the celebration of the Atonement at sundown on Sunday [Friday]

and held over till the going down of the same orb. [Saturday].
Being without a synagogue, the faithful met in the house of one of
our East Temple Street merchants and commemorated the High
Priest entering the holy of holies to make atonement for the sins
of the people. . . .

It is probable that those gathered planned for a more
general observance of the next Holy Day and discussed conditions among their fellow members. Who among them had
prayer books or other items so necessary to the proper observance of the ritual? Who had space to accommodate more than
their own family? Who was in need of medical care?

Basic in Jewish teaching is the love of one's neighbor,
and concern for the poor. Often a Benevolent Society would
be the first formal organization in a Jewish community, and
in Salt Lake City, a way-place between east and west, there
were bound to be travelers in need. One evaluation of Jewish
belief says:

> In the older, traditional Jewish community, enshrined in the
> *shtetl,* learning was considered even more important than prayer,
> and both were incomplete without *zedakah, charity.* In the *shtetl*
> it was customary to hear Jews say: "Praying three times a day does
> not make you a Jew. You have to be a Jew for the world. That
> means you have to do something for other people as well!"[23]

It is not surprising then that a Jewish Benevolent Society
should have been organized before the congregation took a
permanent form. This was also in 1864, with formal
announcements sent to the Jewish press in the following letter:

> Salt Lake City, Utah Ter.
>
> At the meeting of the Israelites of this city and vicinity held on
> Sunday the 15th ult. the first Hebrew Benevolent Society of Great
> Salt Lake City was duly organized, and after the adoption of a
> Constitution and By-laws, the following resolution was carried:
>
> Resolved: That the *Hebrew* and *Hebrew Observer* of San
> Francisco, and the *Israelite* of Cincinnati, be informed of our
> organization and of the election of the following gentlemen as
> officers for the ensuing term:

---

[23]Stuart E. Rosenberg, *The Search for Jewish Identity in America,* originally
published as *America Is Different* (New York, 1965), p. 272.

President, Fred Auerbach; Vice President, L. Levy; Treasurer, Solomon Siegel; Secretary, Theodore Auerbarch [sic]. Trustees — Messrs. James M. Ellis, Harris Aaron, Jacob Ornstein, L. Reggel and S. W. Joel.

One of the sections of the constitution adopted by the Society makes it incumbent upon every member to observe in due manner and form, the two most Sacred Holidays in our calendar, viz; Newyears Day and the Day of Atonement.

Theodore Auerbach, Sec'y.[24]

Encouraged by these beginnings, and also by the enthusiasm and training of some of the young men, the Jews engaged Daft's Hall on Main Street for the observance of the Holy Days of 1865. Their account is eloquent of their satisfaction:

The first Jews who came to this territory settled themselves at once in Salt Lake City. They were but a young couple, Mr. and Mrs. Julius G. Brooks. After a residence of three or four years they went on further west to the coast, but returned in the year 1865, eleven years after their first arrival here, and found instead of in 1854 no Jews whatsoever, four Jewish families and several young, unmarried Jewish men. These were Mr. and Mrs. J. Arnstein, Mr. and Mrs. .... Gans, Mr. and Mrs. .... Levy, and family, Mr. and Mrs. Joel and family, and the Auerbach brothers, the Popper brothers, Ransohoff brothers, S. and E. Kahn, L. Cohn, ... Prag, the Lesser brothers, and A. and I. Watters. These were enough to form a *Minyon* (the necessary Jewish religious quorum for common worship, which demands at least ten male members over the age of thirteen years) for the autumnal holidays.[25]

Now the activities of the Benevolent Society would demand cooperation from all members of the Jewish community. With the shifting population of the frontier, they evidently found themselves taxed beyond their means, as the following communication, dated January 22, 1866, will show:

. . . This society has reason to feel gratified at the interest manifested by its members and . . . proud at the liberality with which all contributed toward defraying the expenses of purchasing a Sepher Torah, Shophar, books, etc. . . . and the readiness with

[24]*The American Israelite,* V. XI (1864-1865), p. 165.
[25]*The Salt Lake Telegraph,* 15 Oct. 1865. Here again the reporter evidences his good will toward the Jews, but does not know their names or understand their ritual.

which appeals for charity have been promptly met; and, whereas
a piece of ground has been donated to the society aforesaid for a
Jewish cemetery; therefore be it resolved that Messrs. J. M. Ellis,
Joseph Siegel, Theodore Auerbach and F. F. Hilp be appointed
a committee to solicit such pecuniary aid of Jewish congregations
and individuals outside of the Territory, for the purpose of raising
means to build a wall and other improvements so much needed. . . .

The expense of the society, owing to its being so remote, has
been more than great; indeed every member has donated more than
the extent of his means. It is . . . essential on this, the thoroughfare
of the great West, to have a resting place for those who may be
called to take that long journey, . . . the estimated expense of fit-
ting up the cemetery is $800 to $1,000. . . .[26]

The spring of 1866 found the Jewish congregation united
and of sufficient numbers to justify the renting of a larger
place for worship. On May 22, 1866, the *Telegraph* reported:

The Israelites of Salt Lake City, as per announcement of
President Nathan Ellis, held divine services at the Masonic Hall in
this city on Saturday evening last, being the inauguration of the
holiday on Shebueth [sic!] . . . On Sunday the scroll was read in
an able manner by H. M. Cohen. . . . The Ten Commandments
were recited; also "akdomous," the particular chant of the day.
From appearances, the feeling is such that at no distant day a
Temple for their worship may be erected in the city.

Of the spring gathering in 1866 word went far and wide,
because at this time, May 31, the first circumcision was performed.

Salt Lake City — Mr. A. Kutner, who lately returned from Salt
Lake City, has kindly placed us in possession of the following interesting facts: The Israelites of that city number about seventy, and
are constantly increasing. They already have a Benevolent Society,
and are now about to establish a Bene Berith Lodge. A very interesting incident took place lately. The wife of Mr. H. Ahrens having
presented her husband with a son, and there being no regular
mohel in the city, Mr. S. Abrams, a private gentleman, offered to
perform the ceremony of circumcision, and succeeded. When the
fact became known, three Jewish gentlemen also had their children
(some of them a year old) circumcised by Mr. Abrams. Although
liberal compensation was offered to this gentleman, he declined

---

[26]*The Occident.* (Philadelphia) Vol. XXIII (1865-1866), pp. 558-559.

receiving any remuneration for his services. Several young Israelites have married Mormon ladies, one of whom has embraced Judaism, and the others are expected to follow. There is an Odd Fellow, also a Masonic Lodge there, the Members of which are mostly Israelites. Great sociability exists among our co-religionists in that place, and they never tire in works of charity, as every needy Israelite who passes through Salt Lake City, can testify to. Mr. T. Auerbach especially deserves credit for his zeal in every charitable cause.

S. F. Hebrew.[27]

Evidently the first child to be circumcised in Utah, Sam Ahrens, did not adhere strictly to his Jewish faith. His unpublished autobiography chronicles his moves from place to place and his adventures in a wild and woolly West. But the word of his proper care as an infant went to far lands as evidence that a Jewish community was establishing roots in Utah, among the remote Mormons.

Word of the organization in Utah and its activities appeared in the press in far distant places. A general summary, evidently mailed in 1866 and published on February 1, 1867, read:

Salt Lake City, Utah — There are in this city ten families and about thirty young men of our persuasion, doing business there. They have united into a benevolent society. President Young presented them with a piece of land, which they improved and arranged into a burial ground. We are told that the Israelites are doing well in point of business, although the Mormons preached against dealing with Gentiles. There are in the Territory 90,000 souls of the Mormon creed, and about 3,000 Jews and Gentiles. There are also four English Jews among the Mormons for the last twenty years, who embraced the new creed.[27a]

Sometime after the above was written, a committee waited upon Brigham Young and secured the use of the Seventies Hall for their New Year's observance. This they felt was a real concession, so they assigned a committee to draft a letter of thanks and appreciation, which said in part:

27Glanz, *Jew and Mormon*, p. 215.
27a*Ibid.*, p. 218.

Whereas the Hon. Brigham Young has never denied any request
made by us as a religious body for our worship, granting us, on
several occasions, the use of an elegant [sic] hall for our worship;
therefore we appreciate his kindness as well as the courteous manner
in which our requests have been granted. . . . We consider ourselves under many obligations to the Hon. Brigham Young and
hereby tender him our sincere thanks. . . .[28]

Records show that services continued to be held in any
available hall, among them Independence Hall, the Masonic
Hall, or the Odd Fellows' Hall, neither of which was as
spacious or appropriate as was the Mormon Seventies' Hall.
One later gathering was held at Richards' Skating Rink, but
more often the new Liberal Institute was used.

By 1866 many Jews were coming into Utah, some to
leave after a short time, others to settle expecting to be permanent. Such an article as the following, with its Chamber-
of-Commerce suggestions might encourage some from far
away:

THE JEWS IN THE WESTERN PART (END) OF AMERICA

. . . In the contemporary correspondence of the *Jew Record* a
letter is brought from one of our fellow Israelites living there. From
it, it seems that up to the year 1864 only three Jews lived there.
And in the year 1864 the number of our fellow Israelites was
approximately 50, most of them without wives. Then they bestirred
themselves to pray publicly [as a congregation] on the days of New
Year and in the Day of Atonement . . . they sent individuals to the
prophet of the Mormons to request him to rent them one of the
Temples of the city to offer prayer in it publicly [as a congrega-
tion]. That prophet granted them their request willingly and permitted them *without payments* to assemble in one of the most beautiful temples of the city to pray in it to the Lord, their God. And
so it was. Then the Jews prayed to God according to their custom
in a Utah city — something that had never occurred there from
the time it had been established. . . . After the holidays had passed,
our fellow Israelites established in their midst a society *"Gemilluth
Hasadim"* [Acts of loving kindness] which still exists to this very
day and it has performed much good in the midst of the community. . . . Likewise they also now have a place of burial set
aside for themselves surrounded by a beautiful fence. The portion

[28]Watters, *Pioneer Jews of Utah,* p. 69.

of land for this purpose was presented to them *gratis* by the officials of the city at the order of Brigham Young, who at all times shows his love for the people of Israel more than to all the rest of the members of other religions. And his saying always is, "That in the end, finally, all the peoples will accept the faith of the Jews."

All of the Jews there are wealthy, through their trade, and they work faithfully, and the Mormons honor them very much and trust them in their words, and their number will increase from year to year, who come there from the four corners of the earth, and everyone finds there his sustenance plenteously either through trade or tilling the soil, for the earth is fertile and blessed like the garden of Eden, and they dwell there securely with none to make them afraid, and the Mormons do not allow any members of any other religious group to dwell amongst them except the Jews whom they respect very much . . . and in their midst is not found even one of the sect of the Reformer. . . .[29]

Except for the report of the fertile and fruitful earth, most of this was true, or almost true. The Mormons did trust the Jews, and Mormon leaders always spoke in terms of praise for these people.

Up to this time, except for Independence Hall, no non-Mormon church had been erected, but such organizations as the Odd Fellows and Masons were active.

Then there occurred a murder which greatly disturbed all the non-Mormon citizenry of Salt Lake City. On April 2, 1866, S. Newton Brassfield was shot and instantly killed by a concealed assassin as he walked down the street in the custody of U.S. Marshal J. K. Hosmer. Brassfield was a young Gentile who had spent the winter here in the employ of Greenhalge, Martin, Dorsey & Scot, freighting contractors. On March 20 preceding, he had married Mary Milam Hill, estranged plural wife of Archibald N. Hill, a prominent Mormon of long standing. The ceremony was performed by Associate Justice Solomon P. McCurdy.

Brassfield was arrested for grand larceny while moving from his wife's residence a trunk which contained her clothing.

---

[29]This letter was found among the papers of Dr. Leon L. Watters. It was labeled a "Free Translation" of an article in Ha-Magid, Lyck, Aug. 4, 1869.

As he was being led away he was fatally shot by a man concealed in an alley. That this could happen in full day and no attempt be made to capture the assassin was a matter of grave concern, especially when Brigham Young referred to it from the pulpit as an instance from which other Gentiles might learn a lesson. That the girl was of legal age, that she had been long estranged from her husband, that the ceremony was performed according to law, meant little to Mormons when weighed in their balance against the fact that her husband had been prominent since the Nauvoo days, that he was one who near Nauvoo had been whipped to insensibility by a mob, that he was at this time on a mission for the Church, and that there were two children from this union. This was not the first "justifiable homicide" committed in the Territory, nor would it be the last.[30]

About six months later another murder, even more shocking, was committed, for while young Brassfield was scarcely known, Dr. J. King Robinson was prominent and popular with Mormons and non-Mormons alike. The 30-year-old physician had come with Connor's command, but after receiving his discharge, had set up in private practice. He married Ellen (Nellie) Kay, daughter of John Kay, well-known Mormon musician and singer, a gunsmith by trade. Dr. Robinson's practice included both Mormon and non-Mormon; he was active in the Sunday School of the non-Mormon Christian church.

His offense was that, in defiance of local officers, he had filed on the hot springs and the land surrounding them to the north of the city, with the plan to erect a hospital and health resort in that area. On the night of October 22, 1866, a messenger came to his home with an urgent plea that he come to the assistance of his brother who had broken his leg in a fall from a horse. Against his wife's entreaties, he set out on this errand of mercy, only to be attacked and killed a short distance from his home on Main Street and Third South. Several men were said to have been involved.[31]

---

[30]This was a period of violence in Utah in which there were a surprising number of homicides, none of which could be traced to any one killer. For the L.D.S. Church account, see B. H. Roberts, *Comp. Hist.*, V. 5, pp.184-188.
[31]*Ibid.*, pp. 194-199.

The whole community was shocked and enraged; large rewards were offered for information leading to the arrest of the guilty, but no one was ever brought to trial.

Now some young Jews became active in the anti-Mormon demonstrations and joined in the street fightings which followed.

The first murder — that of Brassfield — so soon after the organization of the Mt. Moriah Masonic Lodge had caused high anti-Mormon feeling. That and the statements of Mormon leaders about the Civil War then in progress, and the general attitude that, if the North and South should destroy each other, it might be according to God's will, led the Masons to resolve that no Mormon should be admitted to their ranks. "A man not true to his government cannot be a Mason," they said.

By coincidence a second Masonic Lodge, The Wasatch, was organized on the very night on which Dr. Robinson was killed. This cemented all non-Mormon groups into anti-Mormons and stimulated some warm-water Mormons to apostatize. Men now felt that they must stand and be counted.

For a time the two Masonic lodges kept their records in a single ledger, one writing from one side and one from the other. Interesting notations include one that Ira M. Schwartz gave a charity box, Brother Maltise a sword for use of the Tyler, and John Meeks a clock (which was still running in 1935). The Wasatch Lodge held its last meeting September 13, 1867, combining permanently with the Mt. Moriah Lodge.[32]

---

[32]S. H. Goodwin, P.G.M., Freemasonry in Utah, *Thirty Years of Mt. Moriah Lodge No. 2 F. & A.M.* (Salt Lake City, 1930). 57 pages.
Names of officers and members will show the number of Jews:

OFFICERS	MEMBERS	
Joseph F. Nounnan, W.M.	G. B. Moulton	Wm. Showell
William G. Higley, S.W.	N. Boukofsky	Wm. H. Tate
Theo. M. Auerbach, J.W.	D. H. Kingsley	J. M. Ellis
E. Ransohoff, Treas.	J. Ornstein	W. M. Johns
Sol Siegel, Secy.	E. A. Ryan	W. H. Miles
Louis Cohn, S.D.	W. S. Foot	A. C. Sprague
Paul Engelbrecht, J.D.	A. Pepper	
A. Leventhal, S.S.		
Jacob Engle, J.S.		
L. Levy, Tyler		

The combined lodges held their first Masonic Ball on December 27, 1866, in the Social Hall. Tickets were $10.00 per couple. Supper was served by Mrs. A. Greenewald, who operated the Excelsior Hotel. This was the beginning of the annual balls held for years. These were often costume balls, in which fabulous prizes were offered for the best costume. Soon these were taken over entirely by the Jewish Ladies' Benevolent Society.

The first official list of the Jews in Utah comes from the *Salt Lake City Directory,* which was published by G. Owen in 1867. It includes thirty-nine names, most of whom did not sign the letter of protest of late 1866. There were evidently some Jews doing business in Salt Lake City at the time whose names are not on the list.

Auerbach, David	Kahn, Emanuel
Auerbach, Fred H.	Kahn, Samuel
Auerbach, Samuel	Lesser, S.
Auerbach, Theodore H.	Leventhal, A.
Boukofsky G.	Levy, L.
Brooks, Julius G.	Meyer, H.
Cohn, L.	Morris, I.
Davis, H.	Nathan, Samuel J.
Elgutter, Morris	Oberfelder, I.
Elgutter, Solomon	Ornstein, J.
Ellis, B.	Popper, Charles
Ellis, Nathan	Prag, Conrad
Engler, Louis	Ransohoff, E.
Ganz, A.	Ransohoff, N. S.
Glocksmon, M.	Reggel, Louis
Goldstein, S.	Siegel, J.
Greenberg, M.	Siegel, S.
Greenewald, A.	Watters, Ichel
Joel, S. W.	

A comparison of this list with that of 1869 will show that fourteen men have moved away, some of them brothers who have set up branch stores in other towns in Utah, some who evidently left the area. On the other hand the census shows that twenty-one *new* Jewish businesses were established in the intervening two years.

The activities of the Jewish community continued. The Salt Lake *Telegraph* for September 16, 1868, reported the beginning of the Jewish New Year on that date and added that "The services will take place in the Seventies Hall. All the Jewish houses of business will be closed on Thursday and Friday."

That the Jews not only attended to their religious obligations at home, but were conscious of the welfare of their own people in foreign lands is shown by a letter which was printed in the *Deseret News* after having gone all the way to San Francisco, where it appeared in the San Francisco *Hebrew*, October 8, 1869, page 4, column 5. It read:

A GENEROUS GIFT

The following letter, inclosing a draft of $400 — from the First Hebrew Benevolent Society in Salt Lake City, was received by Mr. C. Meyer, President of the First Hebrew Benevolent Society of this city:

Salt Lake City, Sept. 28th, 1869.
Mr. C. Meyers: Dear Sir—

At a meeting of the First Hebrew Benevolent Society, held on the 26th instant, the motion was unanimously carried to send to you four hundred (400) dollars of our funds, for our suffering co-religionists in Western Russia, which I take pleasure in sending you herewith. Please accept the same, and oblige by acknowledging the draft.

Yours respectfully,
Sol Levy

In the name of our suffering brethren far away, we express to the members of the First Hebrew Benevolent Society of Salt Lake City our best thanks.

The American Israelite had evidently received word of the same contribution, but now it would seem that the Mormons shared in the giving. The sum of four hundred dollars is the same and the recipient the same, but the item closes with the statement, "All credit to our Mormon neighbors."[33]

The Mormon people maintained a lively interest in the Jewish activities and might well have contributed to this fund.

---

[33]*The American Israelite* Vol. XVI (1869-1870) No. 17, p. 6.

Another point of conflict between Mormon and non-Mormon came during this same month. Throughout the fall, Brigham Young and others of the Authorities preached against their people's patronizing the Gentile merchants. Why should they give financial encouragement to enemies of the Church? The non-Mormon merchants finally got together and composed the following:

PETITION OF THE GENTILE MERCHANTS
TO THE LEADERS OF THE MORMON CHURCH

Gentlemen: As you are instructing the people of Utah, through your Bishops and missionaries, not to trade or do any business with the Gentile merchants, thereby intimidating and coercing the community to purchase only of such merchants as belong to your faith and persuasion, in anticipation of such a crisis being successfully brought about by your teachings, the undersigned Gentile merchants of Great Salt Lake City respectfully desire to make you the following proposition, believing it to be your earnest desire for all to leave the country who do not belong to your faith and creed, namely: On fulfillment of the conditions herein named: First — The payment of our outstanding accounts owing us by members of your church; Secondly — All of our goods, merchandise, chattels, houses, improvements, etc., to be taken at cash valuation, and we make a deduction of twenty-five per cent from the total amount. To the fulfillment of the above we hold ourselves ready at any time to enter into negotiations, and on final arrangements being made and terms of sale complied with, we shall freely leave the Territory.

Respectfully Yours,

Walker Bros.,	Gilbert & Sons,
Bodenburg & Kahn,	Wm. Sloan,
C. Prag, of the firm of	Ellis Bros., by
Ransohoff & Co.,	J. M. Ellis,
J. Meeks,	McGrorty & Henry,
Siegel Bros.,	F. Auerbach & Bros.,
L. Cohn & Co.,	Oliver Durant,
Klopstock & Co.,	S. Lesser & Bros.,
Glucksman & Cohn,	John H. McGrath,
Morse, Walcott & Co.,	Wilkinson & Fenn,
J. Bauman & Co.,	I. Watters,
Morris Elgutter,	M. B. Callahan,

Thomas D. Brown & Son

Great Salt Lake City, Dec. 20, 1866[34]

---

[34]O. F. Whitney, *Hist. of Utah*, 1892-1904 (S.L.C.) V. II, pp. 164-165.

Brigham Young lost no time in answering this letter. For a long time he had smarted under the barbs and ridicule of the *Daily Union Vedette*, and here was an opportunity to make a public expression. The letter is far too long to reproduce in full, but an excerpt will illustrate its general tenor:

> In the first place, we wish you to distinctly understand that we have not sought to ostracise any man or body of men because of their not being of our faith. . . . To be adverse to Gentiles because they are Gentiles, or Jews because they are Jews, is in direct opposition to the genius of our religion. It matters not what a man's creed is . . . if in his dealings he act in accordance with the principles of right and deport himself as a good, law abiding citizen would. . . .
>
> There is a class, however, . . . who for many years have been the avowed enemies of this people . . . put into circulation the foulest slanders about the old citizens. . . . They have donated liberally to sustain a corrupt and venal press, which has given publicity to the most atrocious libels respecting the old citizens. . . . What community on earth would be so besotted as to uphold and foster men whose aim is to destroy them? . . . There are honorable men enough in the world with whom we can do business, without being reduced to dealing with the class referred to. I have much more to say upon this subject.
>
> BRIGHAM YOUNG
>
> Great Salt Lake City, Dec. 21, 1866[35]

The only two non-Mormon firms that were purchased for incorporation into ZCMI were Ransohoff and Company and L. Reggel, both Jewish. Ransohoff was paid $75,000, and his property on the west side of Main Street became the site of the ZCMI drugstore.[36]

It is interesting to note that neither of these firms signed the public letter, for both had maintained friendly relations through the years. Also, the Ransohoff store was built of a solid stone construction such as would appeal to Brigham Young.

It seems appropriate to close this chapter with the year 1869 and the coming of the railroad to Utah, an event which

---

[35]*Ibid.*, pp. 165-166.
[36]*Ibid.*, p. 168.

changed the manner of life for all in the territory. Goods and people from the East could be transported so quickly and so cheaply that, instead of the shortages of the past, markets were well supplied. Mining had reached a point where money was in circulation so that even farmers and laborers had a purchasing power.

Mining on a large scale was being carried on. Stockton in 1866 was producing silver ore; the Walker Brothers had made shipments of copper ore from Bingham in 1868.[37]

By this time the Jews were established as a community and recognized as a force in society. Although not involved in mining, they found the general influx of capital and of non-Mormon citizens of education and legal training, along with the prosperous economic climate, all favorable. As they could live better financially, so they could live better socially and spiritually.

---

[37]*Utah State Historical Quarterly,* (S. L. City) V. 31, No. 3, Summer 1963. This whole issue is devoted to mining in Utah.

Chapter Four

MORMON-JEWISH RELATIONS

THE DRIVING OF the last spike which connected the transcontinental railroad at Promontory Point on May 10, 1869,
marked the end of an era in Utah, though the real impact
was not felt until the completion of the branch line from
Ogden to Salt Lake City the next January. The mining
boom was already under way; the Emma mine had already
international connections. Descriptive of the conditions is the
note of a mining camp follower, Joseph Rosborough:

> It [Salt Lake City] struck me as the liveliest mining camp I ever
> saw, looking at the number of wagons. There were about two
> miles of wagons coming in every day with ore and bullion. . . .
> The Emma mine and some other mines contiguous were putting
> out great quantities of ore. That was the great period for the
> Emma.[1]

For the next twenty years, the story of mining in Utah
is an exciting one, from the fabulous Emma in the north to
the equally fabulous Silver Reef in the south, while the
Copper Mountain story probably outdoes them all. In addition there were many other productions less spectacular and
shorter lived, which still accounted for employment to thousands of people.

The Gentile population in Salt Lake City doubled and
tripled. The newcomers included financiers, engineers, lawyers, and doctors as well as prospectors, teamsters, miners,
and technicians. Newspapers sprang up in which mining
news and anti-Mormon literature shared the front lines.
Though the Mormon people had been counseled to stay on

---

[1] Robert Joseph Dwyer, *The Gentile Comes to Utah, A Study in Religious
and Social Conflict* (1862-1890) [Washington, D.C., 1941] p. 59. Reprinted
Western Epics (S.L.C., 1971).

the land, they felt the effects of a ready market and good prices paid in coin to replace the earlier barter system.

The census figures for Utah through the first three decades provide an excellent source of information as well as material for study:

1850	11,380
1860	40,283
1870	86,786
1880	143,963

The phenomenal increase through the first twenty years was due largely to the Mormon proselyting program and their efficient immigration and colonization techniques. After 1869 the railroad was responsible for much of the non-Mormon increase. In 1880 the rural areas were still almost 100 percent Mormon, the non-Mormons being confined to Salt Lake City, Corinne, and Ogden. For the Jews, this was especially true.

In a study of the 1880 census, Mr. Nels Anderson found that 35 percent of the adults in Utah were foreign born, and that 55 percent of the total population were under twenty years of age. This gave the territory a young and diverse population, most of them united by the common tie of religion.

This period was filled with conflict between Mormons and Gentiles on many fronts: in the courts, in the market place, in the press. There seemed no middle ground. Each side saw no good in the other, and as the editors hurled invectives and insults back and forth, their constituents cheered or jeered.

GENERAL GROWTH AND EXPANSION

Although the transcontinental railroad missed Salt Lake City, the Mormon leaders at once set about to construct lines of their own. The first to be completed was in 1870, when the Utah Central connected Ogden and Salt Lake City. From this, branch lines were taken out to Coalville and other min-

---

[2]Nels Anderson, *Desert Saints, The Mormon Frontier in Utah,* [University of Chicago Press, 1942] p. 285.

ing districts. Utah Southern Railroad was built along the settlements south to Provo, and later extended to Milford, while Utah Northern connected Ogden with Soda Springs, Idaho, and later reached to Butte, Montana.

Following the bitterness between Brigham Young and the merchants in 1866, some few Jews moved away. Others maintained a central business in Salt Lake City, but opened small branch stores in other areas.

The Mormon cooperative, ZCMI, which seemed the most formidable competitor with Jewish business, opened its doors on March 10, 1869, in the Eagle Emporium, a block below Church headquarters. Here were sold dry goods, clothing, hats, caps, boots, and shoes. A second store in the old Constitution Building carried groceries, hardware, stoves, queens' ware (glazed English earthenware), and agricultural implements. On April 21, 1869, in the building formerly owned by N. S. Ransohoff, they opened the first retail department. Later that year their drugstore was opened.

Their cooperative program was carried to other areas, until by 1870 there were seventy-eight Mormon stores in the key towns of the Territory, and within ten years a total of one hundred and fifty.[3]

Also in 1873, Brigham Young tried to establish cooperatives in some phases of manufacturing and in cattle raising. For a time he advocated the "United Order," a communal form of living in which all shared alike in every phase of economic life. The only place where this ideal met with any degree of success was Orderville, a small community in Southern Utah. Except for this town, the United Order was completely dead by 1874, as were most of the other cooperative attempts. While ZCMI and its tributaries carried on a good business, there was plenty of opportunity for others in many fields. The Jewish merchants who remained had outstanding success.

---

[3]Leonard J. Arrington, *Great Basin Kingdom, an Economic History of the Latter-day Saints 1830-1900,* [Harvard University Press, 1958] p. 303.

The general prosperity was reflected in Salt Lake City as well. Its first streetcar line opened on June 20, 1872, with a mile-and-a-half track down Main Street, on which a heavy, old-fashioned car was pulled by horses. Soon this was extended to seven miles in various directions, with lighter cars drawn by mules carrying the traffic from the Warm Springs and Bath House, now Wasatch Springs Plunge, at Second West and Eighth North to the canyon quarry on the east.

In 1872 also the first gas lines were installed in some of the new homes and buildings; by 1873 the first street lights were put in.

Along with the streetcars and lights, an extensive building program was going on. In 1872 the Walker House, finished at a total cost of $160,000.00, was fine enough to grace any city. This year also Mr. L. Reggel of the Jewish community built a solid line of first-class apartments on Third South west of Main Street. This was called "Reggel's Row," and housed some well-to-do families and most of the government officials. Among them were some bitter anti-Mormons, so that later when feelings ran high between the parties, there were violent street fights in the area.

In 1871 the Liberal Party, organized February 9, 1870, in Corinne, became active in Salt Lake City. They nominated their candidate for Utah's one delegate for Congress and supported him with newspaper publicity and public meetings. Yet on election day he received only 105 votes as against the Mormon candidate's 13,068. Though the number of Liberals increased through the years, the Mormons always voted as a bloc, so that the ratio was always about five to one in their favor.

On July 4, 1871, two celebrations were held in Salt Lake City. The Mormon parade formed north of the Eagle Gate and marched past Brigham Young's home to the Tabernacle, while the Gentiles marched south on Main Street and east to the Liberal Institute on Third East just above the Presbyterian Church. This had elaborate floats and included the government officials, the business and mining men, and their families. On July 6 following, the *Tribune* expressed great satisfaction:

> The moral effect of the Liberal procession on the 4th will be mighty in Utah. While in numbers it was second to the Church turnout, in wealth, influence, and in the social standing of its participants it was equal to the display made by the Theocracy.
>
> The capital never witnessed a gathering, so large as this, free and independent of the Church. . . .[4]

For several years following, the Gentiles led in the celebration of Independence Day, while the Mormons emphasized the Twenty-Fourth.

CORINNE

With the coming of the railroad to Utah in 1869, many businessmen say the possibility for a settlement north on the Great Salt Lake, which would be near the Ogden terminal and could also take advantage of water travel for the transportation of goods. The location seemed ideal, the possibilities unlimited; the frictions in Salt Lake City would not trouble them here, for they would make this a wholly non-Mormon center.

The town, laid out in early February, 1869, by the Union Pacific Railroad Company, envisioned a great metropolis in which one whole block was set aside for a university and another for the Catholic Church. Within two weeks after the survey was completed, more than 500 tents and frame buildings were erected on the site, and the population numbered 1,500, all eager and optimistic. Named among the founders are General Patrick E. Connor, Hiram House, N. F. Ransohoff, Fox Diefendorf, W. T. Field, Charles Dahler, Nat Stein, and many others. Branch firms included the Bambergers, Kiesels, Guthries, George A. Lowe, Auerbachs, Walker Brothers, Scowcrofts, Lewis Jewelry, Tibbals, and others.

A large Opera House was erected in 1870 to match the huge warehouses on both sides of the railroad tracks. The

---

[4]Dwyer, *op. cit.,* p. 124.

city government, set up early that year, planned for extensive civic improvements. Built to establish water transportation, the "City of Corinne," a Mississippi River-type steamboat with three decks, was launched in the spring of 1870 at a cost of $45,000. This was also used as a pleasure boat.

Here also were built the first non-Mormon churches in Utah: the Episcopal Church was first, followed closely by the Methodist in 1871. While the first named is gone, the second still stands (1967). A Presbyterian Church building followed; in fact there were seven different church organizations here, though not all erected buildings. That there were Jews enough to hold a Passover celebration is shown by a reference in the *Corinne Daily Reporter* of Wednesday, April 24, 1872.

But the boom at Corinne was very soon gone. By 1874 the steamship had been sold at a lottery for tickets at $25.00 a chance, the drifting and tent population had drifted on, and most of the business houses had moved over to Ogden or back to Salt Lake City.[5]

The fact that the Gentile city of Corinne died on the vine so early was a source of great satisfaction to the Mormons. For had not Brother Brigham predicted that grass would grow in her streets, and her buildings would be torn down or moved to the surrounding towns to be used for barns and outhouses? They did not fail to note its fulfillment. That Brigham Young helped to fulfill his own prophecy by extending his Utah Northern Railroad far enough into Idaho to secure the freighting business from Idaho mines was, in their minds, all to his credit. To them, Corinne was "The City of the Un-Godly," whose press spilled venom, and whose people were determined to destroy the Mormon Church.

By the middle 1880s most of the Jews had left Corinne, attracted by mining booms in Nevada, Idaho, or Montana. While it lasted, the mining town was a place where money circulated freely, and a sober man with a legitimate trade

---

[5]Bernice Gibbs Anderson, *Corinne, City of the Un-Godly,* n. p. 1959. 19 p. Illus.

could usually garner his share. As the shafts played out, there was usually time to get away without suffering any great financial loss.

SALT LAKE CITY

In general, Mormon-Jewish relations continued friendly, with each respecting the beliefs of the other. While individual Jews might criticize or work against the Mormons, or generally vote against them, there was never any bitterness. On the other hand, Mormon children heard the stories of Abraham, Isaac, and Jacob, with emphasis upon Joseph who was sold into Egypt as their own lineal ancestor. His story was the favorite, although Samson facing an army with the jawbone of an ass, or David killing Goliath with a slingshot were competing ones. Hebrew customs persisted as Mormon customs, as, for example, having the men and women sit on opposite sides of the aisle in church as they did at that time.

A Jewish lecturer in 1870 drew a good audience at twenty-five cents each to hear a discussion of the Holy Land and its people. The press was cordial both in advertising and reporting the activity.[6]

As Orson Hyde had been called on a special mission to the Jews and to the Holy Land in 1842, so now thirty years later a second mission was ordered. This time the travelers would not have to solicit help en route or to earn their way, but would travel by train and steamship and live in comfortable hotels. The group who made the whole trip were Apostle George A. Smith, Lorenzo Snow, Eliza R. Snow, Feramorz Little, Paul A. Shettler, Clara S. Little, and Thomas Jennings.

They spent time in England, France, Venice, Constantinople, and all parts of the Holy Land, in places where they must travel by camelback or horseback, or where they must walk to the sites they set out to visit. Their instructions before leaving were that: "We wish you to dedicate and consecrate that land to the Lord, that it may be blessed with

[6]Rudolf Glanz, *Jew and Mormon, Historic Group Relations and Religious Outlook,* [New York, 1963] p. 290.

fruitfulness, preparatory to the return of the Jews in fulfillment of prophecy. . . ."

They left Salt Lake City on October 15, 1872, and returned July 8, 1873, to be met near Brigham City with a band and large company of friends. In the meantime their letters had appeared regularly in the *Deseret News, The Salt Lake Herald,* and the *Women's Exponent.* These were later collected and printed in a volume called *Correspondence of the Palestine Tourists.*[7]

Though the Jews might view these proceedings with scorn, Mormons were impressed. It was all clear evidence of their interest in the fortunes of God's Chosen People.

Later, in his Quarterly Magazine, Edward L. Tullidge wrote a long, romantic story called "Hadassah, the Jewess," with the subtitle "An historical story of the gathering of the Jews in Europe after their expulsion from Spain." Beginning in the January 1881 issue, where it was given thirty-seven pages, it continued through all four issues, with a total of 145 pages. It was clearly an attempt to idealize a Jewish woman. This was followed in Volume II by "Terese, the Jewish Maiden," which also ran through all four issues. Since Tullidge's reading public was largely Mormon, he must have felt certain of their interest in people of the Jewish faith.

After 1869 other religious denominations increased their activities in Utah, particularly in Salt Lake City, establishing schools, hospitals, and libraries in addition to churches. Through it all the *Tribune* especially kept a constant barrage against the Mormons.

In the exchange of vituperation, the Mormon press had spoken of the Gentiles as a set of marauding villains. In answer, Mr. Ovando J. Hollister, Collector of Internal Revenue for the Territory, compiled statistics. Mr. Hollister was a bitter anti-Mormon. Since his list includes the Jews, it is

---

[7]*Correspondence of Palestine Tourists, Comprising a Series of Letters by George A. Smith, Lorenzo Snow, Paul A. Shettler, and Eliza R. Snow of Utah. Mostly written while Travelling in Europe, Asia and Africa, in the years 1872 and 1873.* (S.L.C., 1875).

interesting to note their comparative numbers and wealth in 1882, as he presents it:

> They have established twenty-six church organizations with a membership of 968 in the Protestant churches (the Catholic population being about 3,000) costing with parsonages $246,100; fifty-four schools with 129 teachers and 3,821 pupils, having twenty-four buildings which cost $149,950; fifty-two Sunday Schools with 2,250 attendants and about 180 teachers; three hospitals (one large Catholic now being built) treating an average of 700 patients yearly, the grounds and buildings costing, estimating the one now building at $40,000 and including some ground purchased but not yet built upon $54,000; eight Masonic lodges, with 422 members and assets, including library of nearly 5,000 volumes, valued at $22,000; six Odd Fellows' lodges, with 309 members, and assets valued at $14,000; three Knights of Pythias lodges with 140 members, and assets valued at $2,000; one Hebrew congregation with fifty members, a Relief and Benevolent Society, with assets valued at $6,000; three Temples of Honor, with 125 members and assets valued at $1,500, and one Reform Club, with 200 members and assets of $50. — in all $495,600, given and raised by the Gentiles, almost within a decade, for religious, educational, charitable and benevolent purposes. . . .[8]

"And this," he concludes, "is the marauding, greedy, scalawag set, who are in Utah only in the hope of ultimately breaking up the Mormons, and getting their lands and houses for nothing."

JEWS IN BUSINESS AND PUBLIC LIFE

The Salt Lake City *Directory* published by Edward L. Sloan in 1874 gives some interesting facts about the Jewish houses of business. The total adds up to ninety-one Jewish establishments, more than three times the number listed in 1869. Of these ninety-one, fourteen had been in business continuously since 1867.

Using the same *Directory*, Dr. Rudolf Glanz makes the the following observations:

> There were already nine Jews among the twelve clothing firms in Salt Lake City . . . in comparison with 1867, when there

---

[8] John M. Coyner, *Handbook on Mormonism.* (Salt Lake City, 1882) p. 71.

were only four clothing firms there, all Jewish. . . . In drygoods
there were four Jews among eleven firms, in fancy goods three out
of five stores were Jewish. . . .

. . . And in 1874 a number of new Jewish names appeared; . . .
1 Cohen, 4 Cohn, 2 Levi, 3 Levy, as well as a number of German
Jewish and Eastern European Jewish names.[9]

There were also Jewish stores in Alta, Bingham, Ophir,
Provo, and Ogden. By 1878 many of the villages throughout
the state had one Jewish store: Adamsville, American Fork,
Minersville, Monroe, Morgan City, Sandy, and Scipio, and
as soon as the railroad reached the southern terminal at
Milford, one was established there.

Thus the fears of 1866 were not well founded. The
increase in population, the steady rise in the economy, and
the natural inclination for people to "shop" and trade where
they find the best bargains made competition possible.

Amid all the babble and recrimination between Mormon
and Gentile, the Jews went quietly about their business on
weekdays and attended their own Sabbath ceremonies with
as many of their members as cared to attend.

Jewish men were also active in public affairs. As has
been noted earlier, they were among the founders of both the
I.O.O.F. and the Masonic Lodges and were always ready to
support all programs for public improvement. In local government, Louis Cohn was elected a member of the city
council in 1874 and again in 1882. He later became fire
chief, and still later police commissioner. Samuel Kahn
was also made a city selectman in 1882, the same year that
Charles Popper was appointed sealer of weights and measures, and recorder of marks and brands.

When the Chamber of Commerce was organized in 1887,
Jews were among the charter members. The articles of incor-
poration were signed by J. E. Bamberger, M. H. Lipman,
Jacob Moritz, Fred Simon, Sam Levy, Henry Siegel, Joseph
Baumgarten, Emanuel Kahn, and Lewis Hyams. Fred H.
Auerbach and A. Hanauer were on the first board of direc-

---

[9]Glanz, *op. cit.,* pp. 240-241.

tors. In 1890 Fred Simon became vice-president, and insisted that any citizen who wished to join might do so regardless of his political affiliations or his religious beliefs. This was a departure, since both the I.O.O.F. and the Masons had excluded Mormons from their ranks.

THE JEWISH COMMUNITY (1869-1881)

That the Jewish people observed their Sabbath and Holy Days is evident from scattered sources before 1881; after that time a careful minute book was kept. Preceding this, their activities must be traced from notations in the current newspapers. Usually the *Tribune* made mention of the meetings, though the reporter seemed totally ignorant of the significance of the various rituals.

The following gives evidence of the 1871 activities:

To the Honorable Mayor and Members of the City
Council of the City of Salt Lake.

Gentlemen: At a meeting of the members of the temporary congregation of the Israelites of this city, J. W. Joelson, Esq., in the chair, the following resolutions were unanimously adopted and ordered spread upon the minutes:

Resolved that the thanks of the congregation are due, and are hereby expressed, to the honorable mayor and members of the city council of this city for the voluntary tender, free of charge, of one of their splendid halls for the observance of our religious services on the holidays just passed.

Resolved, that the Israelites of this city will ever gratefully remember the courtesy thus extended to them.

Resolved, that the foregoing be published in the *Deseret Evening News, Daily Herald* and *Daily Tribune.*

For the congregation,

A. M. Joelson, President
A. Levy, former President
Leopold Arnstein, Secretary

Salt Lake City, Sept. 26th, 1871[10]

---

[10]*Deseret News Weekly,* Sept. 26th, 1871; Also B. H. Roberts, *A Comprehensive History of the Church of Jesus Christ of Latter-day Saints, Century I,* (S.L.C., 1957) v. 5, p. 497.

This carries a special significance from the fact that on the Fourth of July preceding, as discussed earlier, the Mormons and Gentiles of Salt Lake City held separate celebrations. Since this gesture came unsolicited, it seems evident that the Mormon leaders wished to maintain the good will of the Jews.

The *Tribune* of January 30, 1872, reported that Jewish services had been held in the Richards Hall on Second South. The congregation was addressed by the Rev. Dr. Treichenberg, whom *The American Israelite* had called one of the well-learned rabbis in the country. Such a large audience attended that the reporter was surprised. "Jewish services are somewhat a novelty in Salt Lake," he added.

Shortly thereafter Passover was celebrated and the "ancient rite of circumcision of the Jewish Church was performed on the infant sons of Col. S. Kahn and Mr. Heilbronner by Rev. H. Lovenberg of Elko, Nevada. Fortune favored him again in September when he did like services for the sons of Mr. Rosenthal, Joseph Keller, and M. Myers."[11]

On October 2, 1872, the *Tribune* named the principal Jewish firms of the city which would be closed for the services as "Auerbach Bros., Theo Hollander, L. Cohn, Siegel Bros., Watters Bros., L. Reggel, C. Adler, D. Mendelsohn, H. Meyer, Mrs. Goldman, etc." The public was reminded that any person might attend the services if he remembered to keep his head covered. The services were held in the Liberal Institute and the crowd so large that the reporter was impelled to add, "indeed, we were not previously aware that so many inhabitants of this city are of Jewish extraction."

From this time on the Jewish congregation held most of its meetings in the Liberal Institute, which had been built by two of the Mormon apostates, William S. Godbe and E. L. T. Harrison. It was the gathering place for most non-Mormon activities — social, cultural, political, and religious.

During this time the Ladies' Hebrew Benevolent Society, which came to be the oldest of its kind in continuous activity

---

[11]Dr. Leon L. Watters, "Unpublished Notes," p. 7, University of Utah.

in the area, instituted an annual ball as a fund-raising activity
for charity. In 1872, after the announcement, they added that
"All persons wishing carriages for the Hebrew Benevolent
Ball will please call at Watters Brothers Jewelry store."

The New Year's festival of September 21, 1873, was
again held at the Liberal Institute, with readers the Reverend
Mr. Lovenberg (now from San Francisco), M. Levi, and
I. Watters. Very soon thereafter — or perhaps just before,
since no specific date is given — a group met and decided
upon a name for the organization:

> In the year 1873 the late Samuel Kahn, Louis Reggel, Isadore
> Morris, M. C. Phillips, Mr. Gansler, Isaac Woolf, and I. Watters
> assembled at the office of Mr. Gansler in this city and originated
> what is known as the Congregation B'nai Israel: its object was to
> organize a Hebrew Religious and Educational Society, but having
> no funds an appeal was made to the public for aid. A ball was
> given in the Salt Lake Theatre which netted $1,400, Isadore
> Morris selling 200 tickets, M. C. Phillips 150, while Mrs. Reggel
> and Mrs. Kahn, by their determined efforts, sold a considerable
> number more, and aided to make the affair a complete success.
> This was the starting point of the above congregation. . . .[12]

This was just another link in the chain of annual balls,
an activity which assured the membership a small nest egg
to meet emergencies.

In 1874 the officers of the two benevolent associations
were listed as: "President, Mrs. H. M. Cohen; vice-president,
Mrs. D. Mendelsohn; Secretary, Mrs. G. Selig; Treasurer,
Mrs. C. Goldman; Trustees, Mesdames J. M. Joelson, C.
Popper, and Hannack," for the ladies, and, "President,
C. Popper; vice-President, M. Hirschman; Secretary, M.
Wasserman; Treasurer, I. Watters; Trustees, Chas. Adler,
Sol. Levy, and L. Arnstein," for the gentlemen.[13]

The *Tribune* of April 16, 1876, carried the story of the
Jewish Passover, held in commemoration of the final deliver-
ance of the Israelites from more than four hundred years
of bondage in Egypt. The services were held at the home

---

[12]*Salt Lake Herald*, Sept. 13, 1885.
[13]*The Utah Gazetteer*, 1874, p. 174.

of Ichel Watters, with the host officiating. "The Jewish congregation of this city numbers some forty members," it concluded.

Through all the years the ladies kept their organizations active. It was they who in early 1877 visited Brigham Young and secured the deed to the cemetery lot which had been given them thirteen years before, but had never been made legal and final. Their foresight is evidenced by the fact that Brigham Young died in August following.

On July 1, 1877, Rabbi I. M. Wise arrived in Salt Lake City en route to the mining town of Eureka, Nevada, where he was to deliver a lecture. His diary has been published under the title, *By Parlor Car Across the Great American Desert*, and his description of Salt Lake City at that time is astute:

> . . . There are in this Territory about 140,000 Mormons and 10,000 Gentiles, including about 200 Israelites most of them in Salt Lake City. The valley is well cultivated by the Mormons, and the mines are worked by the Gentiles, who are also the principal merchants. The Mormons have cooperative stores, marked Z.C.M.I. i.e. Zion Cooperative Mercantile Institution, one of which, in Salt Lake City, is very extensive. The Mormons do not deal much with Gentiles, although they do some.
>
> Salt Lake City is laid out in regular squares on rolling ground . . . The houses are small, mostly one story high, and stand in large lots set with fruit trees. This is the place for excellent fruit — apples, pears, cherries, grapes, peaches, plums, and berries. There are but few elegant private houses here, and a small number of two-story brick houses. The United States Territorial Offices are in a hotel, and the Legislature meets in an insignificant building. The principal building is the Mormon Tabernacle, a building of one hundred and fifty by two hundred feet, in oval form, with an oval roof and ceiling. It looks outside like a railroad depot; heavy stone columns, twenty feet apart, common mason work, bear the huge roof of one hundred and fifty feet span. Inside it looks again like a railroad depot, with common benches and a gallery, a giant organ and a platform for the choir and the priests in the east. According to my calculation, it seats about six thousand persons, but the janitor says twelve thousand.
>
> Next to the tabernacle they are building a granite temple, one hundred by one hundred and fifty feet, which, if ever finished,

will be a magnificent cathedral. All this is surrounded by a wall twenty feet high, and presents the prospect of a citadel. The other official buildings, including the cottages and residence of President Brigham Young, all surrounded by a wall, look quite insignificant. Opposite, Brigham Young has built a new house, called the Emily [Amelia] Palace, which is a very elegant residence.

Among the other buildings are several hotels, banks, and the business squares on Main Street, which are like those of other large cities. Outside thereof the streets present rather a picture of self-complacent poverty. There are some very extensive business houses here. Among Israelites I saw several houses like Auerbach Bros., Siegel Bros., Kahn Bros., which are very large firms. Others, like Bamberger Bros., are engaged in mining, Charles Popper in wholesale butchery, and other business. All the Jews here are Gentiles. Some of them, like Louis Cohn and Colonel Kahn, are high and zealous Free Masons, Odd Fellows, etc. No Benai Berith lodge and no Jewish congregation yet in the Mormon land.

There are here four newspapers. *The Daily Tribune* is a Gentile paper, and fights Mormonism to the bitter end. One of its able editors is a nephew of Brigham Young. The *Tribune* is a very strong paper and stands perhaps at the head of the territorial press. There exists an implacable enmity between the two factions, and they charge each other with heinous crimes, which I could not discover, of course, being a mere visitor of a day. Mormonism is a social-political religious organization on a small scale, as popery was in the Middle Ages on a large scale. The Mormons must believe that Brigham Young is a veritable prophet, and his aids are all divinely inspired. Consequently his will is law and his command is God's command. Some Mormons actually believe Brigham Young after his death will be a god, and they believe in plurality of deities. There the danger lies. It is all one man's will. This one man is almighty and infallible. A good many men are better than their religion; so it is also among the Mormons. . . .

The Israelites of Salt Lake City treated us very courteously and hospitably. More anon. I.M.W.[14]

Activities evidently continued annually, for the *Salt Lake Tribune* of Tuesday morning, October 15, 1878, noted:

JEWISH ELECTION

At a meeting of the Jewish congregation held on Sunday last at the residence of Col. Kahn for the purpose of electing officers for the ensuing year, the following gentlemen were chosen: Presi-

---

[14]*The Pacific Historian,* Fall 1877, pp. 17-27.

dent, Col. Kahn; Vice-President, Isaac Woolf; Secretary and
Treasurer, M. C. Phillips; Board of Directors, Isadore Morris,
Louis Reggel, and N. S. Ransohoff.

Under direction of the new officers it is expected that the long
contemplated project of building a synagogue in this city will be
carried into effect. A piece of land has already been selected, one-
half block south of the Clift House, and at no distant date the
erection of a suitable structure will be begun. There are said to
be upwards of 150 Israelites in this city and the number is now
sufficiently large to justify the building of an edifice to be used
exclusively for religious purposes.

While this was not the piece of land they eventually
purchased, all these men were on the active roll when the
final decision was made and were instrumental in getting the
first building finished.

It sometimes happens that the fortunes of a people in
one area are vitally changed by conditions far removed from
them, or by global forces of which they are ignorant. Thus
all Jews in America, even those in far-off Utah, were affected
by developments in the year 1880. At that time a program of
oppression and persecution began in Russia, in which families
were taken without warning and transported eastward to the
desolation known as "The Pale." This along with growing
tensions from individual torture cases made the people eager
to escape.

When in 1880 the United States relaxed its immigration
laws and permitted — almost invited — newcomers from all
lands, there began a mass migration of Jews unparalleled in
history. They came not only singly and in families, but whole
villages were transplanted intact. Between 1880 and 1924,
when some restrictions were again made, the United States
had received more than a million and a half Jews from
Russia and the near East. They landed at Ellis Island and
fanned out into New York City and on into other industrial
centers, gradually making their way westward, until even
the most distant areas felt something of their impact. By the
turn of the century, the Jewish population in Utah had made
a definite increase.

Chapter Five

COOPERATION ... AND DISSENSION

No DOUBT THERE were some among the Jews in Utah who had for a long time hoped for a sanctuary, a gathering place where friends might meet for worship in the atmosphere of their own traditions. Gathered as they were from many and varied backgrounds, some were too engrossed in business, others too long divorced from the rituals to care. Nor was there any central organization to bind them together. Perhaps they were stimulated by the sight of other non-Mormon churches as evidence that members had pride in their own particular faith. Even such an item as that in the *Deseret News* in speaking of their Passover of 1874, with its thinly veiled sarcasm, might pique them to action:

> *Jewish Passover* — the Jewish feast of Passover commences tomorrow evening and lasts six days. It will be strictly observed in every part of the globe by orthodox Jews, of whom there is perhaps a few in this city . . . for were it otherwise, it is probable they would make a move in the direction of erecting a synagogue in which to conduct their religious exercizes. . . .[1]

In their historical background, the synagogue building had ceased to be of prime importance. Even the portable ark had been discarded; instead each carried his own scripture along with him. This discarding of the ark dated back to the exile to Babylonia in 586 B.C., during which time they met to read their scriptures together, memorizing some parts and interpreting it to each other.

> When Ezra returned with the Babylonia exiles, he resolved to make Scripture the basis of national life. Ascending a wooden dais, he opened the Torah scroll and read it before the gathering

---

[1]Glanz, *op. cit.,* p. 231.

for six hours, with interpreters explaining the passages to the people. . . . From that time forward, the emphasis shifted from the centrality of the priests to the people themselves; from the place of worship and instruction to the gathering of worshippers, the congregation itself. This was the *edah,* which the Talmud understands as a religious congregation of ten Jews, regardless of its location or its organization structure. Wherever they assembled — in private homes, at the city or water gate — it was their religious purpose, not the place of worship, which was now made paramount.[2]

Whatever their individual or combined motives, they began in early 1881 to consider the feasibility of erecting a building. On March 21 of that year the first Articles of Agreement for Incorporation of the "B'nai Israel" were filed. They are found in Record Book D, pp. 613-617, dated March 28, 1881, J. Malsh, Secretary.[3]

[2]Rosenberg, *op. cit.,* pp. 163-164.

[3]It seems appropriate to copy in full the minutes of the first two meetings in which the organization was effected:

On March 21, 1881, after due publicity, a group gathered to form an organization of the Jews in Salt Lake City. The twenty-three members elected Henry Siegel, president; Leopold Goldberg, vice-President; Julius Walsh, Secretary; Charles Popper, Treasurer; and Samuel Kahn, Alexander Stiefel, and Moses Hirschman as Board of Directors, all to serve until the first Monday in August, when the organization would be effected to serve for a year. The Articles of Incorporation were filed in the County Court of Salt Lake City on 28 March 1881 and entered in Record Book D, pp. 613-617. On March 31, $1,985.00 was turned over to the Treasurer, having been collected by the committee, E. Kahn and N. J. Ransohoff. Charles Popper and Leopold L. Goldberg were appointed to get water for the cemetery and to locate a building lot upon which a school house could be built.

At the gathering on August 1, 1881, the officers elected were Samuel Kahn, President; J. D. Farmer, vice-President; Charles Popper, Treasurer, and J. Malsh, Secretary, with Henry Siegel, M. C. Phillips, and A. Stiefel, directors. The Committee on Ways and Means were Samuel Kahn, M. C. Phillips, F. Auerbach, J. D. Farmer and L. Goldberg.

The membership at the end of the year, arranged alphabetically were:

M. S. Aachheim	Solomon Leebes	N. S. Ransohoff
Frederick Auerbach	J. Leviberg	L. Reggel
Samuel H. Auerbach	Sol. Levy	Henry Siegel
J. E. Bamberger	L. Levy	Sol. Siegel
Joseph Baumgarten	M. H. Lipman	Isadore Spitz
Leopold L. Baumgarten	Julius Malsh	M. D. Sternberg
Alex Cohen	I. Marks	Alexander Stiefel
J. D. Farmer	Isadore Morris	A. Watters
Leopold Goldberg	M. Moritz	Ischel Watters
M. Goldberg	Martin Nadel	Isaac Woolf
Aaron Greenwald	Samuel J. Nathan	Isadore Wurzburg
Emanuel Kahn	M. C. Phillips	Carl Young (Jung)
Samuel Kahn	Charles Popper	

In 1882 Louis Azames, Jacob Behrman, Herriman Bamberger, L. Hiam, Dr. M. Rockman and H. A. Van Prang were added.

On July 9 the Board resolved to purchase the 7½ x 10 rod lot on the corner of Third South and First West streets, owned by John Sharp and known as the "Tanner's Lot." The price was $2,600. Though the report said there were forty Jews in the congregation, only twenty-eight names appear on the list of members.

Even before the formal organization had been effected, the Ladies' Benevolent Society had planned a Grand Ball for February 22, 1881. This they wanted to far exceed anything they had done before, so the press notice read: "First prize $100.00 in gold coin; a gold watch valued at $100.00; a silver tea set; and a fine ring with a diamond, ruby and sapphire. They will be awarded for the best sustained characters, either male or female."

The next year on February 21, 1882, they held another masquerade ball without the elaborate prizes of before. Tickets were $5.00 each. The crowd must have filled the Salt Lake Theatre, for clear of expense they made $1,282.60 to add to the church fund.

Troubles began immediately. There was evidently some opposition to the choice of the lot in the first place, to the price, to the whole proceeding. After the first flush of enthusiasm, there were the usual squabbles, resignations, and re-instatements. Meetings became so heated that a resolution was passed to the effect that "no member shall speak more than once on any subject, except the mover of a motion, who shall have the right to close the argument." At one time it was suggested that the lot be sold and the project abandoned. This was effectively quashed by Mr. Charles Popper, who offered to purchase the property at a profit to the congregation of $1,000.

The group united at last in the determination to proceed with the building, employing Henry Monheim, a leading architect of the day, to draw the plans and specifications. These called for an expenditure of $4,500. After numerous problems of raising money, the building was ready for work on the interior. The group had grown in unity as the work progressed, until they took pride in their accomplishment. The *Tribune* of January 3, 1883 described it:

THE HEBREW SCHOOL

During the past season the Hebrew Society of the City has erected a fine brick schoolhouse on the northwest corner of First West and Third South Streets. The building is 33 x 83 feet, built of brick in one story, there being 20 feet between the floor and the ceiling. The interior is divided into three rooms, one being large, suitable for use as a recitation room, one for holding meetings in, while the other two will be study rooms. Over the vestibule, at the front entrance, a gallery has been provided and will be used by the choir and for a music stand, on such occasion as desired.

The rooms are nicely furnished, having heavy cornices in plaster around the ceilings and the woodwork and plastering are in excellent taste. The interior presents an attractive appearance.

This all the work of citizens who take a deep interest in education and have through their own and donations of others added this improvement to our City at a cost of $14,000. The furniture, consisting of seats, desks, an organ, fixtures, etc. will cost $1,500 and the iron fence will add $500. These articles of furniture have been selected and partly ordered. It is the intention of the Society to dedicate the house sometime in February, but the building will not be used for school purposes until April, by reason of it not being fully furnished.

The building was finally ready for dedication, the Scrolls of the Law installed, and the first service held in March 1883. Here Ichel Watters and Moses C. Phillips officiated. Alexander Stiefel blew the *shofar,* or ram's horn, here and for many years to come. Carl Young likewise led the choir upon this occasion and through the following years. This consisted of volunteer singers — or upon occasion, paid singers. Among them were Harry Joseph, Mamie Morris, Bertha Greenewald, and Joseph Oberndorfer.

The services were Orthodox, as they had been up to this time whenever the group met. The audience all wore their hats, some even removing their shoes to the displeasure of others more fastidious. To the youth who did not understand Hebrew, the Yom Kippur service seemed interminable, lasting as it did for most of the day.

Many of the congregation had come from Germany, where for years there had been adjustments made in the ritual. This group were insistent upon accepting some reforms, some adjustments in the proceedings. Others preferred to keep the service as they had always known it.

After much discussion and dissatisfaction, after a little more than a year of orthodox meetings, it was decided by a majority vote to employ a reform rabbi and use the *Minhag America* of Dr. Wise. Members of the board had some correspondence with Rabbi Leon Strauss of Bellville, Illinois, and on August 27, 1884, sent him a telegram inviting him to "Come on Minister's rate of fare." His salary had been set at $62.50 per month, to be paid in advance, with the understanding that if the services through the Holy Days proved satisfactory, the salary would be paid for one year in advance.

The price of seats was set at $10 to nonmembers, and it was "resolved that hats be removed during the services," a concession which was most unsatisfactory to many of the older members. These people could not sit through the watered-down ceremony with any feeling of satisfaction or reverence — the uncovered heads, the mixing of men, women, and children, the absence of the long Hebrew sections chanted in the familiar cadences, robbed the service of meaning for them. This they could not endure if it were free; certainly they would not pay for it.

Since many who felt this way were among those who had worked hardest on the building, and since all were vocal in protest or defense, the congregation decreased to such a point that Rabbi Strauss left two months before his year was up.

An orthodox member expressed in a long unsigned article in the Salt Lake *Herald* for September 13, 1885, his version of the history of the Hebrew organization up to this date "without malice or ill-feeling in the least respect for anyone whatever." He named the people who had initiated the organization and led in its growth to the erection of the school, to the building of which there was a most generous response.

They finally obtained a sufficient amount by annual entertainments to build the present building known as the Jewish Synagogue; when finished it was dedicated under the old strict Orthodox form and the services held therein up to last year were strictly under the old ritual, as now practiced by all the Orthodox congregations throughout the United States and elsewhere. . . . Through these new revelations discontent set in . . . and from a full attendance it dwindled down to a half-dozen devotees, so that the minister left two months before his engagement expired. . . .[4]

---

[4]Since the feeling between the two branches of Judaism in Salt Lake City was so strong, we include the complete statement of the minority. After having been so active in all the money-raising efforts, they must express their opinion.

THE HEBREW CONGREGATION

One of the Old Rituals Gives a History of B'nai Israel
To the Editor of the Herald:

As the Latter-day Judean Disciples saw fit to exhibit themselves in print, regarding the differences existing among the Hebrews in this city, and bring it to the public, one of the originators of the Congregation B'nai Israel, deeming it just to all concerned, gives a history of the origin and the manner in which the congregation was conducted up to the present date, so that the public may gain a full understanding of the subject.

In the year 1873 the late Samuel Kahn, Louis Reggel, Isadore Morris, M. C. Phillips, Mr. Gansler, Isaac Woolf and I. Watters, assembled at the office of Mr. Gansler in this city and originated what is known as Congregation B'nai Israel: its object was to organize a Hebrew Religious and Educational Society, but having no funds an appeal was made to the public for aid. A ball was given in the Salt Lake Theatre, which netted $1,400, Isadore Morris selling 200 tickets, M. C. Phillips 150, while Mrs. Reggel and Mrs. Kahn, by their determined efforts, sold a considerable number more, and aided to make the affair a complete success. This was the starting point of the above congregation.

A general subscription by our co-religionists and the public was next started for the purpose of raising sufficient funds for building and conducting a school and to this was a most generous response.

Everything went on flourishing under the following named gentlemen, who presided over the congregation at different times: Samuel Kahn, Charles Popper, Henry Siegel, and M. C. Phillips; during these different periods they finally succeeded in obtaining a sufficient amount by annual entertainments to build the present building known as the Jewish Synagogue; when finished it was dedicated under the old strict orthodox form and the services held therein up to the last year were strictly under the old ritual, as now practiced by all the orthodox congregations throughout the United States and elsewhere.

Everything went on harmoniously until Mr. Leon Strauss was engaged to conduct a Hebrew school and act as minister — the Latter-day Judean Disciples, with Mr. Leon Strauss then introduced the latest Judean revelations.

Through these new revelations, discontent set in among the disciples as well as the minister, and from a full attendance at the services, it dwindled to half a dozen devotees, so that the minister left two months before the time of his engagement expired. The holidays being near at hand, the vice-

Left now without a rabbi the leading men of the congregation met to see if they could work out a plan for the observance of the coming Holy Days. After two or three meetings they decided that it was impossible to cooperate, so in 1885 a few of the more ardent Orthodox withdrew entirely, leaving the others to plan according to their own desires.

For nearly four years the group was more or less disorganized, the schoolhouse was rented, and their own observances held under the leadership of private members. In 1885 Samuel Auerbach, always a peacemaker, persuaded them to return to the old ritual for the special days. But the breach could not be healed, and a small group of influential members withdrew entirely.

On June 16, 1889, the president reported that the Congregation had been offered $20,000 for their property, and the committee decided to accept it, glad, no doubt, to be free of the place which had been the subject of so much controversy. From the first, the building had been called a schoolhouse rather than a synagogue, perhaps because they felt that it was not large or beautiful enough to do credit to the title, perhaps because it was more filled with memories of dissension than of rich experiences shared.

Speaking of the development of the synagogue and its history from before the Christian Era, Stuart Rosenberg said:

> . . . the synagogue grew without plan or design, except that it must not try to imitate the temple in any way . . . there could be a *menorah* (candelabrum) but it could not be of seven branches, like that of the Temple, but only five, six, or eight. Even the music could not suggest the majesty of the Temple tones; instruments were prohibited. . . .

president called a meeting of his congregation for the purpose of making arrangements for the services of those holidays, which it was intended should be conducted by some of its members. At the meeting in August last a resolution was introduced to restore the old ritual, and this was carried with some omissions and amendments thereto. A committee for the purpose of arranging the ritual was appointed; but being unable to agree, the president called a meeting the following week, and after calling the meeting to order he announced that the proceedings of the preceding meeting were null and void, and of no effect; thereupon some of the members concluded to withdraw and hold services under the old Hebrew ritual; and this without malice or ill feeling in the least respect to anyone whatever.

[Salt Lake *Herald,* Sunday, September 13, 1885]

> In addition to being a house of prayer and instruction, the synagogue building also served as a public center where matters of public concern were aired. Courts of law met in its rooms, heard testimony, administered oaths and proclaimed judgments. Strangers . . . were welcomed into its hostel, the poor were invited to receive alms there, and community philanthropies were administered by its councils. . . .
>
> The strong emphasis placed by the synagogue upon the human needs of the congregation rather than upon the house in which it met was responsible for the fact that its architecture became a matter of indifference to the Jewish community . . . [It became] a community center, not an ecclesiastical stronghold. It served not only as a place of prayer and study, but as a house of meeting, a *Beth Knesset.*[5]

Charles E. Schulman expressed the meaning even more clearly. "Synagogue originally meant people, worshippers — a consecrated spot where people met to pray. God dwells among people, not in a place."[6]

But this was far back in the first century after Christ, and in the far eastern lands. In the United States of America in 1889 it was a matter of concern that this place of worship be beautiful, dignified, and distinctive, so no one would mistake it for a Christian meetinghouse on the one hand or an ordinary schoolhouse on the other.

So the year 1889 ended on a high note for the congregation of B'nai Israel. The committee had purchased a very desirable site for their new synagogue, and had enough money to proceed at once with building. They also employed a new rabbi, Dr. Heiman J. Elkin, who arrived in late September and at once began activities in the rented Josephite [Reorganized LDS] Chapel on East Second South Street. Rabbi Elkin had just been graduated from the Hebrew Union College that year, so was well trained in the Reform ritual. Their future looked bright.

In contrast, the year 1889 found the fortunes of the Mormon community at low ebb. Most of their cooperatives

---

[5]Rosenberg,*op. cit.,* pp. 165-166.
[6]Schulman *op. cit.* pp. 203.

had failed; federal laws had been passed making the practice of polygamy a national offense.

In order to avoid arrest and trouble, Mormon leaders initiated a new colonizing program in which between 1876 and 1879 "at least a hundred" new settlements were founded outside Utah: in Arizona, New Mexico, Nevada, Colorado, Idaho, and Wyoming. Organized groups were sent in the same pattern which had been used in the early colonization. As the "poly raids" increased in severity, many Mormons moved on to Mexico or to Canada, leaving their holdings for sale. By 1887 the minority report of the Utah commission wrote:

> This year, in the real estate excitement in Utah . . . the Mormons freely sold their city lots and other real estate to Gentiles as well as to others . . . and this notwithstanding . . . that the Mormon Church leaders have . . . remonstrated against their people selling their land to Gentiles. This is another strong evidence of the spirit among the monogamous Mormons . . . to repudiate the authority of the Church leaders, in secular and civil affairs. . . .[7]

This was not in repudiation of authority, but submission to it.

The Edmunds Act passed in 1882 put teeth into the earlier 1862 Act, and began a concerted raid on polygamy, which resulted in 1,300 convictions between 1884 and 1893.[8] By 1885 all the Mormon leaders had left the country or were in seclusion or in prison. On July 25, 1887, President John Taylor died while in hiding. He was succeeded by Wilford Woodruff, who was hiding in the St. George area. With the leading men on all levels out of circulation, business stagnated, and there was widespread suffering and misery.

The Edmunds-Tucker Act of February 19, 1887, dissolved the Mormon Church, confiscated all its property, including the Temple Block, disfranchised all members, and forbade even the printing of circulars or books or pamphlets.

---

[7]Dwyer, op. cit., p. 229.
[8]B. H. Roberts, Comp. Hist., v. 6: 211.

It is worthy of note that the Jews did not join in the
campaign of persecution. Though they did not approve the
practice of polygamy, they recognized it as a tenet of faith
in the Mormon theology, and did not make it a point of
friction in their dealings. Whether or not a man had one
wife or two or three did not matter so much as whether he
met his obligations promptly and whether he was fair and
honorable in his business dealings. Matters of conscience were
private matters.

A few prominent Jews were vocal in defense of the
Mormon right to live their religion, because they knew that
their own people for centuries had been driven and persecuted and executed for practicing theirs.

One of these was Fred Simon, who insisted that Mormons
be admitted to the Chamber of Commerce of which he was
president, and who signed a petition to the United States
Congress asking that they not pass a bill denying a man his
franchise to vote because of his religious convictions. He also
wrote a long letter to Governor Caleb W. West protesting,
saying that "such an argument is making a precedent so
far-reaching that it can only terminate by gradually disfran-
chising the Catholic for believing too much and the Infidel
for believing too little."

Of him the Mormon historian, Orson F. Whitney, wrote:
"But the heart of this man beat not only for family, kindred,
and immediate friends; it throbbed with good will for the
entire community. His purse, credit, and influence could
always be counted upon in aid of any benevolent and worthy
enterprise."[9]

Another member of the Jewish community who went
out actively in defense of the Mormons was Isadore Morris.
He circulated a petition among the influential non-Mormon
citizens of Salt Lake and Davis Counties, asking President
Cleveland to grant a pardon to Bishop William R. Smith.
He went to Washington with the petition and "importuned
the President and the statesmen who were most concerned

---

[9]Orson F. Whitney, *History of Utah* (Salt Lake City, 1904) v. IV: 305.

with special legislation on Utah and polygamy, including Senator Edmunds. They were sensibly moved . . . and a presidential pardon was signed for the bishop. The latter was escorted from the penitentiary by his friend, Isadore Morris.''[10]

[10]Edward W. Tullidge, *op. cit.,* V. II, p. 293.

Chapter Six

A JEWISH TEMPLE IS BUILT

THE DIFFICULTIES which divided the Jewish congregation of Utah in 1885 and caused Isadore Morris and others to withdraw and set up their traditional worship in private homes were the same that had been plaguing similar groups in all parts of the United States. Nor were they peculiar alone to the Hebrew people. Christian denominations were all trying to adjust their ancient interpretations to the new scientific discoveries. The telescope had greatly enlarged the heavens and shown this earth to be not the center of the universe, but an infinitesimal speck in it.

Darwin's theory of the evolution of life challenged the story of the Creation, while modern methods of measuring the age of various fossils made ridiculous the seven twenty-four-hour-days span of Creation. Nor did the "thousand years are as a day with God" explanation help. In this, Christians and Jews alike were forced to look again and with deeper insight into their Scriptures.

The Reform movement had taken an early start in the United States. According to Rosenberg:

> The very first attempt at Reform in America came about in 1824 in Charleston, South Carolina, when a group of forty-seven members of that city's congregation petitioned for certain changes in the synagogue ritual. . . . they requested that . . . the "principal parts [of the Jewish service] and, if possible, all that is read in Hebrew, should also be read in English . . . so as to enable every member of the congregation fully to understand each part of the service. When their memorial was rejected . . . they founded a new group, The Reformed Society of Israelites. . . .[1]

---

[1]Rosenberg, *op. cit.*, p. 191.

Although this early congregation could not maintain itself for lack of competent leadership, it did set a precedent by which groups in other areas made adaptations, as Benjamin II observed as he traveled among his people in the eastern United States. Always he noted whether the service was in German, Polish, Portuguese, Bavarian, or any language other than Hebrew, and he mentioned any cases where the ritual had been modified.

Since Benjamin II gives the first over-all picture of the Hebrew congregations in the United States, it seems appropriate here to insert a brief summary:

> On October 3, 1859, . . . I reached Philadelphia. . . . There are seven Jewish congregations . . . : Mikveh Israel (Portuguese ritual) was founded in 1782. . . . The president of the congregation is Abraham Hart. The cantor and preacher is Sabato Morais, a native of Livorno. . . . Until six years ago, Isaac Lesser, editor of *The Occident,* was the minister. At that time there was a good deal of dissension in the congregation and it divided into two congregations. The seceding group formed a new congregation in 1856 — Bethel-El Emeth. . . .Neuhaus is the president. The vice-president is David Scholes. The third member of the board . . . is Alfred Jonas. Isaac Lesser, mentioned above, is the cantor and preacher. . . .
>
> The third congregation Rodeph Shalom, has a German ritual. It was founded in 1802. . . . Samuel Adler is president of this congregation: the vice-president, Solomon Teller; the cantor, Isidor Frankel. . . .
>
> The fourth congregation, Beth Israel, was founded in 1849. . . . At the head of it are Benjamin Abeles and S. Ezekiel; the cantor and preacher is Gabriel Pape. The ritual is Polish.
>
> The fifth congregation, Bene Israel, was founded in 1847. . . . The members are Netherlanders.
>
> The sixth congregation, Adath Israel, was just recently organized. At the head of it is M. Blumenthal. . . . The ritual is German.
>
> The seventh congregation, Keneseth Israel, is Reform. It was founded in 1847. . . . Abraham Klapper is the head of it. . . . Dr. David Einhorn, editor of *Sinai,* occupies the post of preacher. . . .[2]
>
> On December 8, 1859 . . . reached Baltimore. This is the first city I visited in America that had slaves. There are six Jewish congregations.

---

[2]Benjamin II, *op. cit.,* pp. 302-303.

(1) Nidhe Israel, founded in 1823. . . . The president is B. Himmelreich and the preacher Dr. H. Hochheimer, . . . native of Bavaria.

(2) Aden Street congregation founded in 1845 . . . The president is M. Wiesenfeld. The cantor has been educated as a musician and has introduced choral singing.

(3) Howard Street congregation founded in 1845.

(4) Har Sinai is a Reform congregation. . . . Dr. David Einhorn . . . was the preacher. His efforts were successful in inducing the members of his congregation to keep their places of business closed on the Sabbath.

(5) Key Street congregation, founded in 1852. . . . Its ritual is Polish.

(6) Oheb Shalom, recently founded. . . . sent to Hungary for its preacher — Dr. Szold.

In addition, there is a small congregation whose rabbi is Abraham Reiss, a very pious man with a wealth of talmudic learning. . . .[3]

In the same way Benjamin II reported one congregation in Washington, D.C., founded in 1851, and having a school in which both English and German were taught.

Richmond, Virginia, had three Jewish congregations, all well off. In the first, founded in 1791, the ritual was Portuguese. The second, founded in 1841, had a German ritual, and the third, with a Polish ritual, did not yet have its own synagogue. There was not a Jew in the city in need of charitable assistance.[4]

According to the visitor Cincinnati was then a center of Jewish activity with six congregations among some of which was a yeasty atmosphere of innovation and experimentation:

(1) Bene Israel, founded in 1819. . . . A Polish ritual . . . in all about 200. The congregation . . . is Orthodox; but it has introduced a choir of men and women. Education is taken care of by a fairly good elementary school. The rabbi is D. M. Lilienthal. A delightful community festival was recently introduced by this congregation . . . members . . . send all sorts of food and fruit to the schoolhouse. . . . Then they assemble for a community meal

---

[3]*Ibid.,* p. 305.
[4]*Ibid.,* p. 306.

. . . animated by general conversation and at which all is cheerfulness and gaiety. . . .[5]

(2) Bene Yeshurun, founded in . . . 1840 . . . its synagogue . . . built in 1845. The congregation is well off and consists of 220 German members. . . . They introduced some innovations and since . . . have been called a Reform congregation. They have an organ and a choir . . . , but men and women . . . do not sit together as in other Reform congregations. . . . Dr. I. M. Wise arranged a new Hebrew prayer-book with the title *Minhag America*. It is a shorter version, and those parts . . . are left out that deal with sacrifices and the Messiah. . . . Only the first section . . . has appeared. . . .

Their president is Abraham Aub. They have the best Jewish elementary school in all America . . . under the direction of Dr. Wise. It has two hundred pupils, girls as well as boys. . . .

The above two congregations have a cemetery in common.

(3) Shearith Israel. The members of this congregation formerly belonged to Bene Israel, but withdrew. . . . It has about seventy members and follows a strictly orthodox German ritual. Its president is Nathan Malster. . . .[6]

(4) Adath Israel, founded in 1850, . . . has thirty-five members and follows a Polish ritual. It . . . rents a house for its services.

(5) Beth Hamedrash has fifteen members, some German and some Polish. The ritual is German.

(6) Ahabath Achim (German ritual), founded in . . . 1848, has its services on the other side of the canal that flows through the city. About 120 members belong to it. The congregation has its own cemetery.[7]

Benjamin II clearly was not in sympathy with the Reform movement, for he noted that the *Minhag America,* still incomplete, left untouched the prayers for the New Year and the Day of Atonement so that the old ritual was still in use. But by 1875 the book was finished and the Hebrew Union College was founded in Cincinnati for the purpose of training young rabbis in the expression of Judaism according to American ways.

In an attempt to unify and consolidate the Reform policies, a conference was called in Pittsburgh in November 1885

---

[5]*Ibid.,* p. 309.
[6]*Ibid.,* p. 310.
[7]*Ibid.,* p. 311.

by Dr. Kaufman Kohler. They drew up a definitive statement of their principles and a platform which declared that:

> Judaism presents the highest conception of the "God-idea"; it spoke of the "consecration of the Jewish people to its mission as the priest of the one God" and claimed "that the modern discoveries of scientific researches in the domain of nature and history are not antagonistic to the doctrines of Judaism" . . . "and to maintain only such ceremonies as elevate and sanctify our lives." Finally, they proclaimed, "in full accord with the spirit of Mosaic legislation which strives to regulate the relation between rich and poor, we deem it our duty to participate in the great task of modern times, to solve on the basis of justice and righteousness the problems presented by the contrasts and evils of the present organization of society."[8]

Before this time many congregations in the United States had accepted the practice that what was read in Hebrew should also be read in English, that the congregation might comprehend it, for as they wished to be Americans in other phases of life so they wished to be American in their worship.

It was not so difficult to accept the general philosophy of the One God and the duties attending the administering of charity, but to decide which of the ceremonies were those designed "to elevate and sanctify our lives" was extremely difficult. Though the Reform congregations in Cincinnati and other large centers set up their ceremonies, it remained for the local groups to adapt their own. Such questions as whether or not to wear the head covering and the prayer shawls, to seat the men and women apart or together, to carry the Torah scrolls through the audience, became major points of conflict. These, as well as any basic modification of doctrine caused the first split in Utah in 1885. The division cleared the air and enabled both factions to proceed in harmony to work toward religious observances satisfying to each.

Thus it was that at the close of the year 1889 the retiring president, Moses C. Phillips, reported that conditions in the community were excellent: the members had reached a period

---

[8]Rosenberg, *op. cit.*, pp. 193-194.

of good feeling, of renewed confidence, and financial security.
The sale of the old property for a substantial sum, the engagement of a permanent ordained rabbi, and the prospect of
moving ahead promptly on a new building all served to
bolster the morale. Also, he reported, hydrants had been
installed at the cemetery and water was now available.

In the hearts of the people the cemetery was almost
as important as the temple. Here for twenty-five years they
had buried their dead on dry, sterile soil, with no care for
the graves except such as was given by the individual families
of the deceased. Some of these had planted shrubs though
they must carry water to keep them alive. Now all could
rejoice in the prospect of grass and flowers and trees beneath
which their loved ones might rest.

A careful examination of the burial records up to this
time shows something of the size and general health of the
Jewish community of Salt Lake City. Perhaps the whole
Utah area should be included, for whenever possible Jewish
people brought their dead here.

Up to 1890 there had been only thirty-eight recorded
burials, eight of whom were children younger than five years
of age. No deaths of children between eight and eleven years
were recorded, but of youths between eleven and twenty, six
had died. Only three persons could be counted as old: Sarah
Watters, buried in 1878, was 85; Rosetta Levisburg, buried in
1881, was 70; Louis Wursburg, buried in 1887, was 74 years
old. Of the total, twenty-six were males and twelve were
females. This bears out the fact that there were in most new
areas in America more Jewish young men than women.[9]

New officers elected in the Congregation B'nai Israel in
1890 were Leopold Goldberg, president, Alexander Cohn,
vice-president, Emanuel Kahn, treasurer, and Julius Walsh,
secretary. The Auerbach brothers announced that their
nephew from Germany, Philip Meyer, would draw the plans
for the new temple and present them without charge. He
was the government architect under the Kaiser in Germany,

[9]Watters, *op. cit.*, pp. 177-178.

and would produce a replica of the great synagogue in Berlin. His parents, Gustav Meyer and Rosa Auerbach Meyer, lived in Salt Lake City. That this young man, years later, should become a victim of the Hitler holocaust would further hallow the building in the hearts of its members.[10]

For four years the congregation had been dependent upon its membership for reading the scriptures on the Sabbath and for carrying on the services for the Holy Days. Now in 1889 they were all pleased with their new rabbi, Heiman J. Elkin, who arrived in September, 1889, having just graduated from the Hebrew Union College in Cincinnati the previous June. Trained in the Reform ritual, the young man held services at the Reorganized LDS Church on East Second South Street during the time the new temple was being constructed. Here the first class of pupils was confirmed.[11]

The cornerstone of the new temple on the east side of Fourth East between Second and Third South Streets was laid on Friday, September 26th, 1890, Tishri 12th. 5651. The *Tribune* describes the edifice to be erected as follows:

"The building is remarkable from the fact of its being a facsimile in miniature of the great temple in Berlin, Germany. The size is 55 x 112 feet, including the vestibule. There will be two wings which will seat 500 people. A fourteen-foot gallery over the chancel will accommodate the $3,500.00 organ and the choir. The interior height is forty feet, while toward the rear of the edifice towers a mosque-like dome eighty-eight feet in the air.

"The front is cut Kyune stone, the sides and rear being pressed brick, and the style is Moorish. The cost of the Temple complete will be $37,500.00. The supervising architect is Henry Monheim, the contractors Joy & Black. The building will be an ornament to the city.

"The cornerstone, as is usual with all synagogues, was placed on the northeast corner of the building, a custom dating

---

[10]Philip Meyer died October 15, 1943, at the Theresienstadt Concentration Camp; his wife on July 15, 1946. Records of Myrtle Friedman, Hailey, Idaho.
[11]Watters, *op. cit.*, p. 83.

back from the earliest times. It was neatly cut out in the centre for the 10 x 14-inch tin box which held the souvenirs or mementos of the day. In it were copies of the *Tribune, Herald, News,* and *Times* of the previous day, *Salt Lake Stock Exchange Journal, Salt Lake Advertiser, American Israelite, Cincinnati Free Press,* Cincinnati *Deborah;* also the constitution and by-laws of the Congregation B'nai Israel, a list of officers and members of the congregation, program of the musical exercises of the Yom Kippur, names of members of the choir; photographs of Dr. I. M. Wise, the pioneer Rabbi, of Rabbi Heiman Elkin, of Mrs. Fanny Brooks, the first Hebrew woman in Utah, who came here in 1853; applications for membership and by-laws of the Ladies' Hebrew Benevolent Association of Salt Lake City.

"In back of the Temple is to be built a fine, large parochial school where Hebrews can send their children."

The *Tribune* failed to mention that coins and postage stamps were also deposited in the cornerstone, as it also failed to capture the spirit of reverent rejoicing that characterized the group.

For all its early enthusiasm the Congregation B'nai Israel found that erecting a temple took time and sacrifice. The business of raising the necessary money became so discouraging that the secretary was constrained to enter in his permanent record an unusual complaint:

> In 1889 dues of $25 a year for married men and $10 for single persons were decided upon. Throughout the entire history of the Congregations, difficulties were experienced in collecting dues. Members were dropped for non-payment, generally when the affairs of the Congregation were at a low ebb, and re-instated when its affairs were flourishing. The offenders were not confined to the less affluent, for even the wealthiest and most prominent, including a former president, were remiss. It was, regrettably, a practice of some members to make commitments of subscriptions of liberal size during meetings when audiences were present and later to reneigh [sic] when the treasurer or a committee member called to collect.[12]

---

[12]Minute Book of B'nai Israel Congregation. Entries by date. Microfilm on file.

In spite of difficulties work on the temple did proceed, watched with interest by the general public and reported upon occasionally by the press. The day after its dedication, July 12, 1891, the non-Mormon papers of Salt Lake City vied with each other in their reports, all being lavish in their praise. The *Tribune* gave the longest over-all account.

The dedication services of the new Jewish Temple on Fourth East street were held yesterday morning before an audience which filled the entire house. Among the audience were many prominent non-Jews, including Governor [Arthur] Thomas, Judge [Charles C.] Goodwin, . . . C. W. Lyman and others. The services lasted from 10 A.M. until nearly 1 P.M., and were very impressive and interesting so that the length was not noticed.

The entire interior was attractively decorated with flowers and plants of every kind, the chancel or pulpit platform being fairly surrounded with large potted plants. The general appearance . . . is bright and cheerful; . . . an air of quiet elegance pervading the place, and a more attractive place of worship does not exist in the west. . . .

The musical part was of unusual excellence. It was under the conductorship of Prof. Krouse . . . a picked orchestra of eighteen performers with the following as vocalists in the choir: Mrs. A. Rowe, Mrs. Jos. Siegel, Miss Ada Strauss, sopranos; Mrs. Jack Leviburg, Miss M. Watson, contraltos; Mr. J. P. Wilson, Mr. F. Vollmer, Mr. F. Bennett, tenors; Mr. D. Hirschler, Mr. J. Obendorfer, bassos. . . . The organ is one of the finest in the west. . . .

Those on the rostrum were Rabbis Elkin and Stern, Dr. Schreiber of Little Rock, Arkansas, Simon Bamberger, F. H. Auerbach, S. H. Auerbach, Alex Cohn, Joseph Simon, and the scroll bearers, Ichel Watters and A. Levi.

Rabbi Elkins invoked the blessings of Almighty God for the temple . . . The Jews . . . had been persecuted for centuries, but through them the knowledge of the true God will be disseminated to all the nations of the earth . . . this grand and splendid structure . . . dedicated to His honor and glory.

. . . two sweet little girls, Helen Bamberger, daughter of Simon Bamberger, and Harriet Cohn, daughter of Alex Cohn, presented the keys to the building. . . . Mr. Bamberger received the keys . . . and recounted something of the history connected with the building . . . thanked everybody who had in any manner assisted. . . . Particular credit . . . should be given to Mr. Philip Meyer . . . [who] designed the temple after the one in Berlin.

. . . To the ladies who had raised the money for the stained glass windows and whose fair hands had fashioned and arranged the decorations and had embroidered the curtains in Hebrew designs. . . . For the perpetually burning lamp he thanked Mrs. Sam Lesser, whose husband now deceased, was a pioneer Hebrew in Utah. . . .

Mr. Bamberger then handed the keys to Mr. Siegel, the president of the congregation. . . .

The next ceremony was the reading of the law in Hebrew, which was done by I. Watters, Rabbis Elkin and Stern helping to unroll the scroll.

Rabbi Stern's address was one of the most

POETIC AND PATRIOTIC SERMONS

ever delivered in this city. It was so far outside the beaten track as to be refreshing. It was short, cogent, and conclusive. He said:

"This finished temple and this congregation might inspire any speaker. How beautiful it is! One might be led to exclaim, 'How beautiful are thy tents, O Jacob! and how beautiful are thy temples, Oh Israel!' And this one — what a credit to those who have reared it. Did not David sing, the heavens declare the glory of God. This temple is only an earnest pioneer of the others that are to come. Man himself is a temple to which this is nothing. The bodily temple should be consecrated to God. There is another grand temple, which if properly built, was the labor of a man's whole life. It was the temple of home. It was an American who sang "Home, Sweet Home." Our home temple should be presided over by the father and mother as priests whose mission should be the guiding of their children's feet in righteous paths. The next temple is that of the school where our children are prepared for the battle of life. Do not neglect to make that a perfect structure, for it is there that our children are fitted to become good fathers, mothers and citizens. Then, your business places and trading marts, let them also be temples. If you do not, you ought to, for every act of every man's life should be a sermon. Words may lie, but acts stand for themselves — they always tell the truth.

"There is another temple which embraces all those mentioned before. I fear there may be some who think it should not be mentioned here: it is the temple of good government. We must do all we can to establish this, we cannot delegate this responsibility. We must not think we have done our duty when we have paid our taxes. A man who stays home from an election is a bad man, for he shirks the responsibility of securing good government for his home and his children. Therefore our country must be our temple.

Our large cities are much misgoverned because we do not do our political duty. If we build all the other temples on a firm rock, the last one will rear itself — it will be that grand temple in which will be assembled the people of all the earth worshipping one God."

The scripture lesson was then read by Mr. Fred Auerbach, the selection being I Kings viii Chapter, after which came the sermon of Rabbi Elkins, who retires next month when Rabbi Stern takes his place. He

WELCOMED THE CONGREGATION

as children of the living God. "Ye whose hearts are conjuring up hopes of the future I again welcome you. Israel today sends another greeting to the world. Blessed is everyone who cometh to this house in the name of the Lord. To you, my friends, who many times and oft have tried to show that Israel's hopes, aims and ambitions are identical with those of the rest of the world, I give my greetings. To you, my fellow citizens, it may appear that in extending you this invitation we are boastful, but it is not so. It implies that Israel's God is your God. The existence of Israel only shows that the idea of the Infinite having an abode in us all is the correct one, and that is the rule which renders the reign of justice supreme in the world. For God has said my house shall be a house of prayer for all nations. It is for the inmate of the palatial home and the hovel alike. All of the beauties of the universe were as deep as the ocean, as high as yonder peaks, and no one can realize the joy of man until he realizes the hope of that man. Let us keep on from day to day and from year to year, leaving the consequences to Him who has ruled from the beginning.

"Israel has had and still possesses happy hopes. Remember, fellow citizens, that this temple stands for your own hopes. Happiness is its end and aim of all our lives. May this temple prove to be a blessing to us all."

At the conclusion of the sermon Madame Rowe sang "HEAR YE, ISRAEL" from Mendelssohn; prayer was offered by Rabbi Stern, the dedication chorus was sung by the choir, the benediction was pronounced and the audience dispersed to the music of the postlude (Schubert) by the orchestra and organ.[13]

The Salt Lake *Times* for July 13, 1891, gave special emphasis to the music of the dedicatory program under a large subtitle "MOST IMPRESSIVE CEREMONIES, The

---

[13]For condensations of the program see Watters, pp. 85-86; *The American Israelite,* July, 1891; *Jewish Messenger,* v. LXX No. 5, July 23, 1891.

Beautiful House is Consecrated to the Worship of God With Sermon and With Song." It continues:

> Yesterday was made memorable to the Jewish people of this city by the dedication of their new temple. Services were held for the first time in the synagogue on Fourth East Street. In every sense the event was a successful one — the addresses, the music and the sermon being beautiful and interesting. The music, particularly, was grand, and the programme well arranged. So perfect was the arrangement of everything that the Jewish people may well feel a thrill of pride over the services which consecrated their new temple to the worship of God.

> Invitations had been extended to the prominent men of the city and were generally responded to. The interior of the temple was most beautiful. Soft lights from the jets burning in all the chandeliers filled every nook and corner like the beams from the Aureole. Every sense was intoxicated with the perfume of flowers and of palms which had been wreathed and banked in every point of vantage. The yellow sunlight poured through the stained glass windows blending with that which came from the gas jets and beautifying every face in the audience.

> Long before the time set for the services to begin many feet were turned in the direction of Fourth East street, so that when the music of THE TRIUMPHAL MARCH was played by the orchestra and organ every seat was filled and many were standing. To the music of this grand conception of "Costo's," the officers of the congregation entered the main door of the temple and were followed by the children of the Sunday School, most of whom were dressed in white. The officers of the church marched up the center aisle and took seats within the chancel rail, while the children were assigned seats on the sides. Those in the chancel were: Rabbis Elkin and Stern, Dr. Schreiber of Little Rock, Arkansas, Simon Bamberger, F. H. Auerbach, S. H. Auerbach, Alex Cohn, E. Kahn, H. Bamberger, Henry Siegel, Henry Cohn, Joseph Simon and the scroll-bearers, I. Watters and A. Levy.

> The voices for the occasion were well selected, each vocalist being an artist in his or her line.

> The choir was accompanied by an orchestra of twelve pieces and organ, conducted by Professor P. Krouse. The programme opened by the rendition of "Triumphal March," which was followed by trio and chorus by Gounod, Mrs. J. Siegel taking the solo part. Her clear, high soprano rang out with charming and pleasing effect above the strains of music. The next soloist, Mr. Hirschler, sang "Show Me, Almighty" by Mendelssohn very creditably, his

voice being a superb baritone. After the address of the president of the congregation, Mr. Cohn, "Hymn of Praise" composed by Gounod was sung by Dr. Wilson and the choir, the doctor singing the tenor solo and presiding the Choral part. Dr. Wilson was in excellent voice and he being the tenor soloist par excellence of our city, his effort was much enjoyed. The orchestra next accompanied Mrs. Jack Leviburg who has a rich contralto voice in "Samson and Delilah," her voice showing the careful training and cultivation which she has received in New York during the past five years. Mrs. Leviburg having been an old time favorite in Salt Lake musical circles, her reappearance on this occasion was especially pleasing and gratifying to her former friends. Following Dr. Elkins' thoughtful discourse, Mme. Alberta Rowe sang "Hear ye, Israel," one of Mendelssohn's thoroughly artistic solos. Mrs. Rowe was in excellent voice and her rendition of the foregoing was most happy, her clear, rich soprano notes bringing out the fine acoustic properties of the new temple and winning for herself new laurels.

The "Dedication Chorus" by Hayden, ending the musical part of the programme, was magnificently executed by choir, orchestra and organ.

The decided success of the music was due greatly to Professor Krouse who spared neither time nor skill to make each number the best that has ever been given in any church affair as yet in Salt Lake City.

The great success of these dedicatory services was a source of satisfaction to Jewish congregations throughout the United States. Indeed, it would seem that with such an initiation the work should grow apace, but even here were the seeds of dissension. The *Tribune* comment that during the meeting Rabbis Elkin and Stern sat side by side on the stand and that "Rabbi Elkin . . . retires next month when Rabbi Stern takes his place," implied that the resignation was voluntary and that all was well in the new appointment. Yet the Minute Book shows that five weeks earlier, "Rabbi Elkin was notified that his contract would not be renewed and he was given a five weeks' vacation."

His successor, Rabbi Jacob Ludwig Stern, resigned suddenly before his first month was out. Both events indicate conflicts and power-pulls in the congregation.

The officers acted promptly, however, and by August following had employed Moses P. Jacobson of San Antonio,

Texas, at $2,400.00 a year plus $150.00 travel expense. He also was a graduate of the Hebrew Union College, well qualified by training to conduct the services and by temperament to fit into community activities. He became an effective liaison man with the non-Jewish population, often being invited to speak at civic groups on patriotic themes. To reach an even wider audience, he began to publish a paper, *The Liberalist,* in which to set forth his ideas.

That he was effective in his duties as a rabbi is shown by the increase in membership of the congregation. At the end of 1890 there were sixty-three and in 1892 it had risen to eighty-two members. The record book also reported that "under his guidance the Sunday School prospered greatly." That year his salary was raised to $3,000.00 and his contract extended to cover two years.

There were some signs of discontent in spite of the favorable reports. One entry stated that "Rabbi Jacobson returned his wedding gift of $100.00 as a contribution," which indicates that he had taken unto himself a wife. Soon thereafter he "voluntarily agreed to a deduction of $1,200.00, which was also to be counted as a contribution." Evidently some of the more wealthy members had withdrawn their support.

The handwritten minutes of September 17, 1894, show that the officers were considering whether or not they should hire Dr. Jacobson for their services, but "Owing to certain unsavory articles which appeared in Dr. Jacobson's paper 'The Liberalist' against some of the members of our Congregation, at least 20 members would not come . . . he withdrew from his appointment."

Later in the same meeting they discussed "whether we should allow Mr. M. C. Phillips with his select Orthodox congregation of about 20 families to conduct services in our Temple after his own fashion." Though the subject was dropped without formal action, the answer was "No."

On October 14, 1894, a letter was presented in which Dr. Jacobson claimed that they still owed him $500.00, but the secretary was instructed to say that "we are not in any way indebted to him."[14]

Soon after, it was announced that Dr. Jacobson had accepted a pulpit in Chicago.

Now the congregation was left with a fine, new temple, but with no rabbi and no funds to employ one, even for the Holy Days. Instead, they accepted the services of Mr. Sig. Simon, offered gratis. By 1895 the financial condition was so desperate that a motion was made to dissolve the congregation. This was voted down and Mr. S. Eisman was elected president and J. Boehmer secretary. In April they accepted the offer of Mr. I. Kaiser to conduct a sabbath school without charge. Between fifty-five and sixty-five children attended, so Miss Nagel was engaged to assist at the price of $1.00 per Sunday. Later Misses Sachs, Levitt, and Lichtenstein volunteered their services gratis. The congregation then offered to pay the board of Mr. Kaiser at Greenewalds — $25.00 per month.

A highlight of the year 1895 was the lecture on June 12th of Rabbi Joseph Krauskopf, well-known liberal. He had been one of the first four graduates of the Hebrew Union College in 1883, so was eloquent with the idea that his people should cast off the Oriental cloak and patterns of worship. In describing the Conservative ritual he said that

> . . . He still prays in the language of the East, even though he understands not a word he says. Though far away from the Oriental climes . . . he still repeats prayers that had meaning there, but are out of place here, prayers concerning sacrifices, which he no longer brings, concerning the kind of oil to be used in his Sabbath lamp, neither of which are any longer used by him. He prays for an abundance of rain at a time when a little less than we usually get at that season would not come amiss. He prays for a speedy return to the Orient, without really meaning a word of it.[15]

Nor could Rabbi Krauskopf see any advantage in an antique, handwritten parchment roll over a book in modern

---

[14]All information here taken from the Minute Books under date.
[15]Rosenberg, *op. cit.*, p. 195.

print, intelligible to all the worshippers. Though we have
no detailed minutes of the speech he made before the Congregation B'nai Israel in Salt Lake City in the spring of
1895, it seems fair to assume that it would be in the same
general vein.

On September 1, 1896, the Jewish community suffered
a decided loss in the death of Frederick H. Auerbach. He
had been in excellent health when he left for New York on
business, but was stricken with appendicitis and died following
an operation. Every paper in Salt Lake City carried a head-
line article at the first word of the illness and followed with
details through to the final burial. Long resolutions of sympathy were printed from the Chamber of Commerce, the
I.O.O.F., the Utah Jobbers' Association, The Women's Home
Association, and the Jewish Congregation.

The obituary from the *Salt Lake Tribune* was most complete, though every article spoke of his generosity, his many
charities, and his support of all public improvements. It said:

> He was born in Fordon Province, Posen, Germany, on August
> 22, 1836, and was just 60 years of age. He had never married. . . .
>
> He opened a store in Austin [Nevada], and carried it on suc-
> cessfully until the spring of 1864, when he first came to Salt Lake
> City and at once opened a store of which the mammoth establish-
> ment of today is the natural outgrowth. . . .
>
> At the time of the first Liberal victory here he was asked to
> accept the position of Mayor, but refused. . . . He was president
> of the Chamber of Commerce . . . also ex-member of the Board
> of Regents of the Utah University. In Odd Fellowship Mr. Auer-
> bach was one of the most prominent members, being past Grand
> Master. He was . . . among the first organizers in the Territory.
>
> The firm of Auerbach Bros. of which he was senior partner,
> is one of the heaviest real estate owners and tax payers in the city.
> They own the Auerbach, Progress, part of the Scott-Auerbach,
> Eagle, and the old Cohn block, besides small stores all along Main
> Street and valuable real estate in different parts of the city.
>
> Mr. Auerbach's life insurance policies amount to nearly $150,-
> 000.00, and his fortune is given at $1,500,000.
>
> Among his relatives are his brother, S. H. Auerbach and family,
> his sister, Mrs. Rosa G. Meyer and family, and his cousins, A. L.
> Jacobs and M. J. Friedman, all of this city.

Another brother, Theodore H. Auerbach, and family, live in Boston, and there are relatives in Hailey, Idaho, Reno, Nevada, and Helena, Montana, besides numerous relatives in Germany.

In the meantime Mr. Kaiser had continued his services as teacher for a year, so the officers voted to double his allotment and give him $50.00 a month. He carried on for another full year before his services were terminated in 1897. That year Rabbi J. Korn conducted one service; in 1898 Rabbi "Prof." Schanfeld was engaged for the Holy Day service. On August 27, 1899, Rabbi C. H. Lowenstein was engaged; in 1900 Rabbi Louis C. Reynolds. He remained until the summer of 1903.[16]

[16]Information up to 1900 from the Minute Book, a rich source. After 1903 from the Salt Lake City *Directory*.

Chapter Seven

CONGREGATION MONTEFIORE

FROM THE DAY when Isadore Morris and his friends withdrew from the B'nai Israel Congregation they observed the Sabbath in one home or another. In the fall of 1889 a group of these Orthodox and Conservative Jews met at the home of Nathan Rosenblatt on 8th South and State Street to hold a religious service and to plan future activities.

Although they did not effect a permanent organization at that time, they did discuss a name for their group, tentatively deciding to call themselves "Congregation Montefiore," in honor of the great English Jew, Sir Moses Montefiore. For more than half a century this man had personified devotion and power. His death in 1885 at the age of one hundred and one had made them more conscious of his great contribution to the cause of Judaism everywhere.

Born in Italy in 1784, he early moved to London, where as a broker on the stock exchange he became wealthy. Through marriage he established a close relationship with the Rothschilds and shared their fortune. At the age of forty he retired from business, except that he remained financial advisor to the Queen. Now he devoted his full time to the welfare of the Jewish people.

The Jews concentrated in eastern Europe, the Middle East, and North Africa found him a great benefactor for, as a skilled diplomat, adept at getting access to the appropriate sovereigns, he effectively countered more than one outbreak of anti-Semitism in those areas. In Jerusalem in 1824 he established a close friendship with Mohammed Ali, which was greatly to the advantage of all Egyptian and Syrian Jews.

In 1837 he was knighted, and in 1846 he was made a baronet by Sir Robert Peel, which increased his prestige and power. He became a champion of human rights, so that the oppressed everywhere, both Christian and Jew, benefited by his generosity. A pious Jew himself, he was strictly orthodox in observing all the rituals. Because of this these people felt a special kinship to him.[1]

Though they were still too few in number to form a congregation, they continued to meet and to maintain an interest in the activities of their Reform Jewish neighbors and their Mormon friends. The laying of the cornerstone of the B'nai Israel temple the next year on September 26, 1890, came on the same day that President Wilford Woodruff of the Mormon Church published his statement that:

> . . . Inasmuch as laws have been enacted by Congress forbidding plural marriages, which laws have been pronounced constitutional by the court of last resort, I hereby declare my intention to submit to those laws, and to use my influence with the members of the Church over which I preside to have them do likewise. . . .[2]

This was presented in full to the Mormon congregation assembled in their Tabernacle on Temple Square October 6, 1890, and upon motion of Lorenzo Snow was accepted by unanimous vote.

Thus was cleared away the main point of dissension between Mormons and non-Mormons. True, some Mormons would continue to practice polygamy in Mexico and Canada for many years, but this "Manifesto" marked its legal death and opened the way for statehood. Jews in general rejoiced that this barrier had been removed, those men who had defended the Mormons most of all.

Though nothing current is found of the activities of this conservative group, it is evident that they continued to meet in the homes of those who were established, while temporary

---

[1]An excellent summary of the life of Sir Moses Montefiore is found in *Encyclopedia Brittanica*, Vol. 15, p. 781. Many of the Utah group were devoted to him because of his work in the areas of their nativity.

[2]Church of Jesus Christ of Latter-day Saints, *Doctrine and Covenants*, (Salt Lake City, 1950), pp. 256-257.

residents or Jews who were passing through shared as they could. The name was made official when, six years later in the fall of 1895, "the number of worshipers had increased until there were enough to organize and obtain a charter, designating the congregation as Congregation Montefiore."[3]

Most of these people were relatively new in America, displaced and strange, seeking for opportunities to earn a living and establish a home. Though they had decided upon the name of the congregation in the fall of 1895, it was not until March 20, 1899, that the real organization meeting was held and the proceedings reported officially.[4] It would be four more years before they would break ground for their synagogue.

A study of the list of names of those present at these two first gatherings will illustrate the fluid nature of the population, for of the thirty-four present at the 1899 meeting only eleven were still there on September 4, 1904. They were: J. Appleman, Benjamin Cohn, E. Kahn, I. Levitt, M. Levy, G. M. Lewis, Isadore Morris, Moses Nathan, Nathan Rosenblatt, S. Salmenson, and Joshua Shapiro. The total membership from the 1904 roll book was only thirty.[5] [For full list of names see appendix at end of this chapter.]

As early as 1902 they had planned to build a synagogue. According to Mr. Herman Finklestein, Morris Levy donated a lot at 355 South 3rd East, and Isadore Morris placed upon the table $150.00 in gold dust to lead off with the contributions.[6] Within the next year work began in earnest.

Because of the friendly relations established earlier between the leading members of this congregation and the Mormons, there was a willing cooperation in helping to build the synagogue. The "Journal History" of the Mormon Church notes that: "August 13, 1903, President Joseph F. Smith, accompanied by John Henry Smith, attended the laying of the cornerstone of the Congregation Montefiore synagogue

---

[3]Salt Lake *Tribune*, June 3, 1945. An illustrated article by Zena Potter.
[4]*The American Israelite*, Vol. 45, No. 40, April 6, 1899.
[5]Original Record on file with the Secretary of Congregation Montefiore.
[6]Personal interview with Mr. Herman Finkelstein, May 10, 1967.

and made a brief address." Later, as the need grew for
funds, the same source reports that, "October 4, 1903, the
Mormon Church, at the solicitation of Isadore Morris, contributed initially $500.00 and later $150.00 for the erection
of its synagogue."[7]

An indication that there was a sizeable Jewish reading
public is shown by the fact that almost every issue of both
the *Salt Lake Tribune* and the *Deseret Evening News* carried
items of special interest to the Jews. For example, on November 24, 1903, Charles W. Penrose wrote: "There is some talk
about a general exodus of Jews from Russia. . . . There is
plenty of room here for good immigrants. The Jews will
sometime reoccupy the land of their fathers, but in the meantime, America is a pretty good Zion for the oppressed of all
nations."

The first mention of the activities of Congregation
Montefiore appeared on December 11, 1903, an article in
the SOCIAL AND PERSONAL column:

> A brilliant event of yesterday was the ball and banquet given
> by the Congregation Montefiore at Christensen's. The hall and side
> rooms were handsomely decorated, evergreens, palms, and cut
> flowers being used in profusion, while shaded lights aided in the
> pretty effect. The affair was given for the benefit of the new
> synagogue, and a large sum was realized. The committees who
> had the ball in charge were as follows: Arrangements — M. Levy,
> S. Salmenson, I. Morris, G. M. Lewis, B. Salmenson, J. Shapiro,
> L. B. Mishkend. Reception — Mrs. E. Kahn, Miss Anne Levy,
> Miss Minnie Iseman, S. Salmenson, G. M. Lewis, I. Morris. Floor
> — M. Levy, H. A. Baron, L. Shapiro, D. Kranetz.

The Saturday edition following the next day repeated
under "Society" p. 24:

> One of the largest events of the season was the ball and banquet
> given at Christensen's on Thursday night by the Congregation
> Montefiore, the attendance and all connected with it being all
> that could be desired. Palms, flowers, and shaded lights made the
> hall and refreshment rooms attractive, and the affair was most
> successful from all standpoints.

---

[7]Church of Jesus Christ of Latter-day Saints, "Journal History." Entries by
date.

The *Deseret Evening News* for December 19, 1903, page 7, devoted a section to new houses of worship in the city. It includes some ten L.D.S. Ward Houses, the Catholic Cathedral, the Unitarian Chapel, and in the bottom left-hand corner, "the picturesque Synagogue of the Orthodox Jews cost the Congregation Montefiore $9,000." The picture is blurred, and the building seems to be unfinished so far as steps and yards are concerned.

Although the *Salt Lake Tribune* did not point up the Jews and their activities in the same tone used by the *Deseret Evening News,* it kept its readers informed on world news of general interest. On December 26, 1903, it carried an article on the case of Captain Alfred Dreyfus, a wealthy and prominent Jew in Paris, who had fallen under suspicion in 1893 during a rising and violent wave of anti-Semitism.

Paris, Dec. 25, 1903

> Capt. Dreyfus accused of treason to France, degraded, dismissed from the French army, and exiled to prison on Devil's Island, will have another trial, this time by a civilian tribunal. . . . Court will assemble next month . . . the modified testimony of M. Gribelin, the principal archivist of the headquarters staff, who at the court-martial at Rennes testified that he believed Dreyfus was guilty of treason, but who has now altered his evidence so as to throw the blame upon Col. Henry. . . .

The case had dragged on for twelve years, during which time Captain Dreyfus had stoutly insisted upon his innocence and his friends had worked constantly to prove it. Before the Court assembled Colonel Henry committed suicide. Dreyfus was reinstated in 1904 and decorated with the Legion of Honor in 1906.

The *Deseret Evening News* had followed this case with interest, and on January 2, 1904, carried a half-page spread on "Men Who Fought for the Vindication of Dreyfus," with a three-column-wide picture of the accused.

The *Tribune* for December 27, 1903, gave a summary of items of interest during the year, among them the notice that "August 9, Congregation Montefiore laid the corner-stone of its new synagogue."

In the same issue on page 42, tucked into the middle of a paragraph, is the information that ". . . The Congregation Montefiore are holding services in their new church building, the erection of which was begun early in the summer and completed late in the fall."

Much of the above detail has been included to show that, in all probability, a dedicatory service for the synagogue of the Congregation Montefiore was held. Mr. Herman Finkel-stein, now past ninety [May 10, 1967], recalls that a dedica-tory dance or Grand Ball celebrating the event was held at the Armory Building, Post Office Place, and that Governor Heber M. Wells and lady led the grand march, after which there was a short program and dancing was resumed. The event is especially clear in his mind, he says, because it was on that night that he learned to dance. A shy young man, he had paid his own ticket and the neighborhood girls each paid her own, and then took turns dancing with him. Tickets were five dollars each, so he could not have afforded a partner even if he had dared invite one.

As he remembers it, the synagogue at that time had no basement or central heating plant. He recalled that at some later date — perhaps in the 1920s — a wealthy member from Ogden, evidently Benjamin Cohn, contributed $2,000 with which to clear a mortgage, and there was an impressive cere-mony attending the burning of the papers.[8]

The *Salt Lake City Directory* proved to be a source of some information regarding both Jewish congregations, for each year, beginning in 1904, it listed the addresses of both synagogues, their times of meeting, and for several years all their officers. From 1904 to 1909 no rabbi for Congregation Montefiore is named, but the man in charge, called a

---

[8]The records covering the paying of the mortgage have not been located. As for improvements made later on the synagogue of the Montefiore Congrega-tion, the records of Salt Lake City show: electrical permit April, 1945; building permit, June 11, 1948; building remodeling, June 17, 1952; electric permit, April, 1954; plumbing permit, June, 1961; electric permit, 1963.

"Pastor," is Jacob Brodie, assisted at first by M. Levy. Until 1909 a full list of the officers is given, the positions rotating among Nathan Rosenblatt, S. Salmenson, Isadore Morris, and J. Shapiro, with George M. Lewis the secretary and I. M. Lewis the treasurer throughout the whole period.

To an outsider a Jew is a Jew, whether he belong to the Reform, the Conservative, or the Orthodox Congregation. Only a little association will show the competitive spirit between the congregations, their mutual scorn of each other, and often bitter animosities. After the split in Utah these feelings deepened as each congregation struggled to maintain its organization and to be meaningful in the lives of its members.

Although the Mormon people held all Jews in regard, some of the leaders were more friendly with the Montefiore Congregation, though rank or position did not seem to make much difference. For example, Alexander Stiefel, who had been a drayman for many years, had as long and detailed an obituary as could be desired. From the first he had been active; he sounded the "shofar" in the first gathering and continued to do so for years thereafter. Given a front-page, full-length column, the story details his sudden death as he sat at the table to eat his dinner, and continues:

> . . . The funeral will be held Sunday afternoon next from the residence, 337 West First South Street, according to the Jewish Ceremonial, and also under the auspices of the Odd Fellows, as the deceased was for many years a member of Utah Lodge No. 1. The interment will be in the Jewish Cemetery.
>
> Alex Stiefel was 77 years of age, and came to this country from Baden Baden, Germany, 56 years ago. He settled in Salt Lake in 1871, and has been an active man ever since. He was much respected for his upright and straightforward character, and had a wide circle of friends. The deceased leaves a wife and four sons, Samuel, a resident of California, . . . Maurice, Alfred, and Eugene; the last three being in business in this city.[9]

9*Deseret News,* October 13, 1904.

JEWS IN SALT LAKE CITY
AT THE TURN OF THE CENTURY

An advertising booklet put out by the railroad in 1900 is eloquent of conditions in Salt Lake City at that time. Highly illustrated, on heavy, slick paper, it pictures scenes without a hint of the automobile. Instead are varied horse-drawn vehicles, from the two-wheel, one-horse buggy to the coach large enough for ten to twelve passengers. Bicycles, all having a large front wheel, are prominent; streetcar tracks and an occasional streetcar also form a background. But NO automobile!

The whole publication was designed to attract business and capital to Salt Lake City, and emphasized housing accommodations and business conditions generally. Among the Jewish people are pictured the following, though there must have been many others not recognized by name:

Siegel Clothing Company; Kolitz Candy Kitchen; The Zang-a-Bar in the Walker Building, operated by Charles and Herman Meyer; the Dining Room and bar in the same building, operated by Sigmund Simon; the Salt Lake Brewing Company, run by Jacob Moritz; the Wagener Brewing Plant, operated by Jacob Weisel; and the Krug Brewing Plant. Significantly, these were followed by an advertisement of the Keeley Institute for the treatment of alcoholics.

Clearly, all this is fragmentary. Not until the publication of the *Salt Lake City Directories* in 1904 can information on the Jewish families be found, and then only by those who are able to identify them.[10]

Another source of scattered and varied information was the *American Jewish Yearbook,* which also began publication in Philadelphia, Pennsylvania, in 1904-1905.[11] That year the number of Jews in Utah, based upon an estimate, is given as 5,000. The next year repeats the number, but the following

---

[10]Original booklet owned by Mrs. Naomi Woolley, 5560 Holladay Blvd., Salt Lake City, Utah 84117.

[11]A complete set of the *American Jewish Yearbooks* is in the library at the University of Utah.

Moses Alexander, governor of Idaho, 1914-22
First Jewish governor in the United States

Congregation B'nai Israel

Congregation Montefiore

Fred H. Auerbach, Sr.

Louis Marcus, mayor of Salt Lake City, 1932-36

Philip & Mabel Myer

Four Simon Bros.

The Rausohoff Bros. — Early Jewish Pioneers before the turn of the Century

Samuel Newhouse — Born 1854, New York City. Came to Utah 1896. Mining financier, capitalist, builder Newhouse and Boston Buildings and the Newhouse Hotel, Salt Lake City.

Architect Philip Meyer as a young man

Philip Meyer in 1943

Henry Siegal — Pioneer Merchant of Salt Lake City

Jacob Gadaliah Brodie — The First Cantor and Mohel of Congregation Montefiore

Simon Bamberger — When a Young Man

Charles Popper

Ben M. Roe

Early Governors of Utah
Five state governors of Utah and one territorial governor at the Web
Club in Ogden. From left to right they are Arthur L. Thomas, ter

al governor; Heber M. Wells, first governor of the state; John C.
tler, second governor; William Spry, third governor; Simon Bam-
ger, fourth governor; and Charles R. Mabey, fifth governor.

EIGHTH ANNUAL

Grand Carnival

IN AID OF THE

Hebrew Benevolent and Relief Societies,

—AT THE—

SALT LAKE THEATER,

Tuesday Evening, February 26th, 1884.

Tickets to be had from the various Committees.

Committee of Arrangements:

M. C. Phillips,	S. H. Auerbach,
E. Kahn,	Henry Siegel,
H. Brishacher,	H. Bamberger,

Louis Hyams.

Invitation Committee.

Abram Gould,	Wm Rowe,	Hon J A Hunter,	F Cope,
P L Williams,	Boyd Park,	Gov Eli H Murray,	H Wagner,
Alex Cohn,	L L Baumgarten,	J Barnett,	Geo Culline,
L H Hills,	Wm James,	J Walsh,	S C Ewing,
Chris Diehl,	P H Lannan,	H Monheim,	Jos Siegel,
Col. S. Kahn,	Fred Simon,	James Lowe,	J Leviburg,
M Cullin,	T C Webber,	A Hanauer,	E A Mudgett.
	J H Van Horne,	A Podlech,	

—FORT DOUGLAS.—

Gen A McD McCook,	Capt Munson,	Lieut Witherall,
Adj Groebeck,	Capt Crowl,	Lieut Walker.

The Management have sent East for New Costumes, and Everything will be done to make the event the Grandest of the season.

Siegal Bros. Clothing Store

The Jay Gould Family at the Red Elephant Mine at Hailey, Idaho

Auerbach's branch store in Ogden in 1869

N. S. Ransohoff & Co.

S. J. Friedman Store, Hailey, Idaho

Main Street, Hailey, Idaho

Kahn Bros. Wholesale Grocery, N. S. Ransohoff Wholesale Liquors

Main Street, Salt Lake City

F. Auerbach & Bros. — Wholesale and Retail Store in 1901

Original Charter — B'nai Brith — April 1892

Past Presidents

OF B.F. Peixotto Lodge No. 421.
B'nai Brith.

Salt Lake City, Utah

These brethren have served with dignity, honor, and devotion as President. Intelligently and effectively have they led this lodge toward a fulfillment of the aims and ideals, the mission and traditions of B'nai Brith.

★ Theodore Meyer 1892	★ Herman Bahn 1916	★ Samuel Friedman	Leonard B. Pollock 1963
★ Jacob Moritz 1892	★ Max M. Aaron 1917	Harold Findling 1939-40	Harold Rosenberg 1964
★ Louis Hyams 1893	★ Simon Shapiro 1918	Dal Siegel 1940-1	Ira Tannenbaum 1965
★ Al L. Jacobs 1894	Morris S. Rosenblatt 1919	★ Harry Goldberg 1941	Lu Dornbush 1966
★ Moritz I. Friedman 1895	Frank Caret 1920	Samuel Bernstein 1942	Elliot Bernstein 1967
☆ Albert Graupe 1896	Nathan Horn 1921	Jack J. Weinstock 1943	★ Herbert Levy 1968
★ Isaac M. Solomon 1897	Jack Findling 1922	Myron Finkelstein 1944	Eugene Levetan 1969
★ Joseph Boehmer 1898	Ben Liberman 1923	Maurice Warshaw 1945	Bruce Cohne 1970
★ William Graupe 1899	Joseph B. Arnovitz 1924	Abe Bernstein 1946	
William Watters 1900	James L. White 1925	Alvin J. Smith 1947	
★ Herbert Hirschman 1901	Herbert M. Schiller 1926	A. Wally Sandack 1949	
★ Harry J. Joseph 1902	Ben Rosenblum 1927	Harry H. Sher 1950	
L. G. Reynolds 1903	Nathan Wolfe 1928	Bernard L. Rose 1951	
★ Henry Cohn 1904	★ Samuel H. Gordon 1929	Harold Findling 1952	
★ Charles Loeffler 1905	Charles M. Levy 1930	Robert S. Berman 1953	
Jerome Hirschman 1906	Joseph Rosenblatt 1931	Harry J. Smith 1954	
Isadore Lederman 1907	Frank E. Brittan 1932	Ralph M. Tannenbaum 1955	
★ David Spitz 1908	Ralph M. Kahn 1933	Fred H. Tannenbaum 1956	
★ George Auerbach 1909	Irwin Arnovitz 1934	Richard L. McGillis 1957	
★ Israel Siegel 1910	Abe Cohne 1935	Eric F. Teutsch	
David Levitt 1911	Abe Guss 1936	Victor Kassel 1958	
Ezra Baer 1912	Edward R. Spitzer 1937	Nathan Levine 1959	
Louis Marcus 1913	Joseph C. Girkstein 1938	Mordecai Podet 1960	
Daniel Alexander 1914	William B. Littaker 1939	Herschel J. Saperstein 1961	
Edwin Kahn 1915	Louis Grossman	James M. Roe 1962	

★ Deceased

Plaque of Past Presidents of B'nai Brith

HONOR ROLL

Dr. Isaac Alexander	Milton Levy
Dr. Robert Alexander	Sherman Lowenstein
Fred Auerbach	Walter J. Mayer
Herbert Auerbach	Jerome Mooney
Clarence Bamberger	J. Robinson
Samuel Bergerman	Ben Roe
Abraham Bero	Durant Rohlfing
Abraham Cline	Joseph Samuels
Lawrence Cline	Herbert M. Schiller
Martin Cohn	Ben Siegel
Harry M. Frank	Jules Schayer
David Friedman	Arthur Schayer
Martin Fruhman	Dr. E. M. Silverberg
Henry Garfinkle	Sylvan Simon
Julius Harrison	Milton Smith
Harold Hyams	Reuben R. Smith
Leland Hyams	Benjamin D. Solomon
Carl Lipman	Ralph Tandowsky
Lewis Levitt	Ernest S. Weitz
Robert Lehman	

Plaque of World War I Vets of the Jewish Community

1965—Top Row: Rabbi Stanley Relkin, David Axelrad; 2nd Row: Ruth Steinhardt, Brenda Siegel, Joanne Pedersen

Confirmation Class 1970
Garry Zinik, Barry Dupler, Stephen Goldsmith, Brent Schlesinger, Mark McGillis, Robert Safran, David Bergman, Sandra Segal, Laurie Auerbach, Mr. Norman Rosenblatt, Dr. Mark Littmann, Jan Bournstein, Malka Kassel

Confirmation Class — May 1969

Sitting left to right—Jennifer Marks, Wendy Rosenblatt, Debra Zinik, Karen Faber; standing left to right—Lauri McGillis, Rabbi Frankel, Roger Marcus

Confirmation Class — June 1968

Sitting left to right—Lisa Burnett, Lisa Marguleis, Judith Marks, Susan Sandack, Joyce Altschule; standing, left to right — Craig Schlesinger, Howard Safran, Rabbi Bernard Frankel, Richard Bram, David Bournstein.

1967—*Top Row: Rabbi Stanley Relkin, Barry Mervis, Robert Axelrad, Stephen Marcus, Marshall Smith; 2nd Row: Karen Bank, Jean Goodman, Terri Landa, Marlene Kassel.*

1966—*Top Row: Rabbi Stanley Relkin, Louis Ritz, Joanne Faber, Sharon Connell, Philip Ersler, Stepren Blackman; 2nd row: Carole Katz, Susan Dolowitz, Ronna Siegel, Janet Misner*

Sandra Tannenbaum, Janice Sugar, Susan Finkelstein, Wilma Dolowitz, Jane Ann Lovinger, Rabbi S. Strome

Roger Segal, Rabbi S. Strome, Douglas Bernstein, Joan Levy, Susan Freshman, Judy Ritz, David Burnett, James Friedman, Louis Ershler, Nathaniel Goodman

Howard Landa, Barry Bank, Kay Sugar, Rabbi Sidney Strome, Mark Rudman, Arthur Sandack, Donne Levy

Susan Dickman, Raymond Pederson, Rabbi Mordecai Podet, Tanker Reisman, Roger Sandack, Carol Landa, Richard Sandack, Judith Smith, Michael Feiler, Lorraine Segal

Rabbi Podet, Joan Friedman, Judy Dolowitz, Joan Leslie Leven, Mr. Gerald Gruber, Richard Anthony Sweet, Marilyn Ann Friedland, Martin Bernstein, Nancy Lynne Sandack, Marvin Lee Friedland

Elinor Leven, Janice Finkelstein, Ron Tikofsky, Thomas Bodenheimer, Jeffrey Gillman, David S. Dolowitz, Steven Rosen, Frances Shlafer, Sydney Carson, Marcia Alder, Laura Lovinger, Rabbi Mordecai Podet, Judy Lovinger, Joan Schwartz

Joan Lovinger, Tom Burnett, Neil Smith, Daniel Schwartz, Edna Tannenbaum, Ellen Jean Smith, Rabbi Mordecai Podet, Eileen Segal, Peggy Rosen

Confirmation June 1953
Back Row — Jack Spitzer, David Furth, Donley, Donley, Rabbi Adolph Fink, Michael Roe, ?, Tom Frank, Toby Rosenblatt; Front Row — Susan Wintrobe, Myrna Goldstein, Barbara Finkelstein, Virginia Sweet, Barbara Arnovitz, Bonnie Fink

Eugene Pepper, Roseanne Cline, Rabbi Adolph Fink, Joanne Spitzer, Kenneth Platt, Marilyn Arnovitz, Robert Frank, Francine Tannenbaum, Fred Frank, Valerie Siegel

Dan Tannenbaum, Rabbi A. Luchs, Melvin Finkelstein, Ralph Kahn, Myra Grossman, Kayla Wolfe, Harold Skolnick

Rabbi Alvin Luchs, Rabbi Samuel Gordon, Barrett Brittan, Richard Stone, Dianne Axelrad, Joan Drucker

Dr. Louis Zucker, Alan Cline, Bernard Axelrad, Anatole Zucker, Rabbi Gordon, Nell Grossman, Miriam Rose, Helen Zinik, Eloise Bamberger, Nadine Rosenblum, Evelyn White, Dionne Drucker, Lynn Cohne.

Dr. Louis Zucker, Alan Cline, Bernard Axelrad, Anatole Zucker, Rabbi Gordon, Nell Grossman, Miriam Rose, Helen Zinik, Eloise Bamberger, Nadine Rosenblum, Evelyn White, Dionne Drucker, Lynn Cohne

Rabbi Gordon, Marvin Bloom, Dick McGillis, Ralph Tannenbaum, Jules Frank, Al Klein, Emily Segal, Ruth Wiemer, Barbara Schubach, Jean Wolfe

Dr. L. C. Zucker, Richard Schubach, Robert Axelrad, Rabbi S. Gordon, Donald Rosenblatt, Samuel Grossman, Joel Shapiro, Barney Rosenblatt, Bob Segil, Arthur Sweet, Ruth Glaser, Elinor Kahn, Ruth Cline, Amy Bloom, Betsy Ann Bamberger, Dorothy Cline

Dr. L. Zucker, Marjorie Segal, Marjorie Newman, Hugh White, Rabbi Gordon, Francis Slater, Harold Grossman, Harold Glaser, Helen Herman, Marian Alexander, Howard Marcus, Josephine Clark, Robert Schubach, Barbara Hilson

1st row: *Bernice Rosenblum, Gertrude Schubach, Lenore Lewis, Corinne Finkelstein, Claire Landau, Helen Frank, Helena Rice, Barbara Rosenblatt, Helen Ottenheimer, Helen Hilson, Marjorie Rosenblatt.*

2nd row: *James Lieberman, Daniel Alexander, Irving White, Bernard Wolfe, David Rauitz, Irving Glaser.*

3rd row: *Dr. L. G. Zucker, Stanley Friedman, Howard Collins, Mitlan Newman, Walter Tasem, Rabbi S. Gordon.*

Judy Williams, Linda Siegal, Trudy Pepper, Leslie Bernstein, Pauline Guss, Charlotte Smith, Jerry Lutzker, Louis Grossman, Abe Chiat

Sandra Brooks, Joel Rosenberg, ?, Ronald Turner, Tobby Pepper, ?,
Jon Appleman, Paula Skolnick, Steven Teutch

Jerry Bernstein, Sharon Mednick, Mirl Nord, Sherry Sher, Miariam
Onhouse, Marcia Williams, Gail Bernstein, Richard Golden

Darcey Rosenblatt, Patrice Arent, Franne Einhorn, Paula Block, David Arnovitz, Michael Perlman, Paul Soffran, Nate Bloom, Michael Katz, Rabbi Abner Bergman, Rabbi Nissan Goldstein

Gustave Meyer residence at 315 East Second South,
Salt Lake City, about 1890

Cohn Bros. Dry Goods Store, Salt Lake City

one, 1906-1907, gives the number as only 1,000. The first issue [page 369] gives the names of all the synagogues in the United States dedicated during the year beginning in the fall of 1903 and extending through 1904, but the Montefiore one is not named. Evidently this is a publication of the Reform groups.

An interesting item of each year and something of a barometer of Jewish activity is the list of subscribers to the Jewish Publication Society, given by states, and including addresses of all who subscribe. The numbers fluctuate sharply from year to year, evidently depending upon the zeal of the rabbi or of his appointed subscription agents. The first year, 1903-04, shows only six from Utah belonging: Mrs. S. Siegel of 630 East 1st South, who is a "Patron" here and always hereafter; Samuel Auerbach, J. E. Bamberger, A. Hanauer, Wm. B. Levy, and George Rhode.

The next year there was a sharp increase, probably the result of the arrival of Rabbi Charles J. Freund at Congregation B'nai Israel. He at once initiated a program for renewing the synagogue and of observing on November 24, 1905, a special program commemorating the *Celebration of the 250th Anniversary of the Settlement of the Jews in America.*

At any rate, subscribers increased to thirty-six, each of whom is listed with full address. This serves as a "Who's Who" of active Reform Jews in Utah. [See Appendix]

As has been indicated earlier, the turn of the century — from 1895 to 1905, roughly — marked a period of home-building in Salt Lake City. Many of these were truly palatial in their construction and furnishings.

From the earliest settlement of Jews in Utah, some Jewish citizens built homes to rival the best of any of their neighbors. The ostentatious home of Charles Popper built in 1869 on the east side of West Temple Street just north of Third South has already been mentioned as a center for Jewish activity. Likewise, the apartments called "Reggel's Row" built in the 1870s, had historical significance. Also, Samuel Kahn, known as Colonel Kahn, built a fine home on Main Street between

Fifth and Sixth South, where many visiting dignitaries were entertained. And in 1881 Moses Casper Phillips built a home at 351 East Second South which was still standing in 1951.

In 1966 Mrs. Margaret Shepherd of the Utah State Historical Society office staff, working with Dr. ElRoy Nelson of the University of Utah, made a study of "The Mansions on Brigham Street," now South Temple, beginning at Main Street and moving east to the end of the street. Most of these were built during the period indicated above.

For example, the Samuel Newhouse residence at 165 East South Temple received a long write-up with many pictures in the *Tribune* for Sunday, October 18, 1903, (p. 25) as one of a series of "Palatial Homes of Salt Lake City."

Another which received publicity of the architect's drawings was the large home on the southwest corner of Seventh East and South Temple, (No. 678) which stands today much as it was when it was completed. It was built by Emanuel Kahn, who was in the freighting business with his brother Colonel Samuel Kahn. The architects on this building spared no expense in producing a very complicated, ornate facade.

West of this Kahn home, and on the same lot, are two other three-story homes, not so ostentatious, but still remarkable homes. They belonged to Alex and Louis Kahn, brothers who were in the dry goods business, and were also built during this period.

Still farther east at No. 904 stands the home built by Edward Rosenbaum, wholesale clothier, in 1905. This later became the home of the Moormeister family.

There were at this same time many Jews living in small homes or rented flats, or single rooms attached to their places of business. These people were the later arrivals from the Russian and Near East immigration. Some of them would become affluent in the next decade; others would move to more lucrative fields, for Jewish people adjust quickly to economic conditions.

Business advertisements and new homes built by the more wealthy give only a partial index of Jewish activities at the turn of the century. Certainly the list of subscribers to the Jewish Publications will be more indicative of those who are active in a congregation. In 1904 in Salt Lake City there were thirty-six. In 1913 the list was equally long, but only the five marked here by an asterisk were still on it.

Patron

*Siegel, Mrs. S., 630 E. 1st S.

Members

Auerbach, Samuel, 128 G
Baer, Adolph
Bamberger, J. E.
Barnett, Mrs. H., 128 G
Bergerman, J., 133 S. 1st W.
Boehmer, Joseph, 42 K
Cohen, Henry, Box 467
Cohn, Mrs. Jennie L., 670 E St.
Davis, Mrs. Ben, 354 S. 3 E.
Desky, Mrs. M. H., 624 E. 3 S.
Freund, Rabbi Chas. J., 524 E. 3 S.
Frumpkin, Julius, 135 S. Main
Fulop, Mrs. D. I., 356 E. 3 S.
*Gans, Mrs. Harry, 115 S. 4 E.
Hanauer, A.
Hesselberg, I., 62 E. 2 S.
Joseph, Mrs. Milton P.,
    144 S. 2 E.

Kahn, Mrs. E., 624 S. 2 E.
Kahn, Mrs. Fannie C.
Moritz, Mrs. J., 975 E. 4 S.
Oberndorfer, J., 605 E St.
Rhode, George
Rosenbaum, Mrs. Ed, 624 E. 2 S.
Samuels, Mrs. S., 275 S. 12 E.
*Shapiro, J., 66 E. 2 S.
Simm, Mrs. Teresa, 238 S. 3 E.
Simon, Adolph, 728 E. 2 S.
Simon, Louis, 34 E. 6 S.
*Simon, Sigmund, 24 S. 6 E.
Spiro, Solomon, Box 1073
*Spitz, Mrs. D., 1073 E. 2 S.
Watters, Mrs. I., 253 .... 3 ....
Weil, Max M., 755 S. 12 E.
Weitz, Samuel, 667 E. 2 S.

These annual accounts of the Jewish population of the United States must have been invaluable to Jews having relatives and friends in scattered areas.

APPENDIX

LIST OF NAMES OF CONGREGATION MONTEFIORE AS REPORTED FOR ORGANIZATION MEETING
March 20, 1899

(* Indicates that the name was still on in 1904)

*Appleman, J.
Appleman, S.
Baskin, J.
*Cohn, Benj.
Edstein, H.
Fordonsky, A.
Gebrecht, E. F.
  Secretary
Glassberg, M.
Glaube, S.
Glaubenfeld, L.
Isaachson, J.
*Kahn, E.
Kerenez, D.

Levin, W.
*Levitt, I. N.
  Trustee
Levy, I.
*Levy, M.
  President
Lewis, I. N.
  Treasurer
*Lewis, G. M.
  Trustee
Mayer, M.
*Morris, Isadore
*Nathan, Moses
Pesioritsky, J.

Vice-President
Pink, M.
Rogowsky, F.
*Rosenblatt, Nathan
Sachs, M. H.
*Salmenson, B.
Salmenson, E.
*Shapiro, Joshua
Sheper, A.
Singer, H.
Siler, J.
Wolff, E.
Zerre, J. W.

NAMES OF MEMBERS WHO BOUGHT PEWS IN CONGREGATION MONTEFIORE SYNAGOGUE
September 4, 1904 — from Original Book

(* indicates that member had been present at the organization meeting March 20, 1899)

*Appleman, J.
Appleman, F.
Appleman, H.
Appleman, S.
Axelrad, M.
Busgon (canceled)
Baron, H. A.
Bernstein, D.
*Cohen, Benjamin
  (Ogden)
Claschko, E. (1913)
Eckstein, H. (1907)

Eckstein, S. (1907)
Finkelstein, H.
Geffen, H.
  (Brigham City 1907)
Gaffen, H.
*Kahn, E.
*Levitt, I.
*Lewis, G. M.
  (Transferred to
  J. Rheinshreiber 1909)
*Levy, M. (1907)
Lachman, I.

Mishkind, N. (1907)
*Morris, Isidor
*Nathan, M.
Pasher, M. (1907)
Pepper, Isaac (1912)
*Rosenblatt, N.
Salmenson, S.
*Salmenson, B.
*Shapiro, J.
Shaffer, A. (1907)
Wise, M. (Vernal)

Chapter Eight

EARLY JEWS IN IDAHO

THE MINING FEVER set off at Sutter's Mill in 1848 spread through all parts of the West. Long before state lines were clearly drawn, prospectors were working in areas which would later become Nevada, Colorado, Montana, and Idaho. Among them were certainly some Jews, but like many others of the early comers, their names were lost.

In his *Reminiscences,* W. A. Goulder tells of two Jews who in the winter of 1861-62 were members of a party which was trying to reach the mountain mining center of Oro Pino. The snow was so deep and the weather so bitter that all risked their lives, and each man struggled for himself to reach shelter. The Jews were referred to as Harrison and Haas, with no first names given. Harrison lagged behind while the others, each desperate in his own fight, made their way to Goulder's cabin late at night. Some had frozen feet and hands; all were exhausted and hungry. As soon as daylight approached, a party went back to bring in Harrison He was still alive, but too badly frozen to survive. "Haas, his fellow Jew, returned and with some other Jews helped to bury him."[1]

Here, as in all areas where evidences of gold had been found, men risked their lives to get there, whether it was by freezing in the mountains or by baking on the waterless stretches of sand. Those who survived often neglected to record even the names of those left behind.

The winter of 1864 also saw some tragedies in Idaho, one of which involved a party headed by a Jew. Whether

---

[1]W. A. Goulder, *Reminiscencs of a Pioneer,* (Boise, 1909), p. 227.

or not all the other members were of the same faith, we
cannot know, since no names are given:

> The night we got back to Call's Fort, a man named J. D.
> Farmer came in on foot over the trail from Boise City. He had
> left his party behind him and was the only one to arrive at the
> settlement without help. He had started out from Boise and had
> got snowed up and lost their animals and then started on foot
> from near the present town of Snowville about the same time as
> we were caught at Malad. The next morning we started out with
> sleds and provisions over the Boise trail. We found two of Farmer's
> party at the head of Blue Creek. Then we went on the Rattlesnake
> Pass and there we found the remaining two of his men frozen to
> death, so we took all of his party back to the Fort. We then took
> sleighs from Call's Fort to Salt Lake City, where we arrived about
> the 20th of January, 1864, going by way of Ogden.[2]

Joseph D. Farmer evidently remained in Salt Lake City
for his name is prominent in all the activities of the first
Jewish congregation there. In 1874 he was in business in
Corinne, having gone with others to what promised to be
the great metropolis of the Territory. On August 11, 1882,
he was drowned in the Great Salt Lake, his body not recov-
ered for almost four years, when it was found in a semi-
petrified state, encrusted with minerals from the water. He
left a wife and five children.

Back to Idaho: Oro Pino and Elk City were the first
mining camps. Boise and Silver City developed in 1864.
That year David and Robert Grotstein, Jewish brothers, came
with the army. In 1865 David Falk came to Boise, and with
Joseph Alexander opened a store there.[3]

In March 1863 Idaho was made a territory, the bound-
aries set and J. H. Wallace named as governor. The legislature of twenty members met at Lewiston on December 7,
1863, made the first laws to govern the Territory, and created
Owyhee, Oneida, and Alturas counties.

As early as 1854 some Mormons had settled in Lemhi
Valley, near where Salmon City now stands, but with the

---

[2]Alexander Toponce, *Reminiscences*, (Salt Lake City, 1923), p. 78. Reprinted
1971 — University of Oklahoma Press.
[3]*Universal Jewish Encyclopedia*, (New York City, 1951), Vol. 5, p. 534.

approach of the United States army under General Albert Sidney Johnston they were called back to Salt Lake City, and all Mormon colonizing attempts in Idaho were abandoned for many years.

THE WOOD RIVER AREA

Some prospectors had worked in the Wood River area in the early 1860s, with a general rush in 1865, which brought such a violent Indian uprising that all whites were persuaded to leave. After the Bannock War of 1879, the rush began again in 1880. The district now became known as the "Hailey Gold Belt," though it was not gold but high grade silver and lead that were in abundance there. John Hailey, for whom the principal village was named, was a contractor and businessman who later in his own life would write a history of the state.

By 1881 the rush to Wood River was really on, with a settlement of tents, dugouts, and temporary houses springing up without plan or pattern, as the newcomers competed for places. By June 18 an election was held to determine the county seat of Alturas County, where four or five settlements had already taken root. The *Hailey Times* on June 18, 1931, celebrating the first fifty years in the Wood River Valley, reported the results of an election in which the votes cast in 1881 totaled: Hailey 1,114, Bellevue, 1,087, Ketchum, 306, and Rocky Bar, 251. Hence on September 21, 1881, Hailey was named the county seat of Alturas County, and a temporary government was set up.

The *Hailey Times,* semi-centennial issue, named Charles W. Bates as the oldest living pioneer of the town, for he was then 97 years old. He had come to Hailey a young man with a family and remained to make it his home. A younger pioneer was one Jody Smith, who came with his parents, two brothers and one sister. This was the first Mormon family to arrive and make the town their permanent residence.

The first Jew to really put down roots in Hailey and continue to live there his life through was S. J. Friedman, an unmarried young man who arrived early in 1881 with a mule train of dry goods, boots, and shoes. Born in Germany, April 5, 1846, he had been named Simon Itzig Friedman, but upon his arrival in the United States the clerk misread the initial "I" to be "J", so he accepted the nickname "S. J." by which he was known thereafter. When he received his citizenship papers on September 27, 1880, he made the change legal.

Soon after his arrival in the United States in 1869, he made his way to Salt Lake City, where for a year he found employment in Auerbach's Store. In 1870 he moved to Corinne, the new city of promise, where he did well for a time, but as business declined, he set up in Ogden. As the boom opened in Hailey, he transferred his stock and opened up his business in a 20 x 40 feet tent.

Still another pioneer of Hailey was Adolph Seilaff, who opened a hardware store in 1882, and in 1885 built the first lumber residence on the town site.

Hailey immediately became the typical mining boom town. The Wood River branch of the Union Pacific railroad came there, with the first train arriving on May 7, 1883. A county courthouse, with a jail in the basement, was authorized on February 8, 1883, and accepted as completed on August 1, 1884. The basement was of stone with steel cages for the prisoners, the upper walls of brick.

Hailey boasted the first electric power plant in Idaho, erected at a cost of $22,000. It had also the first telephone system in the Territory. The Alturas Hotel, built in 1886, boasted that it was the finest between Denver and the Pacific Ocean, modern, with eighty-two rooms, well furnished. By this time there were many good residences, schools and "saloons a-plenty," eighteen having been licensed on September 17, 1884, and others later.[4]

Hailey also had a sizeable Chinese settlement, a large red-light district, and open gambling.

[4]George A. McLeod, *A History of Alturas and Blaine counties, Idaho,* (Hailey, Idaho, 1930), pp. 15-16.

Business was so good that in 1882 S. J. Friedman (mentioned earlier) set about to build a permanent store. This he made of stone and brick, 28 by 50 feet in dimension, with a good layer of sod for insulation on the top under the gabled roof. Within a short time he added at the back an extension of rock and stone 30 by 40 feet, under which was a full basement for storage. Over this he also put the heavy insulation. It is likely that he took seriously the fire on September 24, 1883, which wiped out a number of buildings in the east-side business section at a damage of some $75,000.

On April 11, 1886, S. J. Friedman married Miss Luscha Meyer, who had come to Salt Lake City two years earlier with her parents. The wedding was a gala event, and the town reception upon their arrival at Hailey was something unprecedented there. The young couple moved at once into a fine lumber home in the residential area. It had been built and completely furnished during the winter, and is today (1972) still in excellent repair.

Luscha Meyer Friedman came from a well-to-do German family. Her brother, Philip, could not come to live in America with them because he was an official architect for the German government, busy with assignments. Later, when he visited his parents in Salt Lake City, he came on up to his sister's home in Hailey, and while there worked on his plans for the B'nai Israel temple. The family was deeply grieved, years later, when informed that Philip had been killed October 15, 1943, at the Theresienstadt concentration camp, and his wife on July 15, 1946. This sacrifice only deepened the love of the family for Judaism.

Things went well until July 2, 1889, when a disastrous fire wiped out practically the whole business district. The *Hailey Times* told the dramatic story:

> The almost heroic battle of S. J. Friedman with the fire in this city the morning of the second inst., is doubtless still fresh in the memories of the readers of The Times. While every other house on the block was burning and while surrounded with the flames which even burnt the roof off his 90 ft. store, S. J. Friedman

closed his shutters and at the peril of his life, battled with the
destroying elements. No one could reach him through the fiery
furnace, in the midst of which stood his store, and it was impossible
to learn if he was dead or alive. But after the two hours of hell
were over, a knock with a rock on his shutters was responded to,
and Mr. Friedman, his hair and whiskers singed, a few slight burns
on his face, neck, and hands, his clothes soaking wet, his face
black as a charcoal burner, was dragged out of the burned district.
He carried a heavy insurance, but had probably $10,000 worth of
goods over and above his insurance.

Of the disaster to the town, the local paper went on,
"From a prosperous community on Monday we have remaining
one dry goods store, one general merchandise establishment,
one hotel, and two saloons. According to our wealth, the
fire is a heavier blow to Hailey than was the Seattle fire to
Seattle. Our amount of insurance is scarcely $150,000."

For his courageous action during the fire S. J. Friedman
received a letter of commendation from the insurance company, and a silver water pitcher and tray carrying an engraved
tribute. All are still in the possession of the family.

S. J. Friedman was only one of the Jews doing business
in Hailey, but he was probably typical. The 1880 census
said there were 85 Jews in the Territory of Idaho. None
were likely in the Wood River area on that date, but we
can account for several in Hailey before this last disastrous
fire.

A cousin, S. M. (Simon Moses) Friedman, came later,
set up a grocery store, built a home, and raised his family
of three children here. The family of Leon Fuld also came,
but they all joined the Christian Science congregation, so are
lost to Jewish history. Quite a number of single young men
spent some years in Hailey, among them Emil E. Friedman,
younger brother of Simon J. He had worked as a clerk at
Auerbach's in Salt Lake City before coming to Hailey. Jay
Hartman, an orphan raised in Cleveland, was a traveling
salesman out of Salt Lake City, who became ill while on a
regular selling trip in Boise, Idaho, and died there.

Perhaps the greatest tragedy among the Jews here was
the death of Aaron Morris, a brother of Isadore Morris so

well known in the Jewish circles of Salt Lake City. Born in
1854, Aaron had come to Utah in 1879 and to Hailey in 1883.
The brothers had established a bank in Hailey and had also
a business in Ketchum. Aaron was shot from his horse one
night as he rode from Ketchum to Hailey. Since he carried
a considerable sum of money with him, friends had warned
him against this lonely night trip. No clue to the assassin
was ever found.[5]

Certainly the best known unmarried man in Hailey was
Leopold Wertheimer, who opened a men's furnishing store
in 1884. He came to own practically a whole city block and
a store besides. After the fire he rebuilt, and at his death
left an estate worth $100,000. His elaborate funeral and the
press notices all spoke of his generosity to individuals and his
support of all public charities.

There were never enough Jewish men to organize a
formal congregation in Hailey, but S. J. Friedman led out in
the observance of the Sabbath and of the Holy Days. As a
very young man he had promised his mother that he would
not smoke on the Sabbath, and as long as he lived he would
not touch tobacco from Friday night until Sunday. He had
the mezzusah on his door; he owned a beautiful herbstick,
sacramental wine glasses, phylacteries, and prayer books.
While their children were young, the two Friedman families
usually joined in the Sabbath observances, and invited young
Jewish men to join them. Whenever possible they went to
Salt Lake City for the autumn Holy Days.

The disastrous fire of 1889 and the slowing up of the
mining operations brought about a decrease in population
until in 1903 Hailey was listed as a village. Now Jewish
youth went away to school.

GOVERNOR MOSES ALEXANDER

Without doubt the most important Jew in Idaho history
is Governor Moses Alexander. Not only was he first in the
United States to be elected to this high office, but his image

---

[5]*The Salt Lake Tribune,* August 19, 1904, reported this murder.

as a leader in sound and progressive government still persists after more than fifty years.

Born November 13, 1853, in Obrigheim, Bavaria, he was youngest of a family of eight. His father died when he was very young; his mother was an invalid. He did get some schooling, however, for he received an award for proficiency in Latin, the prize a small Latin book inscribed by the King of Bavaria.

At the age of fourteen he decided to seek opportunity in America, for two of his sisters were already living in New York City and he would not be entirely alone. His dreams of quick success were much dampened when upon his arrival he found that neither sister had room for him and he must fend for himself, which meant selling papers.

His fortunes changed when a cousin, Mr. Jacob Berg, came into the city from the Midwest on a routine buying trip and called to visit his relatives. It was at the home of one of his sisters that Moses Alexander met his future employer. The agreement was that he should get transportation, board and room, and ten dollars a month for working in the store. This at first meant janitor work chiefly, and lifting, carrying, filling shelves. But a comfortable shelter and three meals a day meant much to the growing boy, and besides, he found many things of interest in the merchandising business. Within the year he was selling in the men's department, where he put in full time and soon became acquainted with most of the male population of Chillicothe, Missouri, and of the surrounding farms. His genius was partly in the fact that he never forgot a face or a name; a person was individual with him, to be treated with respect, to be understood.

In the first two-and-a-half years of work in the store, Mose, as he was affectionately called, had grown from a boy to a tall gangling youth and risen from janitor to clerk to full time head of a department. When Mr. Berg died, his silent partner, Abraham Wallbrunn, took Mose into the new firm to be called Wallbrunn and Alexander.

During these years Mose met his future wife, Hadwig Kaestner, a German girl who was employed in the Jacob Berg home and later in the Wallbrunn home. The boy was attracted to her at first sight, but there was one serious objection to any marriage with her. She was a Christian. This barrier was removed when in 1876 she began to study with Rabbi Gerstein of St. Joseph, Missouri. After several months of study she was confirmed in the synagogue at St. Joseph and given a new name, Helena. [Copy of certificate of conversion is in the possession of Mrs. William Simons of Boise.]

On November 15, 1876, Helena and Moses were married, and her confirmation dress became her wedding gown.

They settled down to the business of establishing a home and rearing a family. Four children were born to them — three daughters and one son — and Moses built a comfortable two-story house.

His entrance into politics came in 1886, when members of the Democratic party persuaded him to run for a seat on the city council. He was elected and filled the office creditably by being alert to conditions, observing what needed to be done, offering an occasional question or comment, but leaving the leadership role to the older members. At the end of his term he was persuaded to run on a non-partisan ticket for the office of mayor. He won easily in the 1888 election and served his term with such distinction that press and public alike felt that he had saved the town from bankruptcy.[6]

Now, when his stock was high in the community, might have been the time to stay on and try for bigger things. But Mose had other ideas. Tall and thin as he was, he talked to a doctor who advised moving west to a dry climate. At the age of thirty-six, with this bit of political experience behind him, he was ready for new fields and fresh opportunities. Idaho had caught his imagination. He would go there and look things over.

---

[6]*Universal Jewish Encyclopedia, op. cit.,* pp. 175-76.

Leaving his family behind him, he set his face westward to Idaho. He stopped first at Pocatello, where he bought some lots because land was cheap, so cheap that values could go only one way — up. But Boise was to be the capital of the new state, the place where the general policies would be formed. He would go there and literally get in on the ground floor.

He returned to Chillicothe and closed out his business but did not sell his home. His wife and children must remain here until he could get established in Idaho. He returned to Boise via New York and Philadelphia, where he arranged for merchandise to be shipped out on consignment, and in Boise rented a small store on Seventh and Main streets. He opened shop on July 14, 1891.

At first he lived right at the store, but in March of 1892 he sent for his family and rented a home. His business prospered; he employed two clerks and gave the alterations department into the competent hands of his wife, so that within a few years he was firmly established in business.

At this time there were some one hundred Jews in Boise, some second and third generation German emigrants who had been away from the rituals so long that they had lost interest. But others, like himself, sensed that there were enduring values in observing the Holy Days and raising their children in the faith of their fathers. Accordingly, he invited all he knew to be interested to gather at his home for an organization meeting. The officers were appointed for one year, for the opening page of the ledger reads:

CONGREGATION BETH ISRAEL
BOISE, IDAHO

Roll call of officers for term ending Second Monday in January, 1896:

President ....David Falk
Vice-President ....M. Alexander
Secretary ....Charles H. Stolz
Treasurer ....D. Spiegel
Trustees: Nathan Falk, L. Weil
            E. Shainwald

As was stated earlier, the temple was completed and in use almost within a year, with the services conducted in turn by Nathan Falk and Moses Alexander.

But it was in politics where Moses Alexander would distinguish himself. He began first by reading the Congressional Record, by thinking of ways in which the democratic process might bring about improved roads, better sidewalks, equitable water distribution. The true test was to have the people, through their representatives, do what needed doing for the collective good. He traveled the country roads; he saw blear-eyed men drink up their wages while their families lived in want and ignorance. He saw — and he talked about what he saw.

So, as it was back in Missouri, a delegation waited upon him, asking that he be their candidate for mayor of Boise. He had made a practical demonstration of his confidence in government by taking at face value the warrants of city employees. Since these warrants were redeemable only at future dates, other establishments would accept them only at a discount. He insisted that government pay — even local government — must be as valuable as gold in the hand.

He accepted the call to run for mayor in 1897 and won by a comfortable majority. He served his term, accomplished some reforms, but refused to run to succeed himself. But in 1901 he ran again and again was elected. Now with more confidence and with a strong and growing public support, he could make further improvements. Even after he was out of office, he kept in touch with municipal problems.

In 1908 he was nominated as candidate for governor, but due to a bitter party feud he was defeated. Through the following years he was an active and effective party man in the Democratic party, traveling and speaking for its candidates and helping to form its basic policy.

In 1914 he again appeared as candidate for governor, and this time put his whole soul and strength into the campaign. From this battle has come some of the finest Alexander folklore:

. . . he'd stop and address people wherever they gathered. . . .
not far from Caldwell . . . he came upon a cluster of farmers. Inviting himself to address them "on the issues of the day," he spied
a low shed nearby and offered to speak from the top of it. "But,
Mose," one of his entourage protested, "they store manure under
that shed. That's no place for you to speak."

Mose mounted the shed, looked out over his impromptu
audience, and observed: "This is the first time in my life I've ever
spoken from a Republican platform. . . ."

. . . To expose the wastefulness of the state government, he
recounted . . . the story of his visit to the state house. "I found
doors bearing the names of useless boards, slow-motion commissions,
slumbering office-holders," he said, ticking off the articles of extrav-
agance with dramatic one-by-one deliberation. "But not until I
came to an office marked Bee Inspector did I fully realize how
badly the people of this state have been stung."

His hearers ate it up. That story, they commonly agreed, was
a honey.[7]

In this campaign Alexander was elected, but he was
the only one of his party who was, so that he faced a hostile
legislature.

His message pled for reduction of expense, for consolida-
tion of departments, for a comprehensive workingmen's law,
for even a reduction of the salary of the governor from
$5,000 to $3,600 per annum.

Best of all, he closed with the plea that . . . "This is no
time for political strife. . . . Let us both, the executive and
the legislative representatives of the people, seek to work in
full harmony to do the will of those we represent."

The legislature did not respond, with the result that
many laws were vetoed. The whole period was full of strife
and recriminations, but when Governor Alexander ran for
a second term, not only was he elected but carried with him
almost a full slate of the Democratic party.

The election of a Jew to the high position of governor
had been hailed throughout Jewish congregations the world

---

[7]Arthur Wayne, "Great Journey," a manuscript biography of Governor Moses
Alexander, pp. 23-24. Mr. Alexander Simons of Pocatello, Idaho, owned the original. All stories of the campaign come from this source.

over. Now his return for a second term with full party support was a vindication of his personal integrity. His achievements may be summarized briefly:

1. Passage of a Prohibition Law, forbidding import, sale, shipment, transport, delivery, receiving, or having in one's possession intoxicating liquors.

2. Enactment of a Workingmen's Compensation Act.

3. Creation of a state highway system.

4. Completion of the Arrowrock Dam.

5. Dedication of the Dalles-Celilo Canal, creating an open waterway from Lewiston, Idaho, to the sea.

6. Furnishing of Idaho's quota of troops in World War I.

With the close of this term of office Moses Alexander retired from active political life, except as advisor and elder statesman. He died January 4, 1932. History still points to him as an outstanding statesman of the State of Idaho.

Among the stories which have become folklore is one to the effect that during Alexander's last term as mayor of Boise in 1902, Theodore Roosevelt was to visit the city on one of his western trips. It was whispered that Roosevelt would have nothing to do with Alexander, since he was both a Democrat and a Jew. But Moses Alexander outsmarted them all. With a fine outfit, he met the party outside the city limits, and the two men sat side by side in the parade through the city, a recognition and bit of publicity which did not hurt Mayor Alexander in his later campaigns.

Another story is that in his first successful campaign for governor, the opposition waited until Sunday night preceding election to circulate an accusation that Alexander was "Wet" and secretly in league with the liquor interests. Although he had spoken many times in favor of curbing the whiskey interests, he had no opportunity to answer this smear sheet. When the election returns began coming in from Boise, it looked as if Alexander would lose, but he always said, "Wait for the last precinct." He knew that his trips to the rural areas, his extemporaneous addresses to the farmers, his appeals for the use of public funds to improve roads and ditches and schools would not be in vain. And he was right. The rural vote tipped the scales in his favor.

The belligerent legislature of his first term helped greatly in his second election.

OTHER JEWS IN PUBLIC LIFE

By his election to mayor of Boise in 1897 Alexander became the first Jew in public life there. In 1910 Samuel Freund was elected to the state assembly. Charles Himrod was mayor of Boise from 1913-1915; Max Mayfield and Leo P. Greenbaum were in the city council from 1912-1914.[8]

Idaho was made a state in 1890. The census of 1880 had said that there were 85 Jews in the Territory.

JEWISH CONGREGATIONS IN IDAHO

The first congregation in Boise was Beth Israel, organized at a meeting held at the home of Moses Alexander on February 17, 1895. The list of charter members in the group were written as:

D. Spiegel	Louis Stark
L. Weil	David Falk
A. B. Kohny	David Cohen
Leo Spiegel	Leo Falk
L. Boukofsky	Marx Siegel
Julius Grunbaum	Leo H. Seller
George Spiegel	Leo P. Grunbaum
H. Seller	M. Alexander
Sig. Falk	Ben Heymanson
E. Shainwald	Max Mayfield
Max Hardman	Nathan Falk
A. Jackson	Charles H. Stoltz
Joe Spiegel	

By July 24, 1895, they had purchased land for a building on 11th and State Street, and were making plans to build a temple. New members added in 1896 included G. M.

---

[8]*Universal Jewish Encyclopedia, op. cit.,* p. 534.

Simons, Wm. Stark, Wm. Hardman, F. Kahn, J. E. Meyer, L. Hershland, H. Falk, E. O. Lainsvald, I. O. Weiler, and D. Weil.

They evidently worked with dispatch, for the building was first used for the Holy Days of October 1896.[9] The congregation was assisted by contributions from eastern firms with whom they were doing business.

Patterned after one in Illinois, the temple has a full basement with walls of cut stone above ground and large, plain windows. The chapel proper is finished on the outside with shingle in interesting design, with beautiful stained-glass windows, those in the two ends being large and of intricate design.

Minute entries of this congregation are brief and rare, though they do include items dealing with assistance to an indigent family, and a resolution that non-resident members pay dues at $5.00 per year, along with the regular reports of assignments and disbursements.

Though the exact records are not available, the report is that soon after the turn of the century this congregation grew to more than fifty members, but never had a professional rabbi. As the Jewish population declined, the temple was rented occasionally, at one time to the Methodist church and at another to a ward of the L.D.S. (Mormon) Church.

At the present time (1967) the building has been renovated and is no longer available to other faiths; a sprinkling system is installed on the grounds so that the whole place is attractive. Only the annual Holy Days are observed, however, with some members coming in from the military base at Mountain Home, others from Baker, Weiser, and Nampa. Only six to eight families of Reform Jews remain in Boise. Mr. Robert L. Hamersly leads in the rituals. [July, 1967]

"The Jewish part of the cemetery in Boise dates back to 1895, and is at the present time adequate and well kept.

---

[9]Information from the original Ledger Record of Beth Israel Congregation, loaned by Mr. Alexander Simons, of Pocatello, Idaho.

"In 1912 the Orthodox Ahaves (Ahavath) Israel congregation was established with J. Polakoff as Rabbi." This group erected a synagogue in 1949. At the present time there are twenty-one members, who meet weekly. Mr. Martin Heuman is the acting rabbi, or Elder of the Congregation.[10]

"The city of Pocatello formed a congregation in 1924 and elected Myron Porges president."[11]

As was true in Utah, so in Idaho were there Jewish merchants and businessmen in some of the small settlements. Weiser was said to have more Jews in proportion to its population than any other city of Idaho. A letter to Mrs. Sam Emrich brought to light some interesting information.

Sam Emrich arrived in Weiser in 1916, coming by train with his recently widowed mother and his brother, Bertrand, and sisters, Ethel and Elsie (twins), and Rita. They came on the invitation of her brother, Henry Haas, who was in the leather and saddle business there.

Sam was sixteen at that time, and worked for Morris Sommer in the Herman Haas Hardware Building, a general mercantile store, which carried hardware, groceries, and clothing. There were also in business in Weiser Bernard Haas, the banker, Mark Schass, Morris Sommer, Harry Woolf, and Morris Rheinhaus. Marcus Rheinhaus is still operating the shoe firm his mother established there. "There are at this writing Sam, Bert and Belle Emrich — Marcus and Hazel Reinhaus still living in Weiser . . . total — five!"

In 1907 there were reported 300 Jews in Idaho.

In 1966 The Jewish Yearbook [V. 67] lists only 120.

MEYER COHN

Another Jew who deserves a place in Idaho history is Meyer Cohn. Born in Schweutz, West Prussia, June 28, 1844, he came to America as a young man. After some time in New York, he decided to move west. He came first to Utah,

---

[10]Information from Mr. Martin Heuman, Elder of the Congregation, July, 1967.

[11]*Universal Jewish Encyclopedia, op. cit.*, Vol. 5, p. 534.

and later moved north to Malad, Idaho, where he operated a general store. From there he moved into the Marsh Valley and took up a large homestead. This was a new area, modern machinery was not yet available, and one must raise a variety of crops in order to survive — forage for cattle and horses, wheat, vegetables, and some fruit were included.

He was well established before the railroad came through that area. It was he who led out in forming the first irrigation company of that section, making possible the improvement of thousands of acres of virgin land.

He was public spirited, serving two terms as county commissioner, during which time the agricultural production of the area made tremendous strides. Much of the prosperity of the Arimo area was due to his foresight and energy.

He died in 1927 at the home of a son-in-law, Herbert Hirschman.[12]

---

[12]Kate B. Carter, *Treasures of Pioneer History,* (Salt Lake City, 1952, Daughters of Utah Pioneers), Vol. 1, p. 372.

Chapter Nine

UTAH JEWS OUTSIDE SALT LAKE CITY

THE PERIOD OF home building in Salt Lake City over the turn of the century was common to most other parts of the state. In the first settlement of the towns and villages, there was usually among the small, one-story dwellings one large, two-story adobe house built for the bishop — or by the bishop. This was a necessity, for visiting authorities must have a place to stay on their periodic trips. Through travel, though not heavy, also needed points where supplies could be obtained and shelter found when the weather was bad. Many of these houses still remain, standing out prominently in villages like Payson, Mona, Scipio, Beaver, and Parowan. In Cedar City, St. George, and other towns they have been replaced by modern buildings or service stations.

The homes built during the 1895-1905 period in the outlying settlements were mostly of brick. The usual pattern was a basic three rooms, often two stories high, built in an L with a cellar under the back room and the same gabled roof that had characterized Mormon buildings in Nauvoo. Solid and comfortable, they were a decided improvement.

Up to this time, and continuing until later, each village was an almost self-supporting unit upon a base of agriculture. Each family produced its own milk, butter, pork, eggs, vegetables, fruit, and berries, usually its own honey, or in the southern settlements, molasses. Each village was responsible for its own schools and general entertainment. And at this time almost every one had a neighborhood store operated by a Jew.

Any list of the Jews in Utah villages is bound to be incomplete, for sometimes a Jewish merchant would open shop in two or three places in as many years. On the other hand, a few established themselves permanently, each content to do business with all comers, but remaining aloof and private in his religious practices.

Cedar City: Sam Holland operated a hide and junk business there for many years, drawing pelts from a wide area over southern Utah and Nevada. Sam is now in the Holy Land. Al Cline also had an auto agency there.

Milford: At this railroad town in the south there were three Cline brothers, Sam and Harold, attorneys, and Al,[1] who was a distributor of soft drinks throughout the area.

Beaver: Abe and Morris Marcus operated a general store. A. B. Cline ran a "Golden Rule Store" in Beaver also.

Nephi: Louis Frank had a clothing store here.

Richfield: About 1900 Max and Sol Krotki opened a store here called "The Regulator." Later they closed and moved to *Kimberly,* a mining town, where Max Krotki and Charles Skougaard opened a general merchandise store under the name "The K. & S." When the mines closed down, Max went to *Marysvale* and Sol moved in to Salt Lake City.

Also in *Richfield* in the early 1900s J. W. Werner opened The Richfield Clothing Store. When he died, about 1917, he left a thousand dollars to each of the two Jenson boys who had worked for him. He was unmarried.

Minersville: Among the first settlers were Louis Lessing and his wife Henrietta Happeck Lessing, both of whom were born in Germany. They had settled briefly at Pioche, Nevada,

---

[1]Information on the Jews at Milford was incomplete. Additional items:

Before the turn of the century two Jewish brothers came to *Milford:* I. Cline and A. B. Cline. They opened "The Golden Rule Store," a general merchandise establishment. Soon A. B. Cline moved to Beaver and set up another store under the same name.

I. Cline had three sons: Sam, Harold, and Al. Sam and Harold both became attorneys. Al went into business at Cedar City, where he had an automobile agency and also a wholesale cold drink dispensary.

Also in *Milford* Isadore Altman operated a dry goods store. This store is still in operation by younger members of the family.

During the war a refugee Jewish doctor from Germany set up a practice in Milford and remained for three years. He moved to Berkeley, California. (Information from Mrs. Loretta Cline, wife of Harold Cline, deceased.)

but moved on to Minersville in the fall of 1858. Mr. Lessing had interest in a smelter in Nevada, and they did the first smelting done in Utah here. Louis's brother Gus also worked with him.

The Lessings built the Lessing Hotel, for many years the largest building in Minersville. They made their own adobes, burned them into brick, and secured their lumber from the Beaver mountains. They were the parents of five children. Louis died in 1906; Henrietta in 1912. Both are buried in Salt Lake City.

Joseph Dupaix came to Minersville in 1870, put up a store, and operated the post office. His family later moved to Salt Lake City.

William Gressman with his wife and son Joseph operated a business in Minersville also, as did J. C. Semonds.[2]

Gunnison: Max Cohen operated a general store here and also one at *Salina.* At that time there were two banks in Gunnison and another at *Centerfield.* Max became president of the bank in Gunnison. The Jewish peddler who gathered hides and scrap iron in all this area was Harry Polleai.

Price: Harry Lowenstein operated a dry goods store here, with Ben and Sam Stein as clerks. A Mr. Groesbeck, also Jewish, worked for him. Mr. Lowenstein set up a branch store at *Helper,* which Sam Stein operated for a time and then purchased.

Harry Gordon and his young wife, Sarah Bonstik, arrived in America in 1911 and settled in Price in 1914. For the next forty-five years they operated the "Price Hide, Junk, and Metal Company."

Vernal: Morris Glassman opened a mercantile store here in 1905. Soon he had branch houses in *Castle Dale* and *Huntington.*

Here, a little later, Abe Weiss operated a hide, fur, and junk company.

---

[2]Alvaretta Robinson and Daisy Gillins, *The History of Minersville,* (Minersville Centennial Committee) 1962. Copy at the Utah State Historical Society.

Midvale: Charles Poritzky had a general merchandise store here.

Sandy: The Poliner family have operated here for many years.

Garfield: Sam Matz and Sam Glazier both operated stores here during the boom years.

Payson: Nate Horne opened a general merchandise store here, which he operated for a number of years. In 1920 Ben Roe came to work as a clerk, but later bought out the establishment. He tells an incident of how the ten Presbyterian families in Payson formed a club to which all other non-Mormons were invited. When it was Ben's turn to furnish a program for the evening, he invited Judge Herbert Schiller to come down and discuss the beliefs and doctrines of Judaism.

This night the women were also invited, so they had a packed house. Judge Schiller rode down on the Bamberger Line and gave them all an evening to remember, for they all left with some entirely new ideas about what it means to be a Jew.

Soon after this, Ben sold out and moved into Salt Lake City.[3]

JEWS IN PROVO

Samuel and Rosetta Nelke Schwab

The Samuel Schwabs were both American-born Jews, Samuel in Cincinnati, Ohio, February 14, 1858, and Rosetta Nelke in New York City, August 30, 1862. They met in Quincy, Illinois, where Mr. Nelke was a partner in the dry goods firm of Joseph & Nelke. Soon after their marriage in 1886 the couple moved to Dodge City, Kansas, a blustering frontier town at the division point of the railroad.

In 1891 they moved to Provo, Utah, where for twenty-five years they made their home. Their business in men's furnishings was one of the most popular in the city.

---

[3]Ben Roe, personal interview, Dec. 8, 1966.

They were well accepted socially. Mrs. Schwab was active in community life, in the P.T.A., and in various charitable enterprises. She was one of the organizers of "The Nineteenth Century Club." Their sons, Dore and Frank, were also well oriented and popular.

Mr. Schwab also had interest in the mines around Eureka and Park City; he owned an apple orchard on Provo Bench; he was a supporter of the Provo Woolen Mills. He belonged to the Chamber of Commerce and the Elks' Club; he was active in politics, supporting Reed Smoot in his candidacy for the U. S. Senate. He counted among his friends Jesse Knight, Ed Loos, and George H. Brimhall, president of the Brigham Young University.

In 1900 the Schwabs built a beautiful home on University Avenue, one of a number of fine homes that were erected along that street during the early 1900s.

Mr. Schwab retired from business in 1916, and in 1921 moved to Hollywood, California, where Mrs. Schwab died within a few years. Mr. Schwab also died there in 1947.[4]

Miss Miriam Nelke

In the career of Miss Miriam Nelke in Utah we have an example of a Hebrew lady who was dearly loved by her Mormon neighbors. Miss Nelke, born July 27, 1868, in New York City, made her visit to Provo, Utah, in the summer of 1900. As a child she had shown great promise in her ability to memorize, and even then was in demand for reciting in churches, clubs, and social affairs. She had been given university training and attended special schools, until by the time she came to Utah she was a member of the National Association of Elocutionists (later the National Speech Arts Association) and had served on their board for a number of years.

It happened that her "visit" lasted for eight years. She went to the Brigham Young Academy and talked to Benjamin

---

[4]Kate B. Carter, *Hidden Treasures of Pioneer History*, (Salt Lake City, 1952) Vol. 1, pp. 365-366.

Cluff, then president of the institution. He granted her permission to organize classes in Oral English and Dramatic Art. The terms were most liberal: the school provided her with classrooms and she paid a small percentage of her tuition returns to the department.

Her classes grew rapidly. Students enjoyed her work and profited by it. The institution benefited, also, for her trained readers entertained at assemblies and school functions, took out programs advertising the school, and appeared in civic and club meetings. Professor Elbert Eastmond cooperated in helping with stage fixtures and settings; Professor A. C. Lund supplemented her programs with musical numbers by his students. Occasionally Miss Nelke herself would do a full program.

When in 1908 Miss Nelke received a request from Mr. Fred J. Butler to cooperate with him in opening a dramatic school in San Francisco, she could not refuse, for she considered this a great opportunity.

The faculty and students of the B.Y.U. showed much love and respect for her in their farewells. Even Joseph F. Smith, President of the Mormon Church, paid her high compliments. At the farewell party in her honor the gymnasium was crowded. The students presented her with a leather-covered book, containing signatures and sentiments from every one. Best of all, a reading club was named for her — "The Nelke Reading Club." This was organized in 1916. Some people even now speak of her with great affection.

She died December 20, 1942, in Hollywood, California.[5]

Other Jews in business in Provo included the Bukofzer brothers, Leon and Sherman, who operated a shoe store, and Sam Perlman who operated a hide, metal, and junk yard. This was a successful enterprise which is carried on by his son, Phil Perlman. Leven's Dry Goods is also a Jewish establishment. Leven Brothers also have stores in Ogden and Salt Lake City.[6]

---

[5]Edith Y. Booth, "The Early Jews in Utah County," Carter, *Treasures* . . . *op. cit.*, V. 1, pp. 366-367.
[6]Personal interview, Theron Luke, Dec. 12, 1969.

JEWS IN OGDEN

For years after the completion of the railroad Ogden continued to be the clearinghouse for all arrivals in Utah. Usually Jewish immigrants stayed here for a time to look into opportunities before going north into Idaho or Montana, or on to the Far West. Often the businessmen who remained to make this their permanent base had tried their luck in several other places before.

The early Jews mentioned in connection with their first religious observances were Ben Oppman, Sam Rosenbluth, D. and J. Kraines, J. and W. Benowitz. These were Orthodox Jews. Those from Ogden, evidently Reform Jews, who subscribed to the Jewish Publications in 1904 were: Samuel Kline, 315 - 24th Street; Hyman Lewis, 539 - 23rd Street; L. Siegel, 160 - 25th Street; and H. L. White, 2336 Washington Avenue.

These nine men must represent a very small portion of the Jewish people who were living in Ogden. Often the freighters and businessmen, and other who establish industry, go about without leaving any detail of their religious affiliation. For example: Gilbert & Gerrish, pioneers in the area, can be classed as Jewish only by the name "Abel Gilbert" and the record of his helpfulness to known Jews.

Stories of a few of the influential Jews of Ogden follow.

Frederick J. Kiesel

Frederick J. Kiesel was born May 19, 1841, in Ludwigsburg, Wurtemburg, Germany. [Bancroft says Bordenburg, Germany.] He left home in January, 1857, to come to America. For a time he peddled goods in Tennessee, and in 1861 was compelled to serve as a teamster in the Confederate army. He came to Utah in 1863 "to get away from the war."[7]

Mr. Kiesel came to Salt Lake City in one of the Henry W. Lawrence merchants' trains, and upon his arrival was employed by Abel Gilbert, often called the "pioneer Gentile merchant of Utah." The goods arrived in late spring of 1863:

---

[7]"Utah Biographical Sketches," Bancroft Mss. 188, p. 52.

by early fall Kiesel was on his way to Soda Springs, Idaho, with a part of them, since Fort Connor had been set up there as an outpost for part of the California volunteers.

After selling his stock, Kiesel returned to Salt Lake City, but was promptly sent to Manti in Sevier Valley to open a store in connection with Fielding J. Lewis. This was in 1864. By the next spring he had disposed of his goods, so returned to Gilbert in Salt Lake City. Now he was promptly dispatched northward to Cache Valley with a large stock for Wellsville. His second stock for this area was sold in bulk to a Mr. Allen.

In the summer of 1866 Mr. Kiesel brought a stock of goods to Ogden, which he sold in bulk to the Ogden Cooperative, the first store of its kind to be organized in the Territory. In the winter of 1866 he came with another stock from Gilbert & Co. These goods he bought for himself and moved to Paris, Idaho, for the summer of 1867. He conducted a business here for a year, opening also a branch at Montpelier.

He continued his business in the north until his assistant, Mr. Fred Wisner, was killed in the spring of 1869 by some unknown persons, evidently with robbery as a motive. At this, Mr. Kiesel sold out and left the Bear Lake area never to return.

In the meantime Gilbert & Sons had failed in Ogden, and Mr. Kiesel now assumed their business. He managed well for nearly two years, until the smallpox epidemic prostrated all business there. He transferred his business to Ophir, then a booming mining town; at the same time he bought out the business of Isadore Morris in Bingham. Soon he sold both of these to advantage and took a trip to Europe, in the hope that he could find himself a proper wife. He succeeded in this, returning in the fall of 1873 a happily married man.

He went at once to Corinne where he associated himself with Mr. Gumpert Goldberg under the firm name of Fred J. Kiesel & Co. They conducted a wholesale and retail grocery business with considerable success for a time. When the Utah Northern railroad reached Blackfoot, Idaho, they closed out their business there and returned to Ogden to make their head-quarters. Mr. Kiesel and Mr. Goldberg remained as partners for a time. Upon the death of Mr. Goldberg in 1881 Mr. Kiesel took over.

During 1882 he established branch houses at Hailey, Ketchum, Vienna, and Pocatello in Idaho and Ontario in Oregon. Mr. Fred J. Kiesel was sole manager of this gigantic enterprise.

Although he aspired to be only a good merchant, he did become active in politics, supporting the Liberal party in Utah. He took a lively interest in the local municipal affairs.[8]

Gumpert Goldberg

Mr. Gumpert Goldberg deserves a brief sketch here. He was born in Germany in 1832, and came to America as a boy of thirteen. He came west to Colorado, where he met and married Miss Helena Morris. Together they went to the "Last Chance Gulch" in Montana. Here the new city was given her name, HELENA, after the miners could not agree because each wanted it named for his own home town. This was in 1868.

The Goldbergs came to Corinne with the railroad in 1869, and then to Ogden where they became partners with Fred J. Kiesel in the grocery business. Though Mr. Goldberg died while on a trip to Germany, his body was brought to Salt Lake City for burial.

Two Goldberg daughters, Augusta and Theresa, married the Simon brothers, Louis and Fred. The third daughter married Edward Silberstein.[9]

M. Isadore Marks and Louis Goldsmith

M. Isadore Marks was born in Posen, Germany, June 1, 1845, a son of Joel Marks and Adelaide Brock. His father was an agriculturist and merchant, who sent his son to the academy. At fifteen the boy left his studies for other interests, and at eighteen he came to the United States. Arriving in

---

[8]Carter, *op. cit.,* pp. 370-371.
[9]Leon L. Watters, *The Pioneer Jews of Utah,* (New York, 1952) p. 155.

New York City, he found employment as a clerk in a dry goods store. After a few years there he set out for the West, working his way in various places until he arrived in Salt Lake City in 1869. Here he found employment with the firm of Watters Brothers, Jewelers, being sent in December following to open up a store in Ogden.

This did not succeed as well as the owners had hoped, so it was closed and Marks went in 1870 to Corinne where he worked for Louis Cohn in his dry goods store. As business in Corinne declined he secured a small stock and moved to the mining camp of Toano, Nevada, where he set up shop under his own name as I. Marks & Co.

In 1876 he moved to Ogden, where he took up permanent residence and set up in the clothing business. In 1881 he took in as a partner Louis Goldsmith, a native of Bavaria, Germany, and changed the name to Marks, Goldsmith & Company.

Louis Goldsmith had arrived in America as a young man. He had traveled somewhat as a peddler and was finally employed in a business in Baltimore. This firm did business with Nevada, Idaho, Montana, Oregon, and Utah houses, and Goldsmith decided to see some of these places. In Ogden he found his opportunity with Mr. Marks, for the two men worked together over many years and built up one of the largest wholesale and retail establishments in Ogden.

Both men had families. Goldsmith's wife was Miss Esther Siegel of Baltimore, Maryland. Isadore Marks in 1873 married Miss Selina Bornstein of Corinne.[10]

The Kuhn Brothers, Adam and Abraham

In their business life it was the younger brother, Adam, who proved to be the leader. He was born in Weisenheim on the Berg Rhein-pfalz, October 23, 1844, the son of Joseph and Fanny Eichold Kuhn. He came to America alone and went immediately to Des Moines, Iowa, where he was employed in a wholesale clothing and dry goods store belonging to his kinsmen, J. and I. Kuhn. In five years during which he worked for this firm he acquired an insight into the business. In 1862 he moved on west to Denver, where he entered into transporting goods by mule trains to Utah and Montana. In 1869 with the coming of the railroad he sold out his trains and stores and joined his brother Abraham, who was six years his senior, at Corinne, Utah, which at that time held promise of being the metropolis of Utah Territory.

Abraham had been in America two years longer than had Adam, but he had shifted about a great deal from Vincennes, Indiana, to Council Bluffs, Iowa, where he closed out one stock of goods before the Mormons left in 1852. After brief stays in Denver and then in Montana, he arrived in Salt Lake City in 1864. He remained only two years, moved to Montana, made a visit of more than a year to Europe, and returned to America in the fall of 1869. He joined his brother Adam at Corinne at this time, and their business was successful enough that they had branch stores in Evanston, Wyoming, and Ogden, Utah.

By 1880 they decided to concentrate their interests in Ogden, and within a few years had prospered until in 1886 they purchased a large plot on the west side of Main Street and erected one of the finest buildings in the city. It was known as Kuhn Block.

Mr. Abraham Kuhn married the daughter of Abraham and Fredrica Rosenbaum of Germany. They had four sons and two daughters. Mr. Adam Kuhn evidently did not marry. Their names are not mentioned on the early records of the Jewish congregation in Ogden "Ohab Sholem," which was organized in 1890.[11]

JEWS IN LOGAN

There have never been Jews enough in Logan to organize a congregation. Several businesses from Ogden and Salt Lake City have organized branch houses here, operated by Jewish people.

---

[10]Carter, *Treasures, op. cit.,* pp. 371-372.
[11]Carter, *Treasures, op. cit.,* pp. 369-370.

Harry Bonstik, a Russian Jew, settled here with his young wife, Eta Freshman, who was born in Parsavitch, Russia. They arrived in Logan soon after their marriage on March 10, 1914, and opened up the Cache Valley Hide, Metal and Junk Shop, at which they succeeded well. Their son Willis now operates it. Mrs. Bonstik died August 20, 1969; Harry is retired. The family are members of Montefiore Congregation in Salt Lake City.[12]

JEWS IN PARK CITY

Julius Frankel was running a store in Park City before the fire of 1896. His nephew, Blythe Fargo, built a big store there; in 1902 he established a clothing shop and brought in Albert Seaman, his nephew, to help run it. About that time he moved to Denver and set up a business in school supplies, while Seaman took over the clothing store in Park City. In 1924, Seaman took Jim Gwilliam into this establishment.[13]

JEWS IN TOOELE

The Sol Selvin Family

The Sol J. Selvin family came from Russia. Born in a small town in Lithuania, Selvin educated himself and became a teacher in the elementary school. After he served his four-year term in the Russian army, he married a local girl, Fannia Frank, also a schoolteacher. Together they set up a private school, operating it until after their first two children were born. Then they decided to emigrate to America.

They arrived in Murray, Utah, in 1909, but moved soon to Tooele, where Sol found employment in a clothing store. Somehow they managed to live through the lean years and to keep their children in school. Two more were born in America.

The two older ones, a son and a daughter, both graduated from the University of California, and found positions; the younger two would follow their example. Meantime, Sol

---

[12]Logan *Herald,* Obituary, August 20, 1969.
[13]Personal interview, Jim Gwilliam, St. George, Utah, October 9, 1969.

and Fannia wanted to enter into public life. Sol was elected as state representative from Tooele County in 1934 where he served until 1942. Then he was made mayor of Tooele City. In 1944 he was elected to the state senate.

In the meantime, Fannia was working in the public schools, and was succeeding very well when she died of cancer.

Sol's public service included fifteen years on the welfare board, of which he was chairman. He worked as chairman for the Tooele County Chapter of the Infantile Paralysis Board. He also was active in the Scouting program and director of the Tooele County Chamber of Commerce.

JEWISH COLONIZATION

Clarion

Many of the Jews who came to Utah followed a pattern. After a stay in New York City they moved out along the general routes of travel, many going to California or Nevada before they came back to Utah. Often as soon as one member of a family became established he would send for a brother to join him.

The first colonizing attempt in Utah was the result of two agencies: the State of Utah and the Central Jewish Colonization Society of Philadelphia.

For several years California and Colorado and others of the western states had held expositions and fairs to advertise the opportunities each offered to attract new capital and colonists. To these, Utah had sent displays and brochures Now the officials decided to take aggressive action to induce new settlers and business to come to their own state.

Some private companies had undertaken land sales earlier, but now for the first time the State decided upon an active policy of reclamation. The year 1906 marked a peak in the water run-off of the Sevier Valley, and through the years following it continued rather high. So in 1910 the state began construction of the Piute Reservoir, south of Marysvale, to impound water for lands below. About the same time they constructed another dam above Hatch to bring under cultivation some 4,000 acres of land east and north of Panguitch. In short, there was everywhere a spirit of optimism. With plenty of land, maximum use of water would open opportunities for a great increase in population. Accordingly the State Bureau of Statistics was reorganized and called the Bureau of Immigration, Labor, and Statistics, and definitely charged with the business of bringing in new colonists to help vitalize the general economy.

At this same time there was in Philadelphia a Jewish Colonization Society, whose purpose it was to help relieve the congestion of Jewish people in that area and place them upon the land. Representing this group was Benjamin Brown, who investigated possibilities in Utah and persuaded the leaders of his Colonization Society that this would be a good place in which to plant a colony. The *American Israelite* for August 24, 1911, quoting from daily papers of Utah, reported:

> . . . the Jewish Colonization Society early in August became the purchasers of a large tract of land at public auction in Manti. The land was sold by W. D. Crandall, chairman of the state board of land commissioners, who offered in all 8,000 acres. The society will place 500 families on the land, beginning with 200 of these next spring. Later the Jewish colony will number 1,000 families. . . .

The strip of land purchased was an area approximately three miles in width by five miles in length along the Sevier River. It had been appraised at from $3.00 to $25.00 per acre, but the whole tract was sold for an average of $11.20 per acre, with one-tenth of the total as a down payment, and low, long-time annual payments. The Jews did not purchase the entire 8,000 acres; they rejected entirely some of the marginal land. The Jewish Association made a down payment of $6,815.20, which represented an investment by each member of $350.00. One hundred and fifty-two filed for a title and got it. Each member filed a Declaration, giving name, date, and place of birth, and occupation, the originals of which are now on file among the Utah State papers, and form a valuable source for study. It is interesting to note that among them all, only one man listed himself as a farmer. All were from Russia, all were between twenty and thirty years of age.[14]

The State of Utah raised the height of the Piute Dam by eight feet, thereby almost doubling its capacity, and extended the canal thirty-five miles to bring water to this area.

In Philadelphia twelve "pioneers" were selected by drawing numbers from a hat, since all were eager to come. They arrived in Utah in early August 1911, and proceeded to clear, plow, and plant, until within the year they had 1,500 acres under cultivation with crops of alfalfa, oats, and wheat. Though they lived in tents themselves, they had the best of modern equipment for working the land. They also had assistance from faculty and senior students from the Utah State Agricultural College at Logan, so that the beginnings gave hope for the future. As Benjamin Brown said, "They worked twenty-five hours a day to make this venture a success."

This was truly a cooperative undertaking. The young men, supplied with equipment and tools, received $15.00 per week for their labor. By 1912 some fifty-two families had arrived, and the land was surveyed and divided into plots of approximately forty acres each, facing each other along the road. According to the MEMORY BOOK put out by

---

[14]A definitive study of this Jewish Colonization attempt has been made by Dr. Everett L. Cooley, Director of the Utah State Historical Society, and published in the Utah *Historical Quarterly,* Spring, 1968, V. 36, No. 2, pp. 113-132.

"The records of the Utah State Land Board contain the applications of 152 Jews for title to land and water under the Piute Reservoir Project, . . . The Declaration gives place of birth and residence, date of birth, and occupation. For example:

Hyman Dinerstein, factory worker, 77 Second Ave., New York, came to U.S. on the vessel *New York* from Vilna, Russia, arriving July 24, 1904.
Jeremiah Andrews, laundryman from Minsk, Russia . . .
Boris Sxraly, tailor from Tirospol, Russia . . .
Morris Weissenberg, an artist from Jitomir, Russia . . .
Leon Sandrstzy, a machinist from Odessa, Russia . . .
Sam Levitsky, a furrier from Kiev, Russia . . .
Harry Brazin, a mirror maker from Kremcnchuk, Russia . . .
Other trades represented were bricklayer, civil engineer, laborer, trimming dealer, picture-frame maker, cabinet maker, druggist, carpenter, weaver, electrician, book-binder, railroad conductor, cutter, student, and *one* honest-to-goodness farmer, Harry Tucker, 26 years of age, from Walinsky, Russia. pp. 120-121.

the committee to commemorate Gunnison Valley's Centennial in 1959, "Frame homes, corrals, and other improvements on the property were financed by a wealthy sponsor, Harry Joseph." The account goes on to say that the workers had the latest models of farm machinery, and some had good furniture, rugs, china, treasures of art, and other cherished personal belongings, which made their homes comfortable and beautiful. According to this account:

> Near the center of the settlement, a small school house was built. It was used for church and public gatherings. A community well, several hundred feet deep, furnished culinary water. This well is still in use. Shade trees were planted all along the road, but they failed to survive.

> To celebrate their first anniversary, a Harvest Festival was held on August 12, 1912. For this occasion a large bowery was erected, refreshments prepared, and people from all around invited to be in attendance. Governor Spry was the speaker of the day. He praised the colonists for their many accomplishments. . . .[15]

From the beginning, the relation of the Jewish people with their Mormon neighbors was good — as good as it could be when neither spoke the other's language. But the people of Gunnison did invite the newcomers to a public dinner; they gave the settlers fruit from their orchards for the picking of it. Some of the Mormon women helped in the first new venture of "bottling" excess fruit for winter use.

At first the Jewish families had only one team and outfit to serve four homes, and since this was for hauling culinary water, groceries, etc. from Gunnison, it served fairly well for awhile. One cow was supposed to serve four families, but some thought of her as a storage plant from which a quart or so could be taken at a time as needed. More difficult was the sharing of one coal-oil lamp by two families. Yet in spite of it all they did manage to have "Literary Evenings" when they gathered to read to each other or to discuss new stories or old classics.

---

[15]Mrs. Orpha Whitlock, Editor, *Memory Book, to Commemorate Gunnison Valley's Centennial*, p. 93. Book at Utah Historical Society.

As with the Swiss in Santa Clara or the Swedes in San-pete, so the Jews in Clarion have provided some good folklore. One man left his horses harnessed together overnight, because he saw no need to repeat the complicated procedure of har-nessing up again the next morning. Another, driving into the river, wanted his thirsty horses to get a drink, but thought he must jack up the hind-end of the wagon in order to give the tongue the right slant, when he needed only to unsnap the checkline. Still another took the bridles off entirely, and then wading into the above-the-knee-deep water, could not put them back on again, with the result that the team took off without them. Attempts to stop the horses only excited them more, so that the result was a runaway and a wreck of the outfit.

Yet with all their problems, they did do well for the first two years. Mr. Will Barnes of the United States Forest Service visited the colony in 1913. He was much impressed by Ben Brown, who seemed as a modern Moses who had led his people to the Promised Land. Barnes described the lush growth of alfalfa and called Clarion "a land of milk and honey."

The year 1914 began with a promise of even greater success, so that there was such a general feeling of optimism that the government officials felt justified in encouraging more people to share it. On February 14, Governor Spry and a party visited Rabbi Isaac Landman and the Jewish people in Philadelphia and gave a glowing report of develop-ments in Utah. The people had built thirty-three homes; their fields were thriving.

> The conference was held in the Bellevue-Stratford. In the Governor's party were Attorney General A. R. Barnes, W. D. Candland, president of the State Land Board; W. J. Lynch, secre-tary of the State Land Board; Senator Henry Gardner, president pro tem of the State Senate; and W. R. Wallace, Democratic National Committeeman. . . .
>
> Governor Spry and Mr. Candland described . . . the rapid progress the Jewish colonists had made in adapting themselves to

Western customs and adopting modern farming methods, a problem of the latter being the reclamation of the desert by irrigation. Fifty families were sent to Utah two and a half years ago under the auspices of the Jewish Colonial Association. . . . [They] intend to send 100 additional families . . . within a few months; 85 of these live in Philadelphia and the remainder in New York. . . . The average price an acre, including cost of irrigation, is $45.00. . . .

This is somewhat different than the $11.20 per acre which was first quoted. Governor Spry was quick to say that the Jewish settlers were an asset to Utah, but he did not promise too early returns:

"Utahans are pleased with the experiment, and it has been remarkably successful. We regard the colonists as extremely desirable citizens. . . . In a few years they will become independent.

Mr. Candland was even more enthusiastic, for he had personally supervised the distribution of the land. "Their tract," he explained "is one of the most fertile to be found in the West. Taken from the cities . . . they rapidly learned farming and are an industrious, efficient class."[16]

Conditions in August were not so good as they had appeared in February. "The farmers did learn how to build irrigation ditches and control of the flow of water . . . partly from their own ingenuity and partly from help of the agricultural experts of the Utah State Agricultural College. The problem was lack of water. The canal was built and the headgates put in, but there was not enough water, and being at the end of the ditch, the people of Clarion did not get their share."

That this was true is shown further by the fact that the Jewish Association entered a damage suit against the state for failure to supply the promised water, asking $14,250.00 to cover their loss. This was based upon the production of land where the grain received water as compared to the total loss on acreage where the only missing element was water. The

[16]*The American Israelite*, Vol. 60 (Feb. 19, 1949) p. 5.

soil, the seed, the preparation all would show that the suit was justified.

Contributing also to their discouragement was a flash flood, which leveled much of their lush alfalfa crop, burying it under silt and boulders.[17]

The State did vote to extend the time of payment of the annual fee; one or two men had purchased their land independent of the Jewish Association. Others seeking credit from friends in the East found a disposition to doubt an undertaking that had only gone further into debt with each succeeding year. Some few families returned to the East, but on November 15, 1915, the entire remaining population boarded a train for California. Transportation was provided by wealthy Jews of Utah.[18] They felt that opportunities in California were better, the distance was shorter, and the people would not have to face chagrin or shame in meeting their old friends in Philadelphia under the stigma of having failed.

On January 18, 1916, the lands held by the people of Clarion were put up for sale. The one among them who refused to admit defeat was Benjamin Brown, who with his brother, Nathan, remained to make a marked success in the business of chicken and egg production.

The basic reason for the abandonment of this project is very well expressed in the concluding paragraph of Barbara Vogel's paper, "The Clarion Call:"

> Mr. Isaac Isgur offered a thoughtful comment on what appeared to some to be a lack of determination. He observes that in Clarion as in any other undeveloped area, there could be no culture where there was no food. When Clarion colonists saw themselves struggling over the bare necessities of life, often with children hungry and with husband and wife unhappy in their life together because they had to fight so hard for a bare existence, it

---

[17]*Memory Book, op. cit.*

[18]Salt Lake businessmen who contributed to help the Jewish colonists to move to California included Adolph Baer of Baer Mercantile Company, Adolph Simon of Paris Millinery, George S. Auerbach, Louis Cohn, Samuel Newhouse, David Spitz, Nathan Rosenblatt, Edward Rosenbaum, and Daniel Alexander.

seemed that three years were enough. These men and women wanted a fuller life — a life where one would have time for books and music and philosophy. When Clarion seemed unable to provide such a life, the colonists reluctantly gave in to the economic pressures.[19]

So Clarion left only legends and folklore, with one book published which will preserve them. A certain Mr. Bender, totally illiterate himself, was a gifted teller of tales for the community, stories to entertain and to philosophize about. Isaac Friedland, a writer of some talent, asked that Mr. Bender be his working companion, and at night put into writing the stories of the day. These, with experiences of his own, he combined into a book, *The Virgin Soil*. Written in Yiddish, it awaits translation. Through its pages the spirit of the Clarion settlement will be handed on.

One great benefit from the Clarion experiment must not be overlooked. It was the formation of the Utah Egg and Poultry Association. Ben Brown, who had been the moving spirit of the first undertaking, often called their "Moses," would not give up the project. After the others had gone, he and his brother Nathan, with Clyde Edmonds and Bert Willardson, combined to form the Utah Poultry Association, which has now grown into a multi-million dollar operation. Before this time Utah was shipping in both eggs and poultry. Now her market is nationwide.[20]

From this point in history we might conclude that perhaps the Jewish people did not fail; perhaps they just had perception enough to know that no one could succeed under these conditions, so did not waste more time trying. As proof consider the fact that in 1919, just three years after the land was sold, a group of Mormon families moved onto the site.

---

[19]Barbara Vogel, "The Clarion Call!" a story of the Jewish colony near Gunnison. Manuscript at Utah State Historical Society.

[20]*The Deseret News,* March 5, 1943, under the title, OF WHICH WE ARE PROUD, gives details of the organization of the Utah Poultry Producers' Cooperative Association. Beginning on that date in 1923 with a capital of $17,000, a membership of 247 producers and four small plants situated in Ogden, Salt Lake, Provo, and American Fork, it had grown to a net worth of $1,500,000, with 32 plants and 14,000 members.

The village grew to 142 families, with a population of more than 600. Though they had the advantage of all the clearing, leveling, and ditching which had been done by the Jews, they too were forced to move. After fifteen years of labor, they left their holdings in 1934 for the same reason — lack of water.[21]

Closely paralleling the experience at Clarion was that of the town of McCornick, except that the latter was promoted by a private land company rather than by the state. (It was located on Utah 26, between Holden and Delta, 16 miles from Delta.) This company put in the dam and built the cement ditches, surveyed and laid out the lots and fields. These settlers were not Mormons "called" to establish a town. They were Americans all, people of many faiths, seeking opportunity. The town lasted ten heartbreaking years (1919-1929) before the last family left, literally dried out.

At its highest count McCornick had seventy-one families, a population of more than 375 persons, a two-room schoolhouse in which church and other public meetings were held. The records of the Mormon books for the time the ward organization lasted show ninety-five babies born there. In the cemetery ten young children are buried. The two young mothers and two youths almost to manhood grown were taken elsewhere for burial. The story has been written by Mrs. LaVell Johnson under the title, "The Desert Wins Again."

The point to be made here is that while these people held on for ten years, the Jews learned more quickly and did not waste so much time and energy.[22]

---

[21]LaVell Johnson, Delta, Utah, has made a study of these transient towns under the title "The Desert Wins Again," unpublished manuscript at the Utah State Historical Society.

[22]Mention has been made here of the high runoff of the Sevier River in 1906, and of the sharp fluctuations of high and low between that year and 1922. Careful records and continued studies show that in 1966 the Sevier River maintained only one-tenth as much land under cultivation as it did in 1922.

Present-day cattlemen speak of the "70-year drouth," or "the 80-year drouth," depending upon their personal knowledge. One needs only to read the descriptions, not only of Powell, Carvalho, Heap, and other travelers over the Old Spanish Trail, but the diaries of John Pulsipher at Hebron and of A. W. Ivins to know that everywhere there was grass. When Brigham Young named the area below Pipe Springs "Canaan, the land flowing with milk and honey," in 1870, it was a sea of waving grass. True, it was overgrazed, but the real answer to the present barren condition is lack of water.

Nor was Clarion the only attempt of Jews to plant themselves on the land in Utah. In 1914 a group of some one hundred families moved to Park Valley, in the extreme northwest part of Utah, near what was at one time Rosette, a small village. These people settled the large valley, but repeated drought caused them to leave in 1920. The *Tribune* for August 9, 1936, noted that a "Once Prosperous Russian Colony in Park Valley Melts to One Family." The reporter gave Mr. Charles I. Goodliffe, who kept a store in Park Valley, as the source of his information.

Records of the Sevier River Water Association show that seven families of Jews settled on the northwest point of Utah Lake, expecting to provide their water from the source by pumping. They left before the end of the second year. The project was called "Mosida."

In striking contrast is the success story of the two Zuckerman brothers, Maurice and Herbert — Maurice the businessman and financier, and Herbert the geneticist and seed expert. Together they produced the world's best baking potato and ran the world's largest potato farm.

They arrived in Southern Utah in 1944 and took up 4,000 acres of dry land lying north and east of the towns of Enterprise and Modena — the Escalante Desert. They put down artesian wells, which produced plenty of water. They planted the land as they cleared it, into alfalfa and grain, stocking beef to consume the crops until the land should be properly fertilized. Raising beef became a very profitable branch of their industry.

Their potato business grew rapidly. Modern machinery for digging, sorting, sacking, weighing and tagging was not enough. They trucked in loads of laborers from Mexico, furnishing transportation, meals, and lodging besides their wages. All the local manpower was also used.

Their business grew to such volume that in one season they shipped 125 full trainloads of potatoes. One potato pit they claimed to be the largest in the world, holding 120,000 sacks, and it was only one of many.

Herbert died in 1952; Maurice in 1965. After his death the farm was broken up, Jerry Schwartz, a Jewish friend, taking one thousand acres, and the remainder going in smaller units to local people.

By their efforts these men literally made the desert to blossom; an arid waste is now a community of thriving farms.

Chapter Ten

GOVERNOR SIMON BAMBERGER

THE YEAR 1914 was a momentous one. The war begun in Europe that year would soon involve the United States and most of the other major nations of the world. In Utah, the Jewish people were perhaps more concerned than any other ethnic group because so many of them had strong ties with relatives in the warring lands.

Otherwise the general prosperity continued, the Jewish community sharing and supporting it. This year brought them some changes, however. After nine successful years in B'nai Israel congregation, Rabbi Charles J. Freund withdrew. He was replaced by Rabbi Dr. William Rice, who would also continue with success.

The Congregation Montefiore this year employed Rabbi Samuel Beskin of New York, who for the next five years had outstanding success developing a strong *esprit de corps* in his group.

In the civic development of Utah, April 4, 1914, marked the laying of the cornerstone of the new Capitol Building. Twenty-six years earlier, February 28, 1888, the City of Salt Lake had donated to the Territory of Utah twenty acres of land on Arsenal Hill as a site for the official Capitol. On March 8 following, the Territorial Legislature voted to accept the gift and changed the name to "Capitol Hill."

Before statehood, nothing was done toward plans for a building, nor for more than a decade later — nothing other than scattered, pointless talk. Twenty-three years after the site was accepted, and then only after the Harriman inheritance tax of $750,000.00 was placed in the general fund in 1911, were serious plans made. With cornerstone in place, work proceeded at once so that the building was formally opened, although not fully completed, with a reception on the evening of October 9, 1916.[1]

A Jewish Governor would be first to occupy it, and entrusted to him would be the responsibility of completing and furnishing it.[2]

Up to this time a number of Jews had served in public office. Mention has already been made of Louis Cohn, who was a member of the City Council in 1874. Harry S. Joseph served in the State Assembly from 1902 to 1910 and was its speaker in 1908. Simon Bamberger was a State Senator from 1903 to 1907, and Clarence Bamberger was a member of the State Assembly from 1908 to 1910.[3]

The first Governor, Heber M. Wells, who served two terms (1897-1905), was American born; both John C. Cutler (1905-1909), and William Spry (1909-1917) were born in England. All were loyal and active members of the Mormon Church and represented the business interests of the state.[4]

With this background, the election of a Democrat-Jew must be considered a signal personal triumph due to the esteem with which the Mormons regarded this man and their Jewish neighbors in general.

A brief review of the life of Simon Bamberger will help to explain his success. Born 27 February 1845 in Eberstadt, Hesse-Darmstadt, a small village between Frankfurt and Heidelberg, Germany, he received his early education there, and so ingrained was his German tongue that he always retained a distinct accent. At the age of fourteen he came to the United States, joining his older brother, Herman, who had a small clothing store at Wilmington, Ohio. Later they

---

[1]Noble Warrum, *Utah Since Statehood,* (Chicago: J. S. Clarke Publishing Company, 1919) V. 1, pp. 209-233.

[2]For an excellent history of the Utah State Capitol see the account by Dale L. Morgan in UTAH, A GUIDE TO THE STATE, published by Hastings House, New York, 1940, pp. 245-250.

[3]*Universal Jewish Encyclopedia, op. cit.,* V. 5, p. 330.

[4]Up to this time the Mormon voting population was so much in the majority that approval of their leaders was tantamount to election.

moved west to St. Louis, where they greatly enlarged their establishment.

He worked in the various departments, but his first major assignment came when he was sent west to Cheyenne, Wyoming, to collect from a merchant there who had purchased a large stock of goods. He arrived in the fall to find that the man had gone out of business and moved away. Young Bamberger soon found himself snowed in, with no work and little money.

The railroad was building west out of Cheyenne, and because of his experience, he soon got a position as manager of a company store at the "front," or building edge of construction. He established such a reputation for sobriety, honesty, and fair dealing that gamblers, dance-hall girls and laborers began to bring their checks to him to hold. Knowing their own weaknesses and fearing that they would be tempted to throw all the money away in one night, they preferred to take out a little at a time.

As a sideline young Bamberger began to put up tents and shacks as temporary living quarters for the workers and the regular camp followers. These he could break down and transport to each new camp, so that the men could be near their work.

A friend warned him that he might be ripe for a robbery or attack, since it was generally believed that he kept a large sum of currency and silver on hand. Bamberger considered this, sold out, and came on to Ogden, arriving in early 1869.

Here he put up at the "Lester House," owned by Bishop Lester J. Herrick and operated by fellow Jews, Mr. and Mrs. Briner Cohen. He purchased stock in the concern, but an epidemic of smallpox in the town slowed business down until he sold out and moved to Salt Lake City. With Mr. Cohen as partner, he purchased the Delmonico Hotel on the southwest corner of Main Street and Second South. They named it "The White House," and it became the headquarters for mining men who drifted in and out of the city. Other hotels in the city at that time were "The Salt Lake House," "The Townsend House," and "The Valley House."

From his clientele Bamberger became interested in mining, and in 1872 purchased stock in the "Sailor Jack Mine" in the Big Cottonwood District. Later he took stock in the "Centennial Eureka" mine, from which he made a small fortune.[5] For the remainder of his life Bamberger had mining interests in Utah and in DeLamar and Pioche, Nevada. He also built railroads, opened up the recreational center at The Lagoon, and was involved in many other business ventures.

His introduction to public life came in 1898, when he was selected to fill the position on the Salt Lake City Board of Education left vacant by the resignation of Charles Baldwin. Here he served for five years, during which time he distinguished himself as a liberal, with a genuine interest in the welfare of both teachers and pupils. In 1903 when it seemed that the schools must close early for lack of funds, Bamberger took the lead in collecting the money, first by donating one-tenth of the total amount needed and then soliciting among his friends.[6] The money was soon raised. This gesture put him in the public eye, and would stand him in good stead later when he ran for any public office.

In the election of 1902 the Democrats drafted Bamberger to be their candidate for the state senate. His experience in business and his reputaton as a member of the school board were both in his favor. His opponent, Jacob Moritz, was also a German Jew, who had come to Salt Lake City in 1871, and by 1883 had established the largest brewery in the Intermountain West.

The Mormon segment of the population — a very large majority — though nominally Republican, had very strong

---

[5]Before this time Bamberger had not been involved in public affairs. For his moving from the hotel business into mining, see *Salt Lake Daily Tribune and Mining Gazette,* Nov. 22, 1871, p. 3.

[6]Bamberger used this same device several times later in his career. See *Salt Lake Tribune,* May 22, 1903, p. 4.; also May 24, p. 8.

feelings about intoxicating drinks, and the fact that Bamberger himself did not use liquor or tobacco, that he did not employ men who did, that he had been engaged in enterprises which would build Utah and build character in its citizens, all counted heavily with the majority of the voters. The press was quick to use this to his advantage.

> We may be wrong, but Simon Bamberger, compared with Jacob Moritz, looks about as big as an oak tree set up beside a jimpson weed. And that's just about the way the merits of these men measure up.[7]

Simon Bamberger was the only Democrat in Salt Lake County to be elected to any position, and he won by 12,276 to 9,586. Some said this was a vote for the temperance cause against the brewery interests; others said it was the poor folks of the area who had benefited at one time or another from Bamberger's generosity; still others said the schoolteachers had worked for him.

At any rate, when the session opened there were only three Democrats in the Utah State Senate: Simon Bamberger, Harden Bennion, and Alonzo G. Barber, and because their last names all began with *B*, they became known as "The Three Bees."

Although of the minority party, Simon Bamberger distinguished himself as a state senator. He studied and analyzed every proposal and injected into every discussion a fresh and original point of view. He was appointed to eleven committee positions, some of which took him into the rural sections of the state.

One of the bills by which he would be best remembered was to establish kindergartens in the state and to train young women to teach in them. On the day of its passage he received thirteen red roses as a gift from the young women's organization who had worked for this legislation.[8]

Throughout the entire life of this legislature the *Salt Lake Tribune* had been critical, accusing members of spending

[7]*Salt Lake Herald Tribune,* September 30, 1902, p. 4.
[8]*Deseret Evening News,* February 28, 1903, p. 8.

their time on trivia, of mediocrity and ineptness, of "treading water" until the fifty-ninth day when they must finally get to work. It did give appreciation of several of the leaders who had put through some beneficial legislation. Among them the Democratic senator was cited:

> The life of the Senate was Senator Bamberger. He is keen in his observation and a most excellent legislator. . . . His work was forceful and valuable, and he made many a session brighter with the soul of his wit.[9]

The experience of being so far in the minority had been a challenging one to Simon Bamberger, but not one he wished to repeat, so for the next years he turned his attention to his mining interests. These took him often to the East, and it was probably from friends there that he was encouraged to enter politics again, this time on a national level. In 1915 he declared himself available for the Democratic nomination for United States senator. However, after much consideration he decided instead to try for the position of governor of Utah in order to leave the field for U. S. senator open to William H. King.

At the Democratic State Convention held in Ogden, 18 August 1916, Bamberger was elected to be their candidate on the second ballot. That he was nominated by B. H. Roberts, prominent Mormon historian, would mean much to the Mormon voters. To help in promotion, another prominent Mormon, John Henry Evans, circulated a leaflet in which he reminded all members of the laboring class that this man had shown his interest in their welfare by his acts as a legislator, that he always treated his employees as men and not as "hands," that there had never been any need to strike among them. He did not neglect to mention his philanthropies, his support of the schools, and his basic integrity in keeping promises. "A Man of Peace," and "A Builder, Not a Knocker," were coined, and helped to establish a good public image. Perhaps more effective than any of these was the word, not printed, but carefully and skillfully passed

---

[9]*Senate Journal,* 1905, pp. v-vii.

around among the Mormon congregations, that Simon Bamberger was one of those who, during the time of their bitter persecutions, had written a letter to Congress protesting taking the franchise from Mormon men because of their religious beliefs, declaring that in America a man should be a citizen no matter to what church he belonged.

The general Mormon attitude toward the Jews had always been friendly; here was a chance to demonstrate that friendship. A typical campaign story has become folklore:

On a visit to Sanpete County, Bamberger alighted from the train and was met by a local delegation headed by a tall, robust Norwegian with a flowing beard. In contrast, Bamberger, who was short and stubby, heard this towering Norwegian greet him with a menacing threat:

"You might yust as vell go right back vere you come from. If you think we lat any damn Yentile speak in our meeting house, yure mistaken!"

Bamberger looked up into the face of the determined looking leader and slowly replied: "As a Jew, I have been called many a bad name, but this is the first time in my life that I have been called a Damn Gentile!"

Instantly the menacing attitude of the leader of the committee relaxed, and, throwing his arm around Bamberger's shoulders, he exultingly exclaimed: "You a Yew, an Israelite! Hear him, men, he's not a Yentile; he's a Yew, an Israelite!" and then to Bamberger: "Velcome, my friend; velcome, our next Governor."

Late in the campaign the Republican state committee circulated a caricature in which a photograph was changed to emphasize his Jewish characteristics. In answer, the Democrats put out a broadside entitled A CARICATURE THE SUPREME ARGUMENT, showing both the photograph and the caricature, followed by a statement by P. W. Madsen, president of the Western Loan and Building Company. He said:

Having been a neighbor of Simon Bamberger for more than thirty years . . . I feel that I would be failing in my duty as a citizen if I did not publicly resent the insult contained in the vicious and libelous circular issued by the Republican State Committee for the purpose of injuring Mr. Bamberger's candidacy. In this circular Mr. Bamberger is grossly caricatured, though the caricature is put out as an actual portrait.

The evident attempt . . . is to call attention to the fact that Mr. Bamberger is a Jew . . . to arouse religious and racial prejudice against him.

Mr. Bamberger is a Jew, but he is . . . an American . . . incapable of stooping so low as to . . . inject a religious question into a political campaign . . .

I have known Mr. Bamberger for . . . years. He is a good neighbor, a good citizen in the highest . . . sense . . . He is incorruptibly honest, . . . and will carry out to the last letter every promise of his platform.

Hence, I appeal . . . to everyone who wants good government to rebuke the lying libels that are being circulated, and to vote for this man who means what he says and will do what he says.

When the election returns came in they showed Bamberger elected by a plurality of 18,980 votes, and a complete "fusion" ticket elected, in comparison to the straight Mormon-Republican ticket. In his first speech to the legislature, Governor Bamberger set forth clearly what his policy would be. He said, in part:

Our platform pledges are covenants with the people. What we have promised we will do to the best of our ability. But it does not follow because a sweeping change has been made in the political complexion of the Legislature that radical legislation is expected except in those innovations promised to and ordered by the people. Certainly nothing in the way of freak legislation is justified by the platform upon which we were elected. We represent a careful, painstaking and conservative constituency. Our measures should be few, carefully considered, and constructed to stand any test the future may place upon them.[10]

During his campaign he had spoken of the need of a Public Utilities Commission to protect the consumer and do away with special gifts and favors to public officials in the hope of special legislation which would be rewarding. His argument was:

Utah is one of two states — the other one being Delaware — having little or no provision for the regulation of public service

---

[10]Noble Warrum, *op. cit.,* Vol. 1, p. 180.

corporations . . . The members of this assembly are pledged to create a public utilities commission which shall be charged with the duty of establishing and maintaining the mutual confidence and friendly relations of the public and the public service corporations.

This legislation was passed.

Another important innovation was the passage of the Workmen's Compensation Act, which provided indemnities in case of injury or accident. Provisions were also made for a non-partisan judiciary, a state Department of Agriculture, a clear and concise law relating to water rights in irrigation districts. A new compilation of the laws of the state was ordered to be made, and a Board of Control set up to have charge of the penitentiary, the mental hospital, the school for the deaf, dumb, and blind, the industrial school, the State Capitol, and the finances of the University of Utah and the State Agricultural College.[11]

Before the election both parties had favored a prohibition law, so the one passed by this legislature was "state-wide and bone-dry," making it a misdemeanor to buy, sell, or have in one's possession any type of intoxicating drink.

Something of the social nature of the legislation passed is shown by the appropriations that were made. Among them were:

$4,000 for archaeological explorations under the direction of the University of Utah.

$16,000 to the University of Utah for an addition to the mining and metallurgy building.

$100,000 for a monument to the Mormon Battalion, to be erected on the Capitol grounds.

$4,000 for the Salt Lake Free Kindergarten and Neighborhood House.

$2,000 to the Florence Crittenden Home . . . for aiding homeless and destitute women.

$2,000 to the Martha Society, to found and maintain homes for destitute children.

[11]John Eldon Benton, *The Educational Program and Educational Policies under Governor Simon Bamberger, 1917-1921.* Thesis, University of Utah, Department of Educational Administration.

$2,000 for the Children's Aid Society.

$15,000 for the state geologist, the incumbent to be appointed by the Governor and to receive a salary of not more than $5,000 per annum.

The state of Utah had supported Woodrow Wilson for president largely because they approved his policy of "keeping us out of the war." When at last war was declared and we were actually in it, Governor Bamberger spared no effort to support the nation to the fullest. Everywhere he reminded the people that we now had no "hyphenated" Americans — no German-Americans nor Spanish-Americans nor any other "part" Americans. All were now AMERICANS, pledged to support the nation in this war to end war. So ardent was he that voluntary enlistment in Utah in proportion to its population ranked it as second in the nation. The state also oversubscribed in the purchase of Liberty Bonds, and after it had done so, Governor Bamberger and party traveled into neighboring states on a "Liberty Train" to encourage the purchase of bonds among the people there.

Governor Bamberger expressed his pride in the loyalty of Utah on January 13, 1919, when the thirteenth regular session of the state legislature convened in the new Capitol Building in Salt Lake City in joint session:

> It would be superfluous for me to discuss at length the abnormal conditions under which we have labored in this most critical period of the world's history. With pride of an unusual degree I report to you that the people of our state heard and responded to every call of the nation in such manner as to place the name of Utah in the front rank of every movement involving the highest ideals of humanity. With her sister states, Utah has been privileged to do her part in suppressing tyranny which threatened the world and in extending liberty and justice to the oppressed peoples of the earth. In humility we give thanks that a victorious peace is assured to the cause of freedom and humanity.

In the Fourth Liberty Loan, states which promptly oversubscribed their quota were given the privilege of naming one of the ships of the United States. Utah won this distinction largely through the oversubscription of Carbon County on money given by the workingmen. The word "Utacarbon" was coined as the name for the ship. The governor and his party attended the launching, and California set aside July 31, 1919, as "Utah Day."

Miss Margaret Horsley, sponsor of the drive in Carbon County, flung against the prow a red, white, and blue beribboned bottle of California wine, and Governor Bamberger smashed a sparkling bottle of chemically pure Carbon County water.

The Jewish community of Utah supported Governor Bamberger in all his requests, the women in work for the Red Cross and later for CARE. Thirty-nine members of the Jewish congregations enlisted in the armed services, their names today being on a Roll of Honor in the B'nai Israel Synagogue.[12]

In gifts to the American-Jewish Relief Committee, Utah's governor also led out. A large broadside circulated nationally carried headlines and cries of HELP! HELP! HELP! on the bottom. The body of the message asks, "Who is the Julius Rosenwald (of Chicago) of your city, who gives 10% of all the nation will raise?" Under their pictures, Simon Bamberger of Utah, Moses Alexander of Idaho, and Ben Selling of Ogden are named as three of those who will give 10 percent of what their respective states will raise, or three of the forty-five men who will give 10 percent of what their respective cities will raise. The final appeal was that "$10,000,000 must be raised to save 3,000,000 Jews, sufferers from the war."

An incident related by Ben Roe further illustrates the zeal of Governor Bamberger in this cause. A fund-raising dinner was given wide publicity among the Jewish people. On the night appointed, the guests arrived at the building well illuminated on the outside, to step into a large room dimly lighted by candles on long, bare tables. Not a cover of any kind, nor a dish, no food, only rough planks for seats and sawdust on the floor. The "dinner" was an eloquent appeal for fellow Hebrews whose tables were just this bare and whose

---

[12]Their names are listed at the end of this chapter.

surroundings were even more bleak. A generous contribution was raised.

In his last speech to the legislature Governor Bamberger dwelt at some length upon the financial conditions of the state. He said, in part:

> When this administration assumed control of the state government two years ago it inherited a deficit of some $400,000 floating indebtedness. The state's finances were subjected to a further strain by obligations necessarily incurred in the prosecution of war activities.
>
> The report of the state's fiscal condition prepared by the state auditor indicates that by the beginning of the new budget year, April 1, 1919, we will have cleared up not only this old deficit, but will have liquidated practically all the temporary indebtedness incident to wartime activities, besides redeeming the state bond issue of 1898 in the sum of $150,000. . . .

After specifying in detail the amounts, he concluded with the assurance that they would leave the state of Utah with a credit balance of $2,027,209.41.[13]

Simon Bamberger gave himself completely to being a good governor of Utah and a good citizen of the United States. He felt that he had achieved a measure of success in both areas, but did not care to campaign again. In a speech before the Commercial Club in August of 1919 he announced his intention of returning to private life, his immediate project to be the building of a railroad into the Uintah Basin.

He did not live to see the fulfillment of this dream, but after a short illness passed away on October 6, 1926, and was buried in the Jewish cemetery. All his life he had tried to put into practice the highest principles of Judaism, to protect the workingman, to provide for the unfortunate and under-privileged, and to maintain just human rights. He must be counted one of the truly great governors of Utah.

---

[13]Henry Evans, "Simon Bamberger" *Utah Educational Review*, XXV No. 4, (December 1931), pp. 156-157; pp. 189-190.

HONOR ROLL — MEMBERS OF B'NAI ISRAEL CONGREGATION WHO SERVED IN WORLD WAR I

Dr. Isaac Alexander
Dr. Robert Alexander
Fred Auerbach
Herbert Auerbach
Clarence Bamberger
Samuel Bergerman
Abraham Bero
Abraham Cline
Lawrence Cline
Martin Cohn
Harry M. Frank
David Friedman
Martin Fruhman
Henry Garfinkle
Julius Harrison
Harold Hyams
Leland Hyams
Carl Lipman
Lewis Levitt
Robert Lehman

Milton Levy
Sherman Lowenstein
Walter J. Mayer
Jerome Mooney
J. Robinson
Ben Roe
Durant Rohlfing
Joseph Samuels
Herbert M. Schiller
Ben Siegel
Jules Schayer
Arthur Schayer
Dr. E. M. Silverberg
Sylvan Simon
Milton Smith
Reuben R. Smith
Benjamin D. Solomon
Ralph Tandowsky
Ernest S. Weitz

Chapter Eleven

NEW CONGREGATIONS — NEW ACTIVITIES

By 1915 THE great influx of Jews from Russia and the Near East which had begun in 1880 was being felt in Utah. The *American Jewish Yearbook,* mentioned earlier, gave the total Jewish population of Utah for 1917-1918 as 3,737; by 1920 it had risen to 3,940. Likewise it noted that "The Amity Club was formed in Salt Lake City, Secretary, B. L. Cline, 245 Modern Place." According to Ben Roe, the regular members included Barney Fleisher, Ezra Cohn, George Judlewitz, Jack Tannenbaum, Joe Cline, Charles Cline, Dr. Abe Cline, Abe Cline (cousins), B. L. Cline, Martin Fruhman, Sigmund Porizky, Harry Roe, Julius Sprauf, and Louis Kaufman. Visitors were often invited.[1]

Jewish subscribers to the publications of the American Jewish Publishing Company in 1913-1914 were only thirty-five, or five more than subscribed in 1905-1906, but only seven people were included on both lists: Rabbi Charles J. Freund, Julius Frumpkin, Harry Ganz, George Rhode, J. Shapiro, Sig Simon, and David Spitz. From the list in Ogden only Sam Kline is named both years.[2]

Another indication of Jewish activity is found in the work of Noble Warrum, *The History of Utah After Statehood.* Summarizing the general picture of various churches in Utah, he says:

> Referring again to the report of the Bureau of Immigration, Labor and Statistics for 1915, we learn that there were 7 organizations of Seventh Day Adventists with three churches and 205 members; 11 organizations of Baptists with a membership of 1,100

---

[1]Personal interview, Ben Roe at his home in Salt Lake City, Nov. 19, 1967.

members and one colored Baptist with a membership of 70; one
Christian Church with a membership of 225; two colored Methodist
Churches; *three Hebrew Societies;* 3 Lutheran Churches; 6 Chris-
tian Science; and 4 Reorganized Church of Latter-Day Saints.[2]

This account of three Hebrew Societies in Salt Lake
City in 1915 indicates that the split in Congregation Montefiore took place before that time. People who remember the
circumstances say that this was largely a personality clash
and a difference of opinion as to ritual. A strong leader in
the congregation, Joshua Shapiro, dominated. Another strong
leader, Sam Hayden, wished for a more strict adherence to
such practices as seating the women apart from the men,
and observing more closely other points of procedure. As a
result he and some fifty families pulled away and set up their
own congregation, calling themselves *Shaarey Tzedek.*

Dr. Leon L. Watters, writing in the *Universal Jewish
Encyclopedia,* says that this congregation was founded in
1916, and the *Salt Lake City Directory* lists it for the first
time in 1918, with the simplified spelling, *Sharey Tzedek.*
Rabbi Joseph Strinkomsky was named as being in charge that
year, but in 1919 and 1920 Mr. J. P. Berson officiated.

Word of the new congregation did not reach the
American Jewish Yearbook until the 1920-1921 issue where
under the heading of "New Organizations" is given "Salt Lake
City: Sharey Tzedek, Pres. M. Garelick; Secretary C. Salz-
man."

Evidently this congregation worked with dispatch, for
The Salt Lake Tribune of March 28, 1920, gave an account
of the dedicatory services in their new synagogue, located
on Second East between 8th and 9th South. The services
were held at 3:00 p.m., the speakers being Governor Simon
Bamberger, Rabbi William Rice, of B'nai Israel Congregation, and Daniel Alexander. Several musical numbers were
rendered.

For the next four years, 1921-1925, the *City Directory*
lists Joseph Strinkomsky as officiating; after that, 1925-1929,

---

[2]Noble Warrum, *History of Utah After Statehood,* Vol. I, pp. 740-743.

Rabbi Reuben Kaplan came into the office. After 1929 none of the Hebrew organizations are listed, perhaps from a lack of funds during the depression years. Rabbi Kaplan must have remained, for in 1933 he is named in the *Salt Lake Jewish News* final issue as one of the most-loved men.[3]

On the date of the dedication of the Sharey Tzedek Synagogue, *The Salt Lake Tribune* carried a summary of Jewish activities in Utah from the beginning, the source of information being one F. Walleston. This is interesting chiefly in what it does *not* say.

> The first Jewish people settled in Utah in 1862. A congregation was organized in 1866. President Brigham Young of the L.D.S. Church gave his aid in establishing this early church and donated a strip of land to be used as a Jewish cemetery, according to Mr. F. Walleston, who has made a study of the early Jews in Utah. It was not long, he said, before the first church was inadequate to accommodate the increasing congregation, and it was found necessary to erect a larger synagogue.
>
> The temple of B'nai Israel was then constructed and dedicated in 1891. In 1903 the Jewish colony had tripled in size and the synagogue of the Congregation Montefiore was built and dedicated. According to Mr. Walleston, the late President Joseph F. Smith of the L.D.S. church was one of the largest contributors to the fund for building this synagogue. President Smith, he said, also officially represented the church at the ceremony attendant on the laying of the corner stone.
>
> Again it became necessary to increase the church facilities of the Jewish race in Salt Lake and contributions were solicited for the financing of the latest synagogue. There are 100 members in the new church.

This gives no hint of ideological differences among the members but only a grave need of seating space as the reason for the new building. Strangely, no officers or members are named, so that there is no record available as to who the one hundred members of the congregation were.

From interviews with Sam Axelrad, Abe Guss, and others it would seem that for a time the Sharey Tzedek met with

---

[3]Records of this congregation are said to be in the hands of Rebecca Garelick, 918 Edison Street, Salt Lake City.

good success, seating the men in the main hall and the women in the gallery, and carrying out a more strictly orthodox ritual. But because the congregation offered little to young people, it finally died out. The building was sold to the Veterans of Foreign Wars; the funds used to maintain the cemetery.

In spite of the division in the ranks, Congregation Montefiore was able to make major improvements in its synagogue in 1920. These are mentioned in several places without details of all that was done.

Without doubt the most important project sponsored by the more orthodox Jews was the purchase in 1923 of the Colonel Enos A. Wall home at 411 East South Temple as a center for spiritual and cultural activities. It became known as "The Covenant House."

This building had an interesting history.[4] The property was first owned by James Sharp, who had been a member of the city police, a member of the house of representatives, and in 1884, mayor of Salt Lake City. He was also a chairman of the Board of Regents of the University of Utah. He built a substantial home, which after his death in 1904 was purchased by Enos A. Wall, a mining man with interests both in Silver Reef and Bingham.

Mr. Wall proceeded to remodel and enlarge the house; his architect, Richard K. A. Kletting, need think nothing of expense. When completed the home boasted an electric elevator, a built-in vacuum, fireplaces in all six bedrooms, a ballroom on the third floor and several game rooms and guest rooms. Colonel Wall lived in it until his death, and his wife remained there until she too passed away in early 1923, when it came into the possession of the Jewish community. It was a perfect setting for varied group activities, with facilities to fit large groups or small, an ideal gathering place for old and young.

Rabbi E. M. Burstein, who arrived to serve Congregation Montefiore in early 1924, was a wise and able leader.

---

[4]Information on this home was gathered in 1968 by Mr. Margaret (Shepard) Lester of the State Historical Society for use in her illustrated lecture, "The Mansions of Brigham Street."

He called together the young people and let them select their own programs, offering only a suggestion here and there and working quietly in the background. Activities included some study groups and some regular classes in Jewish history and law, but essentially the program was social. At that time young people had few cars, little money for commercial entertainment, and little opportunity to meet socially with others of their own faith. In this congenial setting they could become acquainted and participate in such activities as singing, discussion and debate, and competitive games. Here also they might become a part of an amateur dramatic association in which serious drama as well as hilarious farce and skits were produced. In this environment there developed a camaraderie that was lasting.

Here on May 24, 1925, was organized the Maimonides Club, which united the B'nai Ami and the Junior League to include both girls and boys. Named for the great Spanish scholar, rabbi, physician and philosopher, Maimonides, (1135-1204) the club lent itself to activities of many kinds. Past members, after all the years, grow nostalgic as they remember the Covenant House and recall the happy experiences there. At least eight young couples met and carried on much of their courtship as they participated in the varied projects which were originated here.

The activities which they remember with most pride are the dramatic productions, some of which were of a quality to be presented in the downtown playhouse, "The Hippodrome," usually with excellent financial returns. Sometimes the audience exceeded five hundred people, many of whom came to look forward to these annual events.[5] But most important were the week-by-week gatherings, the informal parties, the fact that there was an attractive place where friends could gather. These combined to make the Covenant House so important.

---

[5]Members at the home of Mr. Ben Roe, Salt Lake City, Nov. 19, 1967, remembered a partial list of the plays presented by the Maimonides Club as: *The Man Upstairs, Kempy, Two Girls Wanted, Under Northern Skies,* and *Patsy.* This list is incomplete.

JEWISH ACTIVITIES IN OGDEN

As has been suggested earlier, Ogden was the clearinghouse for many newcomers to the state. From the earliest times the Jews of the area naturally divided into Reform and Orthodox. In 1916 the *American Jewish Yearbook* reported the formation of a new congregation, Brith Sholem, in Ogden, though organized groups had been meeting for more than twenty-five years.

The best source available for an overall picture of Jewish activities in Ogden was compiled in 1939 by a WPA employee. We reproduce it here in full:

THE JEWISH COMMUNITY IN OGDEN
From a study made by Hugh F. O'Neil

The Jewish congregation Brith Sholem of Ogden was organized in 1890 under the name of Ohab Sholem. Meetings were first held at 352 Twenty-fifth Street in the clothing store of Ben Oppman. The first president of the organization was Sam Rosenbluth, who served from 1890 to 1891. Charter members were D. Kraines, J. Benovitz, W. Benovitz, Ben Oppman, and J. Kraines. The membership soon increased to nine and now (April, 1939) amounts to twenty members.

Subsequent meetings were held at various rented quarters until 1921 when the present synagogue was erected. This one-story building was formally dedicated on August 21, 1921, and is located at 2756 Grant Avenue, constructed of red brick, with an oval roof. Its architecture is mainly American, but shows a slight Grecian Doric influence.

Brith Sholem congregation was incorporated on May 8, 1922, for the purpose of religious worship according to the Orthodox style. Members of the first board of trustees were E. Rosenberg, president; P. Newman, vice-president; I. Gordon, secretary; William Benovitz, treasurer; Joseph Kraines, Sam Miller and S. Silverstein.

Prior to 1917, meetings were held only once each year, on Jewish New Year's Day, which falls in September. There was no resident rabbi until 1917 when H. Alcoff officiated and remained until 1918. A member of the congregation acts as rabbi at the regular Friday night meetings held each week.

Rabbis have been: Ben Alcoff, 1917-18; A. Leherer, 1918-20; Rabbi Finkelstein, 1920-28; Hyman Bariss, 1928-32; Rabbi Blumenstein, 1932-34; Rabbi Friedman, 1934-1935. They have had no resident rabbi since 1935. A rabbi comes from Salt Lake City at the present time, once a week, to prepare meat and perform other services.

Present officers of the organization are: Joseph Benowitz, president; David Lutzker, vice-president; Abe Gordon, secretary; Sam Bruckner, treasurer; Samuel Kraines, first trustee; I. Gordon, second trustee; and G. Medoway, third trustee.

The Torch, a copy of the original ten commandments with their interpretations and applications, and a history of the Jews from Adam and Eve to Moses, who brought the people to the promised land, is read on Holy Days.

Services are held each Friday night at eight and on the high holidays such as Roshshona (New Year) and Yom Kippur (Day of Atonement).

The ladies' auxiliary, an organization within the schule (church) helps needy Jewish people. They meet the second Thursday of each month. Sunday school is conducted each Sunday at ten A.M., at which the Biblical history is taught.[6]

Only in Salt Lake City and Ogden were Jewish congregations organized, and the foregoing is a clear indication of how little is actually known of their doings. The same is true of any accurate census of the Jewish population of the state at any one time. The figures given in the *American Jewish Yearbook* are admittedly "estimates."

Whatever the numbers at any one time, the fact is that they were separated into two groups, each independent and apart from the other. Each carried on its regular Sabbath service and observed the Holy Days according to its own ritual. Each provided as it could social activities for its membership, young and old, and carried on its philanthropies for the needy. Though all appealed to the non-Jewish community for patronage at fund-raising events, each maintained a rigid adherence to its own members. Even the Boy Scout troops were kept separate. Not only was there competition between the congregations, but too often there was a definite bitterness and scorn each for the other. Nowhere could they come to a meeting of the minds.

---

[6]*The Salt Lake Tribune,* April 16, 1939.

JEWISH EDUCATION IN UTAH

Through all the early years in Utah a basic problem for all citizens was the education of their children. Brigham Young placed the responsibility squarely on the ecclesiastical units, the wards. Each was to maintain a school for the children of its members, who were to pay the teacher's salary through tuitions. This posed a problem for poor families with many children and resulted in limited opportunities for many. As soon as they could be useful on the farm, children were forced to leave school; even those old enough to herd cows were taken out in early spring. The result was school terms of from four to five months at best.

Teachers must accept tuition fees in "kind" — that is, whatever the families could supply: flour, potatoes, butter, eggs, lard, stove-wood, hay. Anything, in fact, except cash was brought in. Under these conditions able teachers could not afford to teach. Not until 1890 did Utah have free public schools established.[7]

Most other denominations did offer free schools on the grade level. The Catholics, Methodists, Presbyterians, and Episcopalians, all at one time or another, and some over many years, gave free instruction to children whether of their own faith or not. In some rural areas they set up missions, where the free school was an important asset. A few offered free music lessons to any child who wished to learn to play the organ and could find an instrument on which to practice.

To the Jewish residents the problem of education was felt keenly, for to them learning was of first importance. Educational conditions in Utah, without doubt, formed one of the reasons for the shifting Jewish population. As soon as a family could afford to move, as soon as the children approached adolescence, they felt impelled either to move away or to send the children away to school.

---

[7]Stanley S. Ivins, "Free Schools Come to Utah," *Utah State Historical Quarterly,* October, 1954, pp. 321-342.

THE UNIVERSITY OF UTAH

Utah historians sometimes boast of the "University" in Utah as early as 1850, but this was a name only. Later the "University of Deseret" opened chiefly as a training for teachers in the basic Three R's, in order that they might be more effective in the grade schools. While this was a necessary and valuable training, it could hardly be called a university course.

The growth of the University of Utah was slow and erratic. As late as 1883 the faculty consisted of only three members: Dr. John R. Park, Joseph B. Toronto, and Joseph T. Kingsbury. The highest registration up to that time was 172, a poor showing of a university after thirty-three years.[8]

By the 1890s more teachers were added, new courses were offered, and there developed an *esprit de corps* among the students which resulted in many campus activities and in general zest and enthusiasm. Literary societies, a Barrister's Club, an Open Forum, a Fine Arts Guild, a Modern Language Circle, and student publications brought activities to many members. In 1907 the U was placed on the hill as an emblem for the whole institution, to put a stop to some of the sharp competition between classes.

Extracurricular activities and competition in athletics, oratory, debate, and dramatics, all added to school spirit, and made going to the University the thing to do for all who could afford it. The completion of the Park Building in 1914 helped to bolster the feeling that here was a real university at last, so that from 183 students in 1901 the enrollment grew to 1,644 in 1915.[9]

The year 1915 became one of intense internal strife at the University of Utah. Conditions became so strained that fourteen leading members of the faculty tendered their resignations, all of which were accepted. This was followed by

---

[8]Ralph V. Chamberlain, *The University of Utah, A History of Its First Hundred Years — 1850-1950.* (Salt Lake City, The University of Utah Press, 1960), pp. 107-108.
[9]*Ibid.,* p. 264.

protests from alumni, civic clubs, and the public in general. Now the demand was that the president be asked to resign. This was advocated by members of the Board of Regents as well.[10]

In the end, President Kingsbury was made *President Emeritus* and Dr. John A. Widtsoe appointed in his stead. With the outbreak of World War I, the full facilities of the school were turned to national defense, while the educational offerings were cut to bare essentials. Libraries, laboratories, shops, money, men, were all dedicated to winning the war.

President Widtsoe had come into office under the most difficult conditions; outside events had sidetracked whatever plans he might have had for the school. For two years after the signing of the Armistice, some wartime restraints continued to demand attention. On April 11, 1921, Dr. Widtsoe resigned his position, and the same day accepted an apostleship in the Mormon Church.[11]

Dr. George Thomas was appointed president, his official inauguration being held on April 5, 1922. This date is considered by many to be the real birth of the institution as a full-fledged university rather than an organ of the Mormon Church.

Without doubt there were Jewish young people at the University of Utah before this time, for, "The Upsilon Chapter of Sigma Alpha Mu (S.A.M.) was established on the University of Utah campus in 1919. The original was founded at the College of the City of New York in November 1909, and soon became the largest Jewish fraternity in America."[12]

At an informal gathering at the home of Ben Roe in Salt Lake City, the story was told of four young men who were the first from Congregation Montefiore to enter the University of Utah. This was the fall of 1922. They decided to form a fraternity, selected a name, met often, and kept in close touch with each other. At the end of the year they could boast that their fraternity had set an all-time high

[10]*Ibid.*, pp. 328-333.
[11]*Ibid.*, p. 369.
[12]*The Salt Lake Jewish News*, Vol. I, No. 1, p. 5.

average for scholarship. How could larger groups hope to attain a straight four-point average?

It would seem that, although all Jewish parents who were able financially to do so sent their children away to school, there were some attending the University of Utah each year after 1918. It is interesting to note that in his history of the University, Dr. Ralph V. Chamberlain does not name any Jewish fraternities or sororities on the campus.

THE DEPRESSION YEARS

The Jews of Utah shared the general prosperity of the 1920s, and the straitened circumstances immediately following the market crash of 1929. They did organize at least two mutual assistance groups, however. One was called "The Arbeiter Ring" or "The Workmen's Circle." Members pledged mutual help and attempted to salvage failing business ventures. They also united to provide for needy Jewish families.

A second organization was "Hand-in-Hand." In this group of men each pooled his money in a fund from which loans up to one hundred dollars might be made with only the signature of the borrower and that of the individual contributor. Included was a written pledge that the sum would be paid back promptly in order that it might be kept truly a revolving fund. As soon as it was returned, it would be loaned to another needy neighbor. Although in a few cases a generous donor lost his $100.00, in general the plan was effective in helping to tide many families over this rough period. Folklore says that in one case a secretary, hoping to profit in a poker game, lost the entire principal.

Before the Emergency Relief Administration became effective on a national level, Jews responded to President Roosevelt's plea that they make every effort to provide labor for more people, as the following article shows:

JEWS JOIN NRA DRIVE 100%, SURVEY REVEALS

Jewish concerns, including every type of industrial and commercial endeavor, are co-operating with President Franklin Delano Roosevelt's recovery program 100 percent. . . .

From leading mercantile institutions and department stores to the smallest individual shop keeper, members of the local Jewish community are displaying the blue eagle — emblem of the NRA.

In many instances large Jewish controlled firms have increased payrolls and decreased working hours in accordance with the program outlined by the campaign to effect economic recovery.

But assisting their own people and aligning themselves with government agencies was not enough. Their second law, "Thou shalt love thy neighbor as thyself," meant that any needy person was a neighbor, and every worthy cause deserved support. A striking example is the NEIGHBOR-HOOD HOUSE which had been established in southwest Salt Lake City in 1894. Here, in the poorest area of the city, Miss Emma McVicker, a teacher in the Presbyterian free schools, became keenly aware of the problems of working mothers whose children were left largely to their own devices during the day.

Miss McVicker left the teaching of the "Three R's" to others while she opened a free kindergarten for children from nine months to eight years of age. The mothers left them on their way to work; Miss McVickers cared for them, entertained them, fed them a noon lunch, and had them ready for their mothers after working hours. Soon she had up to forty children daily, and the task was beyond her strength.

A public appeal brought volunteers from women of other denominations. Jewish women were quick to respond, as were Methodists, Catholics, Mormons. It was immediately evident that they needed larger quarters, and that the services must be expanded to take in children of all ages and to provide for them training and guidance. Governor Bamberger and his legislature were generous in providing funds; public consciousness brought a few large contributions, so that by 1925 Neighborhood House sponsored, in addition to the kindergarten, boys' clubs, girls' clubs, sewing classes for mothers, lectures and evening entertainment for adults. Most important of all came to be the annual Christmas celebration, with its tree and its gifts for the children.

The panic of 1929 found the Neighborhood House already in business and a natural center from which to expand further service to more people. New emphasis was placed upon training mothers, both in supplying the needs of their own families by better home skills and in earning money at home by producing saleable articles. In the first, under expert leadership, they were helped in making clothes for their children from the cast-off adult clothing that was gathered. For example, a man's suit, properly ripped apart, cleaned, and pressed, would furnish enough material for an outfit for either girl or boy up to the age of eight. The material would be of a quality which the mother could not afford to buy. In the same way, children's coats were made. Some resourceful women even managed outfits for themselves, or their older daughters, tailored and attractive.

Some of the foreign-born women had skills in needlecraft, netting, knitting, crocheting. They were provided with the necessary thread or yarn, with stamped linen tablecloths and dinner sets on which to work, and the women at the center marketed their finished product for them. For some, this brought a supplement to a meager income; for a few, it was the only income.

That this center existed, that its doors were open to all, regardless of race or creed, that these volunteer workers were willing and eager to help were important. Also helpful was the publicity through which the public was made conscious of the living conditions among the poor. People in fine homes could not be entirely indifferent to the suffering in their midst. The appeals were too insistent, the need too urgent. Now in many ways the Neighborhood House lived up to its name.

Women of all faiths assisted here, prominent among them many Jewish ladies. Measured in terms of hours and days and years of consistent service, Miss Stella Cohn probably made the greatest contribution.[13]

---

[13]Jewish women who served on the Board of Directors for the Neighborhood House included Mrs. Simon Bamberger, Lucille Franke, Mrs. Sol Siegel, Mrs. Anton Boxrud, Stella Cohn, Mrs. Fred Cowans, Mrs. F. C. Schramm, Mrs. Fred Smith, Mrs. Leon Sweet, Mrs. Joseph Rosenblatt, Mrs. Fred Auerbach, Mrs. Joseph Ottenheimer, and Mrs. Ernest Bamberger. Pamphlet, *Fifty Years of Neighborhood House,* 1894-1944, by Lela Horn Richards, pp. 15-16.

Mrs. Gertrude Levin Marcus, widow of Mayor Louis Marcus, sponsored and supervised construction of the Neighborhood Thrift Shop.

On October 25, 1927, the organization of B'nai B'rith Girls, a junior auxiliary to the women's group, was effected. This would continue active for more than forty years. [*Deseret News,* October 25, 1967]

THE ELECTION OF 1932

The election of 1932 was a turning point in Utah political history. The Mormon people, disregarding the preachments from the pulpit, marched to the polls and elected almost a full Democratic slate. They gave Franklin D. Roosevelt a majority; they replaced Reed Smoot with Elbert D. Thomas in the senate, and retained William H. King. Henry H. Blood was elected governor, and among those put into state offices were several Jews: Herbert M. Schiller for district judge, Julian Bamberger for state senator, Irwin Arnovitz for state legislator. Several women were also elected: Mrs. Burton W. Musser, state senator, Mrs. A. C. Lund, Mrs. S. Grover Rich, Mrs. Minnie Harris and Mrs. E. E. Ericksen, state legislators.

In the same year they elected as mayor of Salt Lake City Louis Marcus, a Republican Jew. Whatever else Mayor Marcus had in the way of political know-how, he must have been a man of keen perception and great personal appeal.

LOUIS MARCUS

Mayor Louis Marcus was born in Brooklyn, New York, January 9, 1880, a son of E. A. and Diane Gumpel Marcus. His early education was in the public schools of Delaware and York, Pennsylvania. He came to Utah in 1907 and entered the motion picture business in Salt Lake City, where he acted as operator and exchange manager. In 1912 he married Gertrude Levin of Pueblo, Colorado. They had only one son, Louis Howard.

When he was elected as mayor, Mr. Marcus was president of the United Realty Company, director in Tracy Loan & Trust, Walker Bank & Trust Company, a member of York and Scottish Rite Masons, B.P.O.E., and board member of

B'nai B'rith. His home was at 1371 Second Avenue. He was also president of the Community Chest, a director in the Zoological Society and of the Art Barn Association, as well as an active member of the Salt Lake City Rotary Club.

Because of poor health, Mayor Marcus did not seek a second term. He died July 6, 1936, of a heart attack.

The *Salt Lake Tribune* gave the following summary of his activities as mayor of Salt Lake City:

> . . . One of the principle features of his administration was his attention to the method of handling the city's finances, so that the books would represent the true debt and the true cost of government.
>
> This involved creating serial bonds payable in ten years to pay a deficit of $600,000, which had grown up because the city had spent money on anticipated taxes which were never collected. . . .
>
> During his term as Mayor, he devoted his entire time to city affairs, and placed the city in the national organization created for the welfare of American cities.
>
> He was one of the active organizers and executives of the United States Council of Mayors.
>
> He was also one of the prime movers in the Deer Creek project. After a long investigation with his associates, he decided to place the money and credit of the city behind the Deer Creek Reclamation Project.
>
> He was one of the organizers and the first president of the Provo River Waters Users organization which was organized to contract with the reclamation service for the building of the giant reclamation project. Salt Lake City tentatively subscribed for 40% of the stock in the organization. . . .
>
> He initiated a vote in Salt Lake City which created the Metropolitan Water District. . . .[14]

Thus it was that this man, though he served only one term in the office of mayor of Salt Lake City, adopted policies and set into motion projects which have been of lasting benefit to the citizens of the growing metropolis.

---

[14]*Salt Lake Tribune,* July 27, 1936, p. 1.

Chapter Twelve

SALT LAKE JEWISH NEWS HIGHLIGHTS

By 1933 THE WORST of the depression had lifted, and life in Salt Lake City assumed a more nearly normal aspect. At B'nai Israel, Rabbi Samuel H. Gordon was carrying on with good success. At the Montefiore Congregation, Rabbi Joseph E. Krikstein was eagerly pushing for increased Jewish consciousness. Early in the summer he established a course in the study of Hebrew at the Covenant House. Beginning with five students, the enrollment leaped to twenty in the second week. This was a class on the adult level, and included not only a study of the language but of Jewish customs, institutions, and laws. Classes were held daily except Saturday and Sunday.

The best account of Jewish activities in Utah during 1933 is found in the *Salt Lake Jewish News,* the first number of which appeared on Friday, June 23. Through this publication we catch a general spirit of optimism, pride, enthusiasm — a vital, yeasty atmosphere among the Jewish congregations.[1] Owned by the Jewish News Publishing Company with Harry G. Rosenthal president, the paper appeared every other Friday. W. Donald Rothman was managing editor, H. Harry Hayden, director of advertising and circulation, and Ernest W. Felt, mechanical superintendent, during the entire life of the paper. For issues one and two, Miss Selma Schonfeld was society editor; Barney Rosenblum was sports editor in issue two. After that Miss Miriam Fox took over as society editor, Lester Rich, sports editor, and Samuel A. Herchovitz, Ogden editor. Regular contributors were Rabbi Joseph E. Krikstein and Dr. Louis C. Zucker.

---

[1] A complete file of the *Salt Lake Jewish News* is found in the basement of the Salt Lake City Public Library, 209 East 5th South, Salt Lake City. All citations are from Vol. 1.

The first issue was hailed with congratulations from all parts of the state, with Governor Henry H. Blood leading. Others included Mayor Louis Marcus of Salt Lake City (himself a Jew), Mayor Ora Bundy of Ogden, Mayor Jesse N. Ellertson of Provo, and Judge Herbert M. Schiller (also an active Jew) of Salt Lake City. The lead article, announced in letters two inches high, was MAIMONIDES CLUB DISBANDS.

There followed a vivid picture of the disbandment by a member who, at the climax of the discussion, tore the last match from its brightly colored cover, lit it, and ignited the cover. The group watched while the flame burned brightly, receded to a glow, and melted into ashes in his hand. It seemed symbolic.

A brief history of the founding of the Maimonides Club followed:

> Max Siegel was elected [first] president with Bertha Pepper, Clara Steres, and William Goldberg chosen as vice-president, secretary, and treasurer, respectively. Mayer B. Stone, charter member, who aided in promoting the inception of the society, contributed the club's name. Initiation rituals and a constitution were drawn up and the club became an active group, attracting members from all parts of the state. Plays were presented each year and became annual events of importance to the entire community.
>
> The two members opposing the motion to disband were Max Guss and H. Henry Hayden.
>
> Those voting for disbandment were: Dal Siegel, Cecilia Cohne, Frances Schonfeld, Sylvia Blumberg, Sylvia Pepper, Yetta Friedman, Yetta Hayden, Sonia Siegel, Hyman Guss, Leo Soble, Ted Rosen, Briana Klein, Sam Bernstein, Jackie Zlotnick, and H. D. Rothman. . . .

Although the Maimonides Club had disbanded, others had been organized. On the University campus the *Phi Sigma Sigma,* national Jewish sorority, had been very active. A social-philanthropic organization, it had contributed to the Monrovian Consumptive Hospital near Los Angeles, and had sent money to the National Philanthropical Fund to help needy students through college. Members active on the University campus were named as:

> . . . Dorothy Leon, past president, was vice-president of the Associated Women Students, Senior sponsor of R.O.T.C. and a member of Trotters, honorary riding organization, and Alpha Beta Theta, local literary sorority. Caroline Stein was a member of the women's varsity debate team, Apmin Fine Arts Society, and the Art Guild. Irene Tannenbaum is a member of Apmin Fine Arts Society, the University Glee Club, and a member of the Utah *Chronicle* and Utah *Pen* staffs. Shirley Bromberger was elected to Spurs, national pep organization, feature editor of the Freshman edition of the *Chronicle,* and a finalist in the intermural tennis tournament. Selma Schonfeld has been an officer of Apmin Fine Arts Society, Chi Delta Phi, national honorary literary sorority, feature editor of the Utah *Chronicle,* editorial assistant of the annual publication, *Utonian,* and member of the editorial board of *Humbug,* quarterly humor magazine. She was recently elected to the Order of Acorn, which is the highest honor a junior student can achieve. . . . The officers recently elected for the coming year are: Selma Schonfeld, archon; Janet White, vice-archon; Irene Tannenbaum, tribune; Rose Weiss, bursar, and Hannah Rosenblum, chapter editor.
>
> Chi Chapter is planning active participation in the Regional Convention which is to be held in San Francisco. . . . The Salt Lake delegation will consist of Hannah Ravitz, Frances Schonfeld, Sylvia Blumberg, and Ruth Marks.[2]

The local B'nai B'rith was also active, for they were sending Frank Brittan and J. B. Arnovitz to represent them at the annual District Grand Lodge convention at Santa Cruz, California. This was the B. F. Peixotto Lodge No. 421, whose secretary, Samuel J. Friedman, made the report. In connection with the preconvention requirements of the grand lodge, the local chapter conducted Friday evening services at the Montefiore Synagogue on June 16th. Max Rosenblatt officiated as cantor and Rabbi Joseph E. Krikstein delivered the address.

On the same page was a story naming Jewish youth who had won scholastic honors: Raymond Landau received a scholarship to attend the New York University, and Harry

---

[2]*Ibid.,* No. 1, p. 4.

Smith received a fellowship to Stanford University, one of seven in the nation. Louis Ottenheimer, already a senior at Stanford, had been appointed business manager of the *Stanford Daily,* one of the nation's outstanding student publications.

Also "Word has been received of honors obtained by Miss Esther Rosenblatt and Miss Helena Rice, but details were not available."[3]

As has been noted earlier, the Upsilon Chapter of Sigma Alpha Mu (S.A.M.) was established on the University of Utah campus in 1919. The report of its activities for the year 1932-1933 was stated in general terms:

> In the past year alone, with its scholastic achievements of academic awards from other Universities, positions of merit on important school councils, having members on publication staffs and varsity debate squads, a Captain of the Champion Inter-Mountain Track Team, the Fraternity also engaged in a varied communal program which, under the advisorship of Dr. Louis C. Zucker, has attained civic respect and admiration.[4]

A more definite naming of these students would be good information today, though the readers in 1933 knew well who they were.

More than any other person, Rabbi Krikstein seemed to sense keenly the international situation and to feel that something should be done about the condition of the Jews in Poland and Germany. His article of criticism was very pointed. On July 7, he wrote:

> Nothing reflects more the poverty of constructive Jewish thought and activity in Salt Lake than the fact that this mightiest current issue in Jewish life today does not raise even the slightest ripple in our complacent and apathetic community, not a single national fund box or stamp or flag day or flower day.
>
> I am informed that the disbandment of the Maimonides club has provoked some thought of replacing it by some new youth organization, organized on the basis of a Zionist platform, and dedicated to do the type of work which is so sorely needed in our

---

[3]*Ibid.,* No. 1, p. 5. Miss Rosenblatt was elected to Phi Beta Kappa, Mills College, from which she graduated that year. She also won the annual Literary Prize.

[4]*Ibid.,* No. 5, p. 18.

community, and which only YOUTH, with its energy and idealism, can properly perform![5]

On July 19 at the Newhouse Hotel the first Zionist organization was formed, its object to create interest in the international situation and to do something about it. Officers were Rabbi Joseph E. Krikstein, chairman; Simon Shapiro, treasurer; Norman Nathan, secretary; and charter members Joseph B. Arnovitz, Nat Wolfe, Abe Guss, Ralph Kahn, Sydney S. Fox, Edwin Kahn, Frank Berger, Jack Weinstock, Harry G. Rosenthal, S. M. Greenbaum, Ben Novikoff, and Harry Goldman.

Two days later — July 21 — Rabbi Alkow, Pacific Coast Director of Zionist Activities, of the Temple Emanuel, San Bernardino, was in Salt Lake City. He proposed an organization of *Mazada,* the junior branch of the American Zionist Organization. Lester Rich, H. Harry Hayden, and Donald Rothman were selected leaders. No information further as to the activities of this group has been found.

If the Jewish people had been apathetic before, two front-page articles in the *Salt Lake Jewish News* for August 4 should have stirred them to action. The first was under the heading, SALT LAKE JEWS PREPARE TO JOIN WORLD-WIDE DRIVE URGING ROOSEVELT PROTEST, an effort to stop the atrocities in Germany. More important was the article beside it which stated that Hitler had withdrawn German citizenship from more than 10,000 Jews in his country. This meant that these people would be deprived of their property and considered as criminals in the body politic.

Certainly now the newly-formed organizations would have plenty to do. The great need of their kinsmen and friends in Germany would demand their united effort. They all denounced Hitler in the strongest terms; their real business was to extend financial aid to people trying to escape his wrath. Rabbi Krikstein's charge of "Apathy" must be changed to action.

[5]*Ibid.,* No. 2, p. 4.

Not only new clubs but permanent ones must be activated and growing. On June 12, 1933, initiation ceremonies brought into *A.Z.A.* Dan Alexander, Max Marovitz, Walter Roth, Harry Ravitz, Milton Newman, and Irving Glaser. Officers were Abe Miller, president; Morris Epstein, vice-president, Sam Henteleff, secretary; Morris Pepper, treasurer; Lester Salmenson, reporter; Abe Wagner, sergeant at arms. Outgoing president was Avrom W. Sandack.

On August 18 a new youth club was organized. Designed to promote better and friendlier feelings, it pledged the support of Jewish youth to every worthy endeavor. Dr. William Bernard Lutzker presided, members of the committee being Dr. Milton Pepper, Harry Goldberg, Sam Bernstein, Abe Guss, William Goldberg, Dr. Lutzker, and Ben Pepper. No name was given.

Since the *Salt Lake Jewish News* closed with the next issue, it is not known whether or not this club succeeded.

The fall issue — September, 1933 — was sponsored by the Congregation Montefiore as a fund-raising project. It was much larger than the preceding ones, was done on heavy, slick paper, and carried many advertisements along with the stories of Jewish accomplishments. Everywhere was echoed Max Baer's earlier statement that, "I'm proud to be a Jew! I'm very proud to be a Jew. You may tell the readers of the *Salt Lake News* — tell the world — that nothing brings me more joy than my Hebrew descent."[6]

A review of the activities of the past year (1932-1933) of the Peixotto Lodge No. 421, B'nai B'rith was given by Samuel J. Friedman, with pride in its program:

> . . . under the able leadership of Warden Brother Abe Guss . . . obtained the applications of thirty candidates who were initiated at one time as the Jack Findling Memorial Class. . . . Educational features provided by the Intellectual Advancement Committee included such speakers as Senator Wm. H. King, who spoke on conditions in Europe; Dr. Fellows of the University of Utah who gave an illustrated lecture on the Dreyfus Case; Rev. J. Trapp who

---

[6]*Ibid.,* No. 3, p. 9.

spoke of "The Philosophy of Spinoza," Professor Clapp on "Past and Present." The Maimonides Club presented a playlet.

Social functions included a Grand Ball in November, a Fathers' and Sons' banquet, a suggestion of Bro. Rabbi Gordon.

Bro. Simon Shapiro took contributions from the Wider Scope Committee. . . .

All lamented the loss of two great leaders during the year, Brother Daniel Alexander and Brother Jack Findling, also members Max Daniels, Louis Jacobs, Mark H. Desky, and Sig Simon.

Members serving as officers of Peixotto Lodge No. 421 were Ralph Kahn, president; Irwin Arnovitz, vice-president; Frank Brittan, monitor; A. Cohne, assistant monitor; Samuel J. Friedman, secretary; Louis Grossman, treasurer; Abe Guss, warden; Edward Spitzer, guardian; and Julius Rosenberg, N. Rosenblatt, N. Block, trustees.

This New Year's edition contained several innovations. One was a section in which were named most beloved people, most tragic or humorous events, and "most" or "best" in several categories. Selection was made by opinions collected by random samplings. While this is most pleasant and for us today very informative, there were then, no doubt, several other people eligible in each category, all of whom would be dissatisfied and critical.

Much more profitable would be the list of greeting cards printed for distribution through the paper. These constitute only a small segment of the congregations, but seem worth listing. In almost every case the entry is given as Mr. and Mrs. and Family:

J. B. Arnovitz	Sam Guss
L. Block	William Jacobson and family of
W. Collins	Chicago
I. Isen	E. Levinson
Herman Finkelstein	Charles W. McGillis
Arthur Frank	Harry Monsey
William Gallenson	J. Monsey
Morris Goldberg	M. Marks Ottenheimer
William Goldberg	F. Pepper
Abe Gross	M. Pepper
Abe Guss	B. Ramo

Will Rees Plumbing	Shapiro Market & Delicatessen
Nathan Rosenblatt	Fritz Sirstins Cleaning & Tailoring
Ben Rosenblum	P. Soble
Harry G. Rosenthal	Jack Tannenbaum
Herman Rosenthal	Harry Wax
Hyman Rosenthal	H. Werber
S. Salmenson	H. White
Nat Segil	J. L. White

The glimpse one gets here of Jewish life and activity in Salt Lake City in 1933 is very brief, but it is most illuminating.

SALT LAKE PICKS

Being a selection in General of the Leading Persons and Events in Salt Lake this Past Year.

EDITOR'S NOTE:—Jewish citizens, called at random, were asked their selections, which follow. There are, probably, many worthy persons not mentioned here. However, we feel that the list below offers a representative picture of the thought we intend to convey. Names of those called will not be divulged.

(This publication may, or may not, agree with the opinions obtained.)

JEWISH CITIZEN NUMBER ONE—Mayor Louis Marcus, because he is an efficient, capable, aggressive public leader.

MOST MOMENTOUS HAPPENING—Initiation of Jack Findling Memorial Class of thirty candidates into B'nai B'rith Lodge.

MOST TRAGIC EVENT—Death of revered Jack Findling.

MOST HUMOROUS EVENT—"Battle of Ballots" at recent election of AZA Sweetheart.

MOST INSPIRING SERMON—Any of Rabbi Samuel H. Gordon's Sabbath Morning discourses at Temple B'nai Israel.

MOST INSPIRING WRITTEN MATERIAL—Rabbi Joseph E. Krikstein's Current Comments editorials in the Salt Lake Jewish News.

MOST BELOVED JEWISH MEN—Nathan Rosenblatt, Lewis Block, Julius Rosenberg, Joshua Shapiro, H. E. Schiller, Reuben Kaplan.

MOST BELOVED JEWISH WOMEN—Mrs. Charles Ottenheimer, Mrs. Charles Levy, Mrs. M. Nathan, Mrs. Mose Lewis, Mrs. Sig Porisky, Mrs. Jacob Bamberger.

JEWISH YOUTH NUMBER ONE—Alfred Klein, whose international fraternity achievements have brought him many honors.

JEWISH YOUNG LADY NUMBER ONE—Satirical, witty Selma Schonfeld, whose literary accomplishments and sorority leadership at Utah University are well known.

YEAR'S MOST MARKED DISAPPOINTMENT—Salt Lake Jewry's reaction to the German situation.

YEAR'S MOST MARKED NEED—(a) A modern gymnasium and recreation room at the Community Center.
(b) Synagogue and Temple attendance, Jewish consciousness

EDUCATIONAL LEADERS—Dr. Louis C. Zucker, Mrs. M. K. Baer, Dr. Charles M. Blumenfeld.

BEST JEWISH ATHLETE—Fleet-legged Herman Goldstein, U. of U.

MOST ACCOMPLISHED YOUNG MAN—Virtuoso Simon Ramo.

YOUNG MEN MOST LIKELY TO SUCCEED—Avrom W. Sandack, Buddy Wolfe, Dan Alexander.

MOST JEWISH INSTITUTION — The Congregation Montefiore "Chader."

YEAR'S BEST JEWISH MOVIE—"Symphony of Six Million."

YOUTHFUL HEBREW SCHOLARS—Charles Holland, Fred Rosenthal.

MOST TYPICAL JEWISH SCENES—(a) Thursday afternoon at the Kosher butcher shop (b) Tisha B'ab ceremonies at the Congregation Sharey Tzedik.

YOUNG MAN WITH FINEST CHARACTER—George Provol.

MOST BELOVED INSTITUTION—The Jewish Community Center, the Covenant House.

MOST BINDING JEWISH ELEMENTS—Synagogues and Temple.

GREATEST INJUSTICE—The boycotting of German as an expression of retaliation against Hitler.

BEST INNOVATION—Weekly Fraternity luncheons at Sigma Alpha Mu.

SALT LAKE JEWISH NEWS WISH—That this will be accepted in the spirit it is offered.

UTAH PARTICIPANTS IN WORLD WAR II

Killed: Harold Glazier, Lieut. U.S.N.R.
        Morris Romick, Pvt. USA
        Sherman Pomerance, Lt. jg U.S.N.R.
        Edward Cherenik

Shirley Appleman	Arthur Weiss	Leroy Goldberg
Wilford Arnovitz	Isadore Werber	Stanley Goldberg
Louis Aronovich	Hugh White	Herman Goldstein
Bernard Axelrad	Sheldon White	Myron Gould
Robert Axelrad	Irving White	Ralph Green
Hans Baer	Daniel Wolfe	Walter Green
Herbert Belmonte	Verner Zinik	Edward Greenband
Don Bercu	Fraydel Zlotnick	Lawrence Greene
Marlan Bercu	Anatole Zucker	Max Grobstein
Robert Bercu	Hyman Davidson	Harold Grossman
Herman Bernstein	Jules Dreyfous	Howard Grossman
Marvin Betnum	Edward Eisen	Alfred Gruber
Paul Block	Joseph Eisen	Hymie Guss
Marvin Bloom	Max Eisen	Morris Guss
Robert Bloom	Morris Epstein	Oscar Guss
Hal Boehmer	Arthur Evdasin	Walter Hahn
Willis Bond	Herman Feinstein	Louis Hayden
Harry Booth	Edmund Feldman	William Hayden
Leonard Brittan	Myron Fox	Edward Herscowitz
Harold Chesler	Alan Frank	Marion Hersh
Alan D. Cline	Boris Frank	Eugene Hertz
Don Cohen	Jules Frank	Herman Hertz
Morris Cohen	Abe Freshman	Charles Holland
Ben Cohen	Mark Freshman	Fred Kant
Howard Collins	Albert Friedman	Ira Kaye
Emanuel Swersky	Jordan Friedman	Al Kramer
Fred H. Tannenbaum	Seymour Friedman	Raymond Landau
Ira Tannenbaum	Stanley Friedman	Robert Leon
Jack M. Tannenbaum	Charles Gallenson	Joseph M. Leven
Louis Tannenbaum	Leon Gallenson	Nat Levine
Ralph M. Tannenbaum	Ben Garelick	Eugene Levitan
Isidore Wagner	Erwin Garelick	Lee Lovinger, Jr.
Harry Wax	Jerome Garfield	Wm. B. Lutzker
Morris Wax	Peter Garfield	Sidney Marks
Louis Weiner	Irwin Glazier	Calvin McGillis
Sidney Weiner	Charles Goldberg	Richard McGillis
Victor Weiner	Harry Goldberg	David Mednick

Ernie Mednick
Irving Mednick
Jack Mednick
Joseph Mednick
Melvin Mednick
Abe Miller
Harry Miller
Paul Miller
Alan Moll
Sam Moll
Arthur Monsey
Max Morovitz
Richard Movitz
John Muller
Milton Newman
Robert Osterman
Louis Ott
Irwin Ottenheimer
Milton Ottenheimer
Jerome Paver
Sherman Paver
Jerome Pepper
Dr. Milton Pepper
Leona Poliner

Lester Poliner
Saul Poliner
Leonard Pollock
Albert Popham
Stewart Porizky
Dr. Leon Ramo
William Rice
Earl Rich
Lester Rich
Isidore Richmond
Irving Robinson
James Roe
Bernard L. Rose
Kurt Rose
Herbert Rosenberg
Bernard H. Rosenblatt
Donald N. Rosenblatt
Bernard Rosenblum
Frank Rosenblum
Burton Rosenthal
Irving Rosenthal
Walter Roth
Harris Safron
Saul Safron

A. Wally Sandack
Joseph Schoolman
Richard Schubach
Robert Schubach
Irvin S. Sedwin
Adrien Segil
Mayer Segil
Robert Segil
Joel B. Shapiro
Sam Shapiro
Harry Sher
Dal Siegel
Leo Siegel
Harry Simon
Aaron Skolnick
Irving Skolnick
Alvin I. Smith
Leo Soble
Bernhard Stein
Daniel Susman
Milton Susman
Arthur D. Sweet
L. Jack Sweet

Chapter Thirteen

RECOLLECTIONS AND OBSERVATIONS

by

Dr. L. C. Zucker

IN THE LATTER 1920s, the Jews of Salt Lake City were inclined to think of those Jews in Germany who discussed Hitler and his Nazi movement as ridiculous patrioteers. The race between Herbert Hoover and Al Smith to reach the White House was taken much more seriously. The Zionist movement languished; the ideological bickerings sounded remote. Both Reform Jewry and Orthodox Jewry (for Congregation Montefiore was still ruled by the now aging immigrants from the townlets of Eastern Europe) placidly followed the established routine.

The B'nai B'rith lodge meetings were largely spent in parliamentary skirmishes and tempests about nothing of far-reaching importance, nothing serious. Jewish parents were, in the main, making a nice living at their various businesses; the youth were in high school or going to college (Wharton School, Smith, Stanford), only a few to the U of U; Sigma Alpha Mu, the fraternity, and Phi Sigma Sigma, the sorority. These were American youth, their horizon limited to the campus and their little Jewish world. The Reform boys and girls were confirmed; the Orthodox were Bar Mitsvah.

The two rabbis were militant ideologues, not too ecumenically related. Rabbi Joseph Krikstein of Montefiore (Chicago Theological College) was intellectual, erudite, concerned chiefly for the faithfulness of his people to Rabbinic Judaism. Rabbi Samuel H. Gordon of B'nai Israel (Hebrew Union

College) was Classical Reform, the popular and esteemed "ambassador to the Gentiles."

There were two Jewish physicians in Salt Lake City, Dr. Sol Kahn and Dr. Robert Alexander, and three Jewish lawyers, Herbert M. Schiller, Ben Liberman, and Daniel Alexander. In the early 1930s there would be a third physician, Milton Pepper, and several more Jewish lawyers, Alfred Klein, Samuel Bernstein, Irwin Arnovitz, Alvin Smith, and one Jewish dentist, [Dr. William Bernard] Lutzker. Temple B'nai Israel continued to take its tone from the German Jews or those others assimilated to the Germans — Sweet, Kahn, Schiller, Ottenheimer, Rosenbaum, Bamberger, Sig Simon. Men like Jack Findling and Simon Shapiro were leaders in the management of the Covenant House and in B'nai B'rith.

The Depression did not begin to hurt here until late 1930. The youth away at the name colleges were called home to continue their education at the U. of U. About 1932 S.A.M. appointed Dr. L. Zucker as faculty adviser, and almost every meeting was chiefly a session of Judaic learning. The apex of this learning effort was a classical slide lecture on the Dreyfus case given by Prof. George E. Fellows of the History Department of the U of U, and shared with a crowd from the Jewish community. Socially, the apex was its participation in the Panhellenic dance of the spring of 1933. Then it vanished, as did the Phi Sigma Sigma, apparently never to return.

Business failed: for instance, Herbert Hirschman's shoe stores in Salt Lake City and Ogden, and Charles Ottenheimer's factory in Provo. And there were personal tragedies, such as the suicide of Daniel Alexander. Yet, paradoxically or significantly, the B'nai B'rith lodge, under the chairmanship of Rabbi Gordon or Ben Liberman, presented to the Jewish community, at the Covenant House, a series of "adult education" lectures by Elmer Rice, playwright from New York, Selig Perlman of the University of Wisconsin Department of Economics, and other distinguished out-of-staters. In 1929-1931 Ludwig Lewisohn and Chaim Bialik were introduced to the University and general community by Dr. Louis C. Zucker in a series of lectures sponsored by the University of Utah Extension Division.

Then came Hitler's seizure of power and his anti-Jewish orations heard round the world. Instantly the climate changed from ominous to worse. The Nazi threats were no longer a joke. The Joint Distribution Committee, the Hebrew Immigrant Aid Society (HAIS) at once communicated with every Jewish community in the United States to inform, to obtain affidavits for refugees to get admitted into this country and to prepare jobs and housing for them. The colossal task was to raise the amount of money needed to move and reestablish an unlimited number of refugees from Nazi Europe.

Ottenheimer said, "Call them *emigrés*." Culturally, this wavelet was on a much higher level than the earlier German immigration. After the war, the Edgar Bodenheimers, both lawyers and professors in law schools, came to Salt Lake City from Germany via Washington.

The Jewish Telegraphic Agency and the American Jewish Congress and the Zionist organizations, Hadassah and the others, kept up a stream of information throughout the American-Jewish body politic. No Jew in Salt Lake City or in all Utah remained uninformed, unconcerned. Both rabbis, James L. White, Max Siegel, Abe Guss, Ben M. Roe, and others took hold, to succor and save the condemned Jews in Germany, then in Austria and Hungary, then Czechoslovakia and Roumania, in cooperation with Jewish leaders in Idaho — Boise and Pocatello in particular — under the direction of the able and vigorous leadership, rabbinic and lay, in New York. It was in this atmosphere that the United Jewish Council of Salt Lake City, and its instrument, the Salt Lake Jewish Welfare Fund, were founded in 1936, thanks chiefly to the vision and force of Rabbi Krikstein.

The Nazi regime was not slow to issue decrees evicting the Jews from business and the professions, from German society and the schools; and, in almost instant reaction, "refugees" started coming to Salt Lake City, to relatives —

like the Harts, two generations, to the Sweet (Leon, Arthur, Jack) family. Max Lehmann, pioneer in Germany in the canning of fruits and vegetables, after searching for a new location in Africa and South America chose to try a partnership with Harold Fabian of Salt Lake City. Here Mr. Lehmann, like the younger Harts, began to learn the English language and to look around for a broader area of opportunity. But by 1940 the Lehmann family and these Harts had departed to the West Coast.

By 1936-1937 we began to get old and young from the concentration camps. The resident Jews, both men and women, tried their best for all of them. Some made loans available to start a business, such as a gas station, to eke out wages, or to provide transportation fares. The resident Jews felt, "These are our brothers; we cannot let them go to ruin."

The newcomers, who in the past had looked on the East European Jews and the American Jews with a certain condescension, were unhappy to find themselves the beneficiaries of American Jews who were, to a large extent, of East European origin. Every businessman among them claimed that, in the old country, he had been somebody of substance and importance. They were demanding; they made the adjustment with difficulty. In general, one might say that those who stayed long enough to see their children become Americans and progress toward a dignified place in business or the professions mellowed.

The professional men were more modest. On the other hand, the latter have not remained, with two exceptions: one, Sigmund Helwig, Ph.D. from the University of Vienna, who soon proved himself a first-rate certified public accountant; the other, a younger man, Walter Hahn, who is an able professor of languages and education at the University of Utah.

The neo-Germans, who may be so termed to distinguish them from their predecessors of the mid-19th century, affiliated not with the Reform congregation, but mostly with Congregation Montefiore, liking neither Orthodoxy nor Reform. They are live members of the Jewish community, but hardly leaders. A few neo-German families were settled in small towns, such as Milford and Fillmore; but no Jews at all live any longer in the countryside of Utah. Concern for the Jewishness of the children and a need for cosmopolitan culture made this outcome certain.

What of the Mormon "peril?" When the Jewish husband of a German Gentile arrived in Salt Lake City in 1940, the wife's Mormon relatives long established here hoped to convert him and her. In vain. Conversion on the part of the neo-Germans to Mormonism has been practically nil.

So Utah and Idaho Jewry was clearly aware from 1933 on that the New Order in Germany gave no quarter to the Jews in their power, and subjected them as Jews to extreme cruelty. The worse fears were entertained for the fate of the Jews of Poland, or wherever the Nazis overran. Was anyone here asked to implore the Mormon Church to intervene or intercede, to stop the descent to genocide, the extermination of the Jewish civilian population in Nazi Europe? I don't know. The genocide of the Six Million was not discovered until after the war, and then we in Utah and Idaho were told about it, too.

But however concerned the Jews out here were for their brethren overseas, they pitched into the business of providing for the leisure time of the Jewish servicemen and women sent in masses to the Air Force bases newly opened in these states. From the summer of 1942 to the fall of 1945 Jewish people were active in activities in Utah as far away as Wendover and the hospital in Brigham City. There were interfaith dances and Jewish dances at the Covenant house; there was much home hospitality, especially on the Jewish holidays, "Jewish" food taken to the bases, Jewish services held there, usually under Max Rosenblatt or Louis C. Zucker. Programs of Jewish music were presented there as well as at the Covenant House. The temple and synagogue were never so jammed on High Holy Days as in those years; Covenant House never so frequented by youth at play or by young intellectuals as in those years; Jewish life in Salt Lake City was exciting in those years with so much Jewish youth, and so varied, around, wherever you went.

The resident Jews not only wanted to make these young people in uniform, a great many of whom had never been away from their native neighborhoods before, feel better, feel wanted and appreciated, but also enjoyed them because they carried a breath from the great Jewish centers, chiefly New York, and many of them still adhered to the old world Orthodox way of life. Also there was the feeling that, through them, we were actively participating in the struggle to bring down the Third Reich and, incidentally, to liberate the Jews.

Perhaps this home activity reduced the anxiety over the Jewish hell in Europe. At the same time the thought was strong that ministering to the servicemen was related to the world-wide struggle to rid the world of the Nazi monster as quickly as possible. Sons were willingly, if not joyfully, sent forth to war because the defeat of Amalek was one thing the war was about.

Although practically every Jewish woman who was able shared the work, Claire (Mrs. Abe) Bernstein was perhaps the outstanding hostess at the Covenant House. Several of the neo-Germans served wholeheartedly, and Hans A. Illing diligently set up concerts of highbrow music and sought to be useful around the Jewish Welfare Board Director's office and in the field in all sorts of ways. From the beginning to the end, the National Jewish Welfare Board had a director stationed in Salt Lake City. These were able men, of large, sophisticated outlook, who were adopted by the Jewish community, without whose willing labors they could have accomplished nothing. There were also Jewish chaplains.

Of course, numerous of the more permanent Jewish service personnel, especially the intellectuals, did not limit their acquaintance to the resident Jews, just as the Jewish women did not limit their services to the Jewish service personnel: they met the trains at all hours along with their

Mormon and other Christian sisters, and they joined in making the interfaith dances a success.

After the war, when there was not room for them in colleges they would normally have chosen, much the largest number of Jewish students the University of Utah has ever seen enrolled here. They came from New York and California, even Colombia, and two brothers from Jerusalem came after the UN resolved to partition Palestine. Thanks to their numbers and their vital Jewishness, however varied it was, "Hillel" started on the U. of U. campus in 1946 — the only one that has ever been in Utah and Idaho. It had a vigorous, if troubled, career that was the high water mark socially, culturally, and ecumenically. Rabbi Alvin S. Luchs, of Temple B'nai Israel, versatile and exact scholar and sparkling, provocative conversationalist, who would magnetize a company of intellectual Jewish servicemen, was the counselor until he left Salt Lake City in the spring of 1948.

There probably always were some Zionists in Salt Lake City since the first Congress in Basle in 1897. Salt Lake Hadassah was organized in 1903. Zionists included Rabbi Krikstein, Simon Shapiro, Edmund Feldman, L. C. Zucker, Ben Roe, and a few others. We were exercised over the 1936 anti-Jewish riots in Palestine and by the British White Paper of 1939. Rommel's victories in North Africa caused anxiety for the Jewish settlement in Palestine. After the war, 1946, Rabbi Arthur J. Lelyveld came to Salt Lake City, in the name of the newly formed Committee on Unity for Palestine, and organized the Salt Lake District of the Zionist Organization of America. First officers: Simon Shapiro, president, Dr. L. C. Zucker, Ben Roe, and Simon Rosenblatt, committee members.

In the meantime, L. C. Zucker had used his influence and pen in forwarding the movement, first, with a long editorial in the *Deseret News* on the impending World Congress and another on the assassination of Chaim Orlosoroff in Palestine. An article on Jewish books followed in the *News*, besides a number in the community publications.

The next year — 1947 — were elected the officers who still are serving. This year was held a great meeting in honor of James G. Macdonald, later American Ambassador to the state of Israel. Held at the Hotel Utah, this was probably the largest and most representative Jewish-sponsored community-wide meeting in the history of this Utah-Idaho, or whole intermountain area.

By now James White was on the Zionist side, although not a member of the Salt Lake Zionist District. Simon and son Joel Shapiro, Ben Roe, Louis Zucker now went to work trying, in a letter, to persuade President George Albert Smith of the Mormon Church to throw the weight of the Church behind the struggle in the United Nations to achieve a Jewish State in Palestine. There was no answer at the time, but some months later President Smith called L. Zucker to explain the silence, and to assure him and his associates of the Church's sympathy.

(Back in 1942 or 3, an ardent Zionist of New York had spent several weeks in Salt Lake City holding conversations with the high authorities of the Church and then extended these in letters. Perhaps President Smith had become sympathetically oriented at that time.)

Upon the birth of the state of Israel in May, 1948, the District held a meeting at the Covenant House as a mark of rejoicing. Elihu Salmon was here from Jerusalem and gave a thoughtful speech.

The Salt Lake City Jewish community continues to respond liberally to appeals for aid to Israel, in the annual United Jewish Appeal drives, and Hadassah is healthy, but the Zionist organization cannot be gotten on its feet again.

The American Friends of the Hebrew University, Alex Berner and L. Zucker, and officers, however, are in constant touch with New York City, Los Angeles, and Washington and carry on "political" work.

During the spring of 1952, at a meeting in the new social hall of Temple B'nai Israel, men from the University and businessmen, along with the first officers, made a good start to support the work of A.F.H.U., the American public relations agency of the Hebrew University in Jerusalem. Occasionally we provided the Hebrew University with a laboratory instrument; we also sponsored lectures on life in Israel by Stephen Spender, Isaac Stern, and others. We sent L. C. Zucker as a delegate to the historic Princeton Conference in 1954, presided over by Albert Einstein. Although the local organization does not meet any more, individuals still support the national organization.

Chapter Fourteen

POSTWAR YEARS — 1945-1954

THE END OF World War II in 1945 was the occasion for nationwide rejoicing, in which the Jewish community of Utah joined heartily. One hundred and eighty Jewish boys from this state had served in the conflict, and all but four had returned to their homes. These were Lieutenant Harold Glazier and Lieutenant j.g. Sherman Pomerance, both in the U.S.N.R., and privates Morris Romick and Edward Cherenik.[1]

That the two congregations in Salt Lake City were alert and active is shown by newspaper articles written by Zena Potter, each featuring a large picture of the meetingplace and of the rabbi. Since the Montefiore group were celebrating the 50th anniversary of the date on which they received their charter, their story appeared first:

> Of the original 27 charter members of the Congregation Montefiore, three survive, Nathan Rosenblatt and Moses Nathan, both of Salt Lake City, and Joshua Shapiro of Los Angeles, Cal. Mr. Rosenblatt came to Salt Lake City in 1899 on the first excursion train from Denver.
>
> . . . Rev. Oscher Goldman, present head of the synagogue, came here in November 1939, with his wife and three children. Rev. Goldman was born in the holy city of Jerusalem, Dec. 24, 1910, and was educated there. . . . He came to the United States in 1930. Prior to coming to Salt Lake City, Rev. Goldman occupied pulpits in Philadelphia, Pa. and Atlantic City, N.J.
>
> Synagogue activities include Hebrew school classes, Friday night and Saturday services, Sunday School classes and educational and religious discussions by auxiliary groups.
>
> Present officers of the organization, whose membership now numbers about 100, are Joshua Shapiro, honorary president; Ben Pepper, President; Henry Ungerleider, vice president; Herman

[1] See complete list of names attached.

Finkelstein, honorary secretary; Sam Bernstein, secretary; Nathan Rosenblatt, treasurer; Abe Guss, assistant treasurer.[2]

The article on the Congregation B'nai Israel, which appeared a month later, gave a brief historical summary and a statement that "B'nai Israel's congregation has given to Utah a governor, Simon Bamberger, to Salt Lake City a mayor, Louis Marcus, and to the state, county, and city other prominent men." It went on to elucidate some differences in doctrine:

> . . . The Reform Jew prays todays, as he has always prayed, for the ability to see and welcome all truth, whether shining from the annals of ancient revelation, or reaching us through the seers of our own time. To Judaism, there is neither an infallible book nor an infallible man.
>
> . . . There is, however, the belief in the messianic age to come, and when it comes all humanity will be involved in it, for the salvation of the Jew is inextricably bound up with the salvation of humanity.
>
> . . . Stern reality and the logic of the situation caused the rabbis to look upon scattered Israel, no longer as a nation, but rather as a congregation or religious fellowship. Without common country, state or language, Israel . . . continued and has persisted as a unique people, held together by common ties of tradition and future hope. . . . Reform Judaism is and wants to be nothing else than Judaism revitalized — Judaism translated into the language and spirit of our age.[3]

The membership was given as ninety-two in August of 1946, and the officers for the year 1947-8 were listed as:

> Pres., Irwin Arnovitz; vice-pres., Max Siegel; sec., Sigmund Helwig; corresponding sec. & treas., Alvin I. Smith. Board members: Simon Frank, Sam Axelrad, Myron Finkelstein, Fred Provol, James L. White, J. J. Weinstock, Dr. Milton Pepper, Corrine Sweet. Sunday School committee, Wally Sandack, Chairman; Ritual Committee, Ben Roe, chairman; cemetery committee, J. A. Kahn, chairman; Committee on Temple repairs, Max Seigel, Chairman; Committee for erection of New Temple, James L. White, Chairman; Membership Committee, Fred Provol, Chairman.[4]

---

[2]*Salt Lake Tribune,* June 3, 1945.
[3]*Salt Lake Tribune,* July 1, 1945,
[4]B'nai Israel Minute Book, August 16, 1945.

Some mention has been made earlier of the fact that many Jewish families sent their teen-age children out of the state to school. THE JEWISH YEARBOOK FOR 1946 lists the numbers of Jewish students attending state schools over the nation. For Utah, it is:

Total enrollment in Universities	17,091
Jewish enrollment in Universities	40
Total in Colleges	367
Jewish in Colleges	0
Utah Junior Colleges total	2,774
Jews Junior Colleges	3

This seems conclusive evidence that the Jewish youth were being sent outside the state during their maturing years. While there are no numbers for the attendance in the last years of high school, there is no way to tell how many sixteen- to eighteen-year-olds are out of state, nor is there any indication that the forty who are attending universities — specifically the University of Utah — are upperclassmen. Though forty is a good number, there would likely be more than that if all freshmen were in attendance and all four years counted. The three in junior colleges could well have been in Ogden or Cedar City.

During the war the Jewish ladies of both congregations worked diligently to further the war effort and to keep up the morale of the boys. Many of them had boys in the ranks, and so were glad to help sons of other mothers. Now united in a common cause, they became truly sisters, without the aloof coldness which had prevailed between them before.

Besides the CARE boxes and the hospital supplies they sent out, they met every troop train, no matter what the hour or the weather. They invited boys who were stationed near into their homes or sponsored public entertainment for them.

So genuine was the cooperation between them that one was heard to exclaim, "Thank God, the barriers are down! Down at last."[5] Though they might not have been entirely

---

[5]Personal interview, home of Ben Roe, November 19, 1967.

down, there was a cordial, cooperative spirit among them, an
achievement after long years.

The activities of Utah Jews during the war received
national recognition when James L. White, Salt Lake City
attorney, was made Regional President of B'nai B'rith, the
Jewish service organization. There was no opposing candidate. At the same time Mrs. Dal Siegel also of Salt Lake
City, was made first vice-president of the Regional Ladies'
Auxiliary.[6]

These two were present in Washington, D.C., on February 5, 1946, when General Dwight D. Eisenhower gave
B'nai B'rith a special citation for their work in behalf of
the morale and welfare of the army personnel. During the
war B'nai B'rith had furnished and equipped 1,507 recreation
facilities in 227 different camps, 81 aid bases, 53 hospitals,
22 training schools and WAC barracks and five induction
and separation centers.[7]

Then came the happy day when Israel was made an
independent state. Such a rejoicing as went up all over the
land! May 14th, 1948, was certainly a date to remember!
In Salt Lake City there were other demonstrations, but the
gathering at the Covenant House most fitted the gratitude
and joy of many dedicated Jews who had long hoped for
this day.

On May 21, 1946, Salt Lake City was visited by Rev.
Karl B. Justus of New York City. Rev. Justus was a former
Methodist minister who had served in the navy as chaplain;
he told the Utah audience that of the three and one-half
million Jews in Poland before the war, only 80,000 remained
alive and seven out of every eight of them would need help if
they were to survive. The United Jewish Appeal asked the
Jews of Utah to contribute $150,000.00 as their share. The
committee was set up with Joseph Rosenblatt and Mrs. Max
Siegel as co-chairmen to raise that amount.[8]

---

[6]*Salt Lake Tribune,* June 20, 1945.
[7]*Salt Lake Tribune,* February 5, 1946.
[8]*Salt Lake Tribune,* May 26, 1946.

Perhaps the most dramatic appeal came during a "Salute to Israel" on December 5, 1948, when two young veterans told some of their experiences during the war, in an appeal for orphaned children. They were Captain Yehuda Koppel and Corporal Alisa Pnueli, and their account of the underground operations of getting children out of the concentration camps and their own involvement in the actual combat brought to their fellow Jews a whole new concept of the holocaust in Europe and of the need of the welfare fund. James L. White was made chairman of this project.[9]

By October 23, 1952, the Congregation Montefiore had finished a two-story addition at the rear of their synagogue. This included six classrooms and a kitchen, in addition to a spacious room in the basement for use as a social hall. This was the second addition to the building since its construction in 1903. The first was made in the early 1920s. Mrs. Milton Pepper and Abe Bernstein had served as co-chairmen of a large building committee which spearheaded the renovation.

> Members of the two Hebrew congregations in Salt Lake City —Congregation Montefiore and Temple B'nai Israel — will hold a joint service at the synagogue of the former, 335 - 3rd East, at which time the recently completed addition to the synagogue will be dedicated.
>
> The service will be conducted by Rabbi E. Louis Cardon of Congregation Montefiore, assisted by Cantor Harry Sterling. Participating will be Rabbi Adolph Fink of Temple B'nai Israel and Hymie Guss, president of Congregation Montefiore.
>
> A reception will be held after in Dupler Hall, part of the remodeled building.
>
> The Sisterhood of Congregation Montefiore will sponsor a Family Festival and Dance Night Saturday at 9 p.m. in Dupler Hall Ballroom, square and Israeli folk dancing will highlight the entertainment. Refreshments will be served.
>
> Mrs. Manny Pepper is chairman of the festival.[10]

Two months later the Congregation Montefiore received from a former prisoner of war, Leo Brody, a valuable religious candelabrum for use in their eight-day festival.

---

[9]*Salt Lake Tribune,* December 5, 1948.
[10]*Salt Lake Tribune,* October 23, 1952.

An ornate silver candelabrum, fashioned 200 years ago by an Israeli craftsman, will play a part Thursday in the Salt Lake celebration of Hanukkah, Jewish "Festival of the lights."

The relic, which is fronted with eight tiny oil lamps . . . was one of the few family treasures smuggled from behind the Iron Curtain by Leo Brody, now with Radio Station KDYL.

Mr. Brody came to Salt Lake City three years ago from Red Czechoslovakia. Prior to and during World War II, his family went through severe persecution. . . .

During this time . . . the historic candelabrum, appraised by U. S. experts at thousands of dollars, was buried underground. He managed to salvage it, . . . after being released from a concentration camp.

The altar of Congregation Montefiore synagogue . . . will be the resting place of the treasured art piece during the festival.[11]

In the meantime, the B'nai Israel Congregation had also enlarged and improved their facilities with a new temple house dedicated May 24, 1953. Present was a capacity audience of members and friends. The rites, in which leaders of several religious faiths participated, were held in the temple itself, and the new facilities were opened for public inspection at a reception afterwards. These provided classrooms, a large multi-purpose area with a stage, a lounge with fireplace, a kitchen, and a rabbi's study.

The Rev. Eric N. Hawkins, Zion Evangelical Lutheran Church Pastor and Salt Lake Ministerial Assn. president, congratulated the congregation for its enterprise, commending the new structure to the furtherance of "the religious tone of this community."

Others who spoke briefly were the Rt. Rev. Arthur W. Moulton, retired Episcopal bishop of Utah; Richard L. Evans, member of the First Council of Seventy, Church of Jesus Christ of Latter-day Saints; Rabbi E. Louis Cardon of Congregation Montefiore, and Dr. Harold Scott, First Unitarian Church pastor.

Dr. Walter Teusch directed the choir.

Congregation members only will attend the dedication banquet and dance Saturday at 7 p.m. in the new hall. There will be a children's service and entertainment Sunday at 11:30 a.m. under the direction of Mrs. Ted Burnett, Sisterhood Religious School chairman.[12]

---

[11]*Deseret News,* December 8, 1952.
[12]*Salt Lake Tribune,* May 24, 1953.

For the Succoth Festival that fall, the sisters of B'nai Israel erected a booth around the pulpit and decorated it with crops of the harvest, reminiscent of the agricultural life of the ancient Hebrews. The committee was Mrs. Daniel Schwartz, Mrs. Alvin Smith, Mrs. Marvin Herman, Mrs. David Alder, Mrs. Jerome Feiler, Mrs. Irving Ershler, and Mrs. Sam Axelrad.

It was well that they had a good photograph of Rabbi Fink in this setting, for within six months he was dead and buried.[13]

On January 6, 1954, Salt Lake City was visited by Dr. Everett Ross Clinchy and Karl B. Justus, president and division vice-president of the National Conference of Christians and Jews. President Levi Edgar Young of the L.D.S. Quorum of Seventies arranged the meeting at the Hotel Utah, and representatives of the Catholic Church and several Protestant Churches, as well as Mormons and Jews, were in attendance.

> Dr. Clinchy told the group that the conference's main business is to enlist the support of such agencies as churches, schools, trade and industry groups, civic organizations, and the mass media in promoting brotherhood.
>
> He emphasized that the NCCJ does not seek an amalgamation of creed or doctrine or compromising of anyone's principles.[14]

Dr. Clinchy visited fifteen cities in the interest of the brotherhood movement before leaving for Asia with Nobel Prize winner, Arthur H. Compton, on a Ford Foundation lectureship. While his appeal met with approval and an organization was effected, there was little immediate activity or follow-up on his suggestions.

On September 11, 1954, the *Deseret News* heralded the official beginning of the Centennial Year with a two-column spread, illustrated, carrying the caption, THE JEWISH TERCENTENARY.

---

[13]*Salt Lake Tribune,* photograph September 29, 1953; burial March 12, 1954, as recorded in the cemetery records.

[14]*Deseret News,* January 7, 1954.

The Tercentenary Banquet was held November 18, 1954, at the Hotel Utah, with Philip M. Klutznick, national president of B'nai B'rith, as speaker.

> Mr. Klutznick heads the oldest and largest Jewish group in America. B'nai B'rith was established 111 years ago. Today it has lodges in 33 countries with a total membership of over 500,000.
>
> Welcoming Mr. Klutznick to Salt Lake City were Harry Smith and Ben Roe, President and Vice-president, and Dal Siegel, Tercentenary banquet chairman.[15]

Another activity in celebrating this 300th anniversary of the arrival of the first Jews in America was the Utah Symphony, under its new conductor, Maurice Abravanel, in a program of Jewish music. This was financed by the Jewish community and given free to the general public, a rare cultural gift long to be remembered.

The Jewish congregations of Utah did not take the Centennial Year as a time to look back and assess their achievements; instead, they looked forward to their needs. What could be more important than a Community Center where there would be facilities for all — a building which would be worthy the best efforts of both congregations? But how to begin and where to build?

James A. Hogle, Sr., answered the last question by donating an acre and three-fourths of land on the bench at 2400 East on 17th South, an ideal location with ample room.

On December 21, 1956, ground-breaking ceremonies were held, with Simon Shapiro turning the first shovel of earth. Present also were many dignitaries, among them Phillip M. Stillman, executive director of the United Jewish Council; also Alvin I. Smith, President of the United Jewish Council; Abe Bernstein, former Council president; Rabbi E. Louis Cardon, Congregation Montefiore, and Rabbi Mordecai Podet, Temple B'nai Israel.

On September 8, 1958, the cornerstone of the building was placed by Simon Shapiro, the oldest member, with Dal

---

[15]*Deseret News,* October 18, 1954.

Siegel, president of the Center's Board of Directors, officiating. Again both Rabbis attended, with Harry Sterling, cantor. Abe Bernstein, chairman of the building committee, was master of ceremonies. Mrs. Sarah S. White, widow of the man whose name the building bears, guided the stone into place as it was lowered by a winch, as Simon Shapiro listed its various contents.[16]

It was another year before the final dedication of this first monument to two-congregation cooperation. Spacious enough for all needs, with meeting rooms, game rooms, swimming pool, it is a constant source of pride and a center for fostering Jewish tradition.

While Jewish parents might have problems of assimilation, of intermarriage, and of indifference to some requirements, this building is still a strong unifying force in their society.

---

[16]Both the *Salt Lake Tribune* and the *Deseret News* carried stories of this event on September 8, 1958.

Chapter Fifteen

RECENT ACCOMPLISHMENTS

THE BUILDING OF the Jewish Community Center at 2416 East 1700 South, named after community leader James L. White, gave opportunity for leisure-time cultural and recreational programming, principally for the Jews of the city but also for interested non-Jews. Opened on 15 March 1959, it became the center of many and varied activities, all tending toward better relationships between the two congregations, B'nai Israel and Montefiore.

In the meantime gradual changes were being made in the lay personnel of both congregations. There was practically no change in numbers, both receiving new members from the Jewish families moving in as a result of government projects in the area, added personnel at the University of Utah, and specialists in various professional fields. But there were deaths and moving away enough to keep the overall population about constant. It was a change in basic personnel which moved toward professionalism. For example, the age-old Relief Society became Jewish Family Services. Now, instead of volunteer help for the needy, they had the services of a paid professional. As one person aptly put it, "Therapy replaced chicken soup."

Also there was a move to upgrade the help; teachers were paid more, part-time administrative aids were also paid.

By 1969 the congregations decided to combine their religious education for children, thereby being able to have a large enough group to pay for a competent teacher. Under the name, United Jewish Religious School, this school graduated its first class in 1971.

Uniting the religious schools of Congregation Montefiore and B'nai Israel not only upgraded the quality and quantity of Jewish education in the city, but it was the forerunner of the eventual merger of the two Synagogues. The new one, named Kol Ami, marks the most significant development within the community. It is too early yet to evaluate clearly, but it should be the most unifying force Salt Lake Jewry has yet experienced.

Salt Lake City Jews have an outstanding record in charitable fund-raising. While not a wealthy community, Salt Lake City has always been among the top cities in per capita giving. During the years we are discussing, millions of dollars have been raised and given to support Israel's nonmilitary needs such as education, hospitals and immigration of refugees from other lands, including their housing, sustenance, and rehabilitation. Other monies have been directed to the numerous charities necessary to a better life in the U.S.A. and overseas countries other than Israel.

Giving has increased in recent years and must be classified as a major accomplishment of the past two decades. The principal fund-raising agency is the Salt Lake City Welfare Fund, an arm of the United Jewish Council of this city. Excellent work has also been done by Hadassah and B'nai B'rith women, and to a lesser extent by the National Council of Jewish Women.

As a result of the efforts of a few men, a professorial chair over a department of Jewish studies has been promised by the University of Utah.

Additional interest in Judaism and the State of Israel is reflected in the curricula of the colleges of the state, especially the Brigham Young University, where a dancing troupe presents an Israeli repertoire, the Hebrew language is taught, and teachers of Hebrew and Judaica are developed.

Jewish men of Salt Lake City who have gained national recognition are: businessman Maurice Warshaw in the field of philanthropy in aiding the handicapped and underprivileged;

Maestro Maurice Abravanel in the field of cultural attainment for bringing Salt Lake City international fame with the excellence of our Symphony Orchestra; and

Doctors Max M. Wintrobe and Louis Goodman in the field of medicine for their unsurpassed work and contributions in the subject of hematology.

The organizational structure of the Jewish community has been largely responsible for the worthwhile accomplishments that have thus far been realized. Good things do not usually happen by accident. It takes thinking, careful planning, and devotion to goals to bring them about. There are a few people who have been more responsible than others for keeping things moving, and possibly rate mention, but since so many complications are involved we will desist.

Judaism in Utah is a living, growing organization, responsible for much that is good in our society.*

---

*Much of the information in this last section was supplied by Mr. Dal Siegel, Mr. Joel Shapiro, and others.

Addendum

BEN M. ROE

IN 1966 BEN M. ROE was singled out to receive the coveted Chai award, which made him one of a minyan (ten men) in the United States, for his contribution to many Jewish and humanitarian causes. Theodore R. McLelden, former Governor of Maryland, made the presentation. This signal honor had been well deserved, as a list of Ben's activities would show.

Born June 7, 1898, in Serie, Lithuania, Ben came to Salt Lake City in 1913. His older brother Harry was living here, so Ben had some security until he could get oriented and learn the language. By 1915 he had employment in a store in Pioche, Nevada. As World War I progressed, Ben felt that he should help his adopted country to "make the world safe for democracy" and was one of the first to enlist in Pioche. He was strong and tall and could pass for 21, though really he was two years under age.

Ben served with distinction through the conflict. He was wounded several times, for which he received the Purple Heart. Upon his return he served as commander of his American Legion Post, and later as president of the 91st Division, in which he had served.

Ben's second call to render distinctive service came during World War II, while Hitler's holocaust was wiping out the Jewish community in Germany. By a miracle a way of escape was open to some of the Jews, who found temporary shelter in Shanghai. After a while a way was found to bring many of them to the United States. Many Jewish communities assumed responsibility for helping these new Americans. We received a number of those families in Salt Lake and Ben was asked to be chairman of providing employment and many other services, which required tact and insight. He met this challenge with much success. The Jewish community opened their doors and hearts in a most generous and heart-warming way. The refugees soon became a part of the community.

The third noteworthy contribution of Ben Roe was his early concept, in cooperation with Dr. L. C. Zucker, of a Judaica Library at the University of Utah. On January 13, 1941, celebrating their anniversary, Ben surprised his wife Berniece with a gift in the form of a contribution in their name to be used for the purchase of suitable books for a Judaica collection. Each year following they have continued to contribute to the library. That same year Ben started contributing toward Hebraica collections at Brigham Young University, Utah State University, and Westminster College, and has continued over the years.

In 1965 as chairman, and with the help of Doctor L. C. Zucker, he initiated a drive to raise $100,000 to be used for the purchase of Hebraica and Judaica for the University. Today the Judaica and Hebraica collection at the University of Utah is among the outstanding collections in the Inter-mountain West.

Additional Achievements and Contributions
of
BEN M. ROE

1—Initiated and supported the writing of this book.

2—One of the founders and supporters of the Alberta Henry Education Foundation for Underprivileged Minority Groups. Treasurer for many years.

3—One of the founders and supporters of the American Civil Liberties Union (Utah Affiliate) and treasurer for many years.

4—Member National American-Jewish Public Affairs Committee.

5—Chairman American-Jewish Tercentenary Committee for Utah (1654-1954).

6—Past President of Temple B'nai Israel.

7—Board member of Friends of the University of Utah Libraries.

8—Board member of American Cancer Society of Utah.

9—One of the founders and supporters of the model U.N. at the University of Utah.

10—Board member and social service chairman Utah Chapter Hemophilia Foundation.

APPENDIX

LIST OF RABBIS
CONGREGATION B'NAI ISRAEL

Sept. 1889 - July 1891	Rabbi Heiman J. Elkin
July - August 1891	Rabbi Jacob Ludwig Stern
Aug. 1891 - June 1894	Rabbi Moses P. Jacobson
July 1894-1900	No Rabbi. Services read by Sig. Simon and I. Kaiser
1900-1903	Rabbi Louis G. Reynolds
1904-1913	Rabbi Charles J. Freund
1914-1920	Rabbi Dr. William Rice
1921-1925	Rabbi Adolph Steiner
1926-1943	Rabbi Samuel Gordon
1943-1953	Rabbi Alvin S. Luchs
1953-1954	Rabbi Adolph Fink (Died March 11, 1954)
1954-1961	Rabbi Mordecai Podet

LIST OF RABBIS

CONGREGATION MONTEFIORE

Information here has been taken from the Salt Lake City *Directory* beginning in 1904. It was listed under the general head of CHURCHES, and in alphabetical order as HEBREW.

1904   Congregation Montefiore, 365 South 3rd East: Pastors, Jacob Brodie and M. Levy; president, N. Rosenblatt; vice-president, G. M. Lewis; secretary, I. M. Lewis; treasurer, J. Coppel; trustees, S. Salmenson and J. Shapiro.

1905   Pastor, Jacob Brodie; president, S. Salmanson; vice-president, Isadore Morris; secretary, G. M. Lewis; treasurer, I. M. Lewis; trustees, S. Salmenson, D. Draines, B. Appleman.

1906   Rabbi, Jacob Brodie; president, S. Salmanson; vice-president, Nathan Rosenblatt; secretary, G. M. Lewis; treasurer, I. M. Lewis.

1907   No information on this congregation this year.

1908   Rabbi, Zorach Bielsky; president, M. Levy; vice-president, Isaac Levitt; secretary, G. M. Lewis; treasurer, H. Zieler.

1909   Rabbi, Zorach Bielsky. [No other officers' names here or hereafter.]

1910-1912   Rabbi, Joseph Hevesh

1913   Rabbi, Dr. Leon Album

1914-1918   Dr. Samuel Beskin

1919-1920   Rabbi, Moses Klerman

1921-1922   Rabbi, David Aronson

1923   Rabbi, M. Z. Levine

1924-1926   Rabbi, E. M. Bernstein [Burstein?]

1927   Rabbi, Joshua Bach

1928   Rabbi Hyman Krash

After 1928 the *Directory* did not carry this information. The Salt Lake *Tribune* for June 3, 1945, gave a summary article in a different format. It stated that:

Joseph Krikstein served until 1938

Benjamin F. Groner served 1938-1939

Oscher Goldman came in Nov. 1939 and was still serving.

From other sources: Abraham L. Rosenblum arrived in 1946; E. Louis Cardon in 1952; Maurice Schwartz in 1962.

LIST OF RABBIS
CONGREGATION SHAAREY TZEDEK

1918   Rabbi Jos. Strinkomsky

1919   J. P. Berson

1920   J. P. Berson

1921-1924   Jos. Strinkomsky

1925-1929   Rabbi Reuben Kaplan

After 1929 the *Directory* gave no information, but Rabbi Kaplan is mentioned as being active in the *Salt Lake Jewish News* of 1933. He was buried February 5, 1950.

DEATHS IN B'NAI ISRAEL CONGREGATION
1922-1954

1922
2/18	Sarah Kahn
8/20	Clarence Ache Cohn
10/10	Saeul Auerbach
10/24	Helena Goldburg
11/13	Emiel Moses Freedman

1923
1/17	Gertie Desky
5/29	Sarah White Korublum
7/28	Jacqueline Lorraine Kaufman
11/23	Carrie Mooney Kalue
11/26	Joseph Cohn
12/10	Xaunie Hananer

1924
1/31	Jonas Braun
3/2	Herman Bamberger
5/1	Samuel Kohie
5/22	Rachel Brodie
5/28	Edna Cohn
7/27	Bernard Uhlfelder
8/20	Cristine Minstain
11/15	Eveline B. Auerbach
12/16	Adolph Lochivitz

1925
3/2	Isador Braun
4/28	Martin Nadel
5/12	Clara Wainstein
8/1	Sidney McGillis

1926
2/8	Robert L. Simon
10/6	Simon Bamberger

1927
2/23	Morris Eisner
6/29	Myers Cohn
7/23	Jacob Gottstein
10/21	Isadore G. Meyer

1928
3/13	Hermine W. Friedman
4/28	Emil A. Friedman
6/28	Augusta Watters
9/14	Jacob Bergerman

1929
4/1	Johanna Eisenberg
8/19	Samuel Weitz
10/5	Lemuel Cohen
11/14	Sol Rosenbaum
12/21	David Auerbach
12/6	Mark Ezekiels

1930
4/6	Jerome Cohn
7/31	A. L. Jacobs
11/13	Beverly Wilenski
11/16	Belle Gottheimer
7/5	Caroline M. Strass
12/27	George Symores

1931
2/23	Ella Tothschild
7/22	William Baruch

1932
6/13	Isaac Bernstein
6/23	Abram Harrauer (Hanauer?)
7/6	Ben Falk
8/2	Ida Hanauer
12/3	Fannie Blaum

1933
3/27	Max Daniels
4/14	Isadore Findling
4/12	Mark Desky
8/16	Sig Simon
9/25	Harold E. Schiller

1934
2/21 Fannie Theobald
8/16 Simon Lewis

1935
7/30 Annie W. Spitz
8/1   Henry Segil
8/2   Carolyn Bloom
9/18 Barney Baron

1936
2/24 Aaron Symors
5/21 Ida Bamberger
6/23 Morris Glickman
7/27 Louis Marcus
8/26 Max Hanauer
11/27 Max Kevitch

1937
2/8   Minnie Spitzer
4/18 Albert J. Auerbach
7/27 Samuel Levy
8/14 Jacob Meyers
9/10 Barney Gesas
11/12 Movitz Bamberger
12/14 Mary Levy

1938
5/28 Fred S. Auerbach
6/13 William Graupe
7/11 Sarah Lovinger
8/5   Johana Braun

1939
3/11 Eugene E. Kahn
5/22 Sarah Cline
6/21 Josephine J. Ottenheimer
6/23 Adelheid Mayer
7/6   Felix Falk
9/25 Ella Leone Rosenblum
12/4 Palmyre C. Offer
12/5 Louis D. Bercee
12/8 Samuel Spitz

1940
2/12 Joseph Bumgarten
5/12 Hymare Cline
10/26 Cora L. Simon

11/6 Harry Levy
11/7 Esther Bergerman
11/24 Dena Levy Tannenbaum
12/15 Julius Rosenberg

1941
1/10 Rose Friedman
1/14 Mathelda S. Cohn
3/31 Charles Ottenheimer
4/22 Benjamin Koven
4/23 Nate Segil

1942
1/8   Aimee Mae Bloom
2/17 Mollie Glaser
2/25 Harry Falk

1943
11/30 David Spitz

1944
3/29 Natalie Spitz
8/20 Fred Horwitz
9/2   Jacob A. Greenwald
11/21 Samuel J. Friedman

1945
2/4   Melissa Mandel
3/19 Herbert S. Auerbach
3/23 Bertha Garfinkle

1946
1/5   Ethel Parver
1/31 Dora Zarne Rich

1947
4/10 Emma G. Leven
6/16 Adolph L. White
9/9   Mary G. Lewis
10/24 Harold B. Leven
11/11 Esther Cohen Jacobson
12/2 Harry H. Roe

1948
2/2   Luscha Friedman
4/10 Gertrude Levitt
5/3   Mose Lewis
12/12 Lillian G. Oberndorfer

1949
2/27 Jennie Auerbach
7/14 Samuel Glaser

1950

5/28	Max Ottenheimer
10/12	Herbert Hirschman

1951

1/20	Lee Lovenger
3/14	Rosena Cohen
5/27	Ernest S. Weitz
8/13	Nathan Rosenbaum
10/9	Betty June Gottstein
1/6	Irene Simon
11/14	Hattie Cohn Rosenberg
12/2	Jeanette Wolfe Jacobs
12/27	Moritz J. Friedman

1952

4/11	Sam Goldberg
5/3	Louis Frank
6/20	Paul S. Newman

8/11	William N. Collins
8/14	Paul Wintrobe
10/22	Mina Rose
11/20	Morris Spitzer
12/9	Nate Morgan

1953

1/25	Sara Levy
2/2	Julius Wolff
9/10	Arthur Frank
12/7	Jack Garfield

1954

3/12	Adolph H. Fink
4/9	Lillie Rose Kahn
4/10	Stella Roth Spitz
9/5	Nellie G. Lewis
9/6	Hannah Rosenblum
11/11	Arnold A. Wolf

THE JEWS OF UTAH: A HISTORY 1854-1954

DEATHS IN CONGREGATION SHAAREY TZEDEK
1926-1954

1926
9/28   Golda Rosenthal

1928
4/30   Gashia Zlotnick
9/1   Bertha Shafer
9/20   Fannie Udelavitz

1930
2/20   Samuel Wilson

1931
3/6   Abraham Grobstein

1932
3/14   Sophie Garelick
8/8   Rachael Garelick

1934
4/15   Meyer Harris

1936
2/29   Arnie Kanvitz

1937
2/23   Max Landau
12/17 Abraham Moskowitz

1938
5/21   Annie Frisco

1940
5/19   Aaron W. Sheffer

1942
2/7   Judith F. Grobstein

1943
6/3   Rose Klein

1945
12/8   Jacob Rosenthal
12/11 Jacob Udelavitz

1948
1/27   Max Isenberg
7/4   Rebecca Grobstein

1949
8/20   Morris Garelick

1950
2/5   Reuben Kaplan
9/4   Annie Kaplan
12/30 Louis Rosenthal

1952
6/27   Louis Karrvitz
11/13 Rachael Isenberg

THE JEWS OF UTAH: A HISTORY 1854-1954

DEATHS IN CONGREGATION MONTEFIORE
1922-1954

1922

2/16	Joseph Slater
2/20	Bessie Kaplan
2/20	Bert Rosenthal
3/13	Marcus Sduartz (?)
3/26	Leonard Martin Rosenthal
5/5	Israel Siegel
7/15	Aaron Ben Cohn
9/19	Jan Zeiles
11/29	Blanche Moss

1923

3/3	Joseph Reinshrilur (?)
3/13	Sigmund Aruscd Appleman
4/1	Ida Strauss
8/23	Pearl Cohen
10/24	Sarah Mastrow
12/18	Beckie Glakuran
12/29	Abraham Sharon

1924

1/17	Dern Rosenthal
3/25	Max Greenstein
7/20	Samuel Ruthbard
7/29	Leah Goldberg
10/29	Samuel Lorn
11/10	William Berry Bergman
12/28	Jennie Berkovitz

1925

3/17	Gertrude Segal
4/29	Hannah Altman
5/12	Betty Ovenstein
7/18	Morris Silver
11/18	Emma Segal

1926

4/8	Infant Goldberg
4/30	Edith H. Liberman
6/16	Paul Friedman
8/16	Rebecca Chone

9/7	Pearl Friedman
10/2	Isaac Steres
12/15	Herman Eckstein
12/15	Shilsom Eckstein
12/30	Bertha Feldman

1927

1/24	Narhab M. Rosenblum
5/1	Hannah Pilger
10/8	Elias Wolfe
10/18	Sabevia Markowitz
12/15	Max Hecht

1928

3/11	Isaac Pepper
5/1	Ben Pilger
5/8	Morris Bostik
7/11	David Kofman
8/21	Infant Goldberg
10/25	William Bandeland

1929

2/25	William H. Berkovitz
4/28	Jacob Shurwitzkin
6/27	Bertha Epstein
7/2	Sam Fischgrund
8/5	Infant Goldberg
11/1	Minnie Brisk

1930

5/4	Joseph Sprinher
5/29	Yetta Doctorman
7/15	Ester Wilenski
9/5	Maurice Barnett
10/20	Hyman Mayrowitz
11/8	Bernard Salenson
11/29	Wudger Porizky

1931

2/26	Ethel Sheinberg
3/9	Hilda Scheinberg

3/26   Infant Golberg
3/31   Rose Arnovitz
10/7   Abraham Steier
11/10 Joseph Zimmerman
11/11 Joseph Ruthbard
11/22 Rose Glassman
12/31 Morris Arnovitz

1932
6/19   Sophia Guss
7/13   Sophia Mishkind
7/14   Aaron Goldberg
8/3   Harry Wagner
11/18 Benjamin Steim

1933
4/2   Max Weiss
6/7   Max Weiss
7/19   Louis Cohen
8/13   Freida Stein

1934
5/7   Donald Lutzker
6/3   Abraham Mishkind
6/24   Pearl Davis
7/3   Morris Bonstik
7/26   Joseph Bernstein
11/7   Sam Guss

1935
5/3   Nathan Richmond
6/24   Joseph Zwilling
8/23   Louis Smith
9/13   Abraham Guss
12/3   Harry Rose

1936
2/6   Stella Rosen
2/23   Jennie Goodman
5/1   Fannie Zwilling
6/22   Clara A. Gordon
7/10   Tillie S. Rosenblatt
7/29   Etta Geffen
9/4   Jake Lukton
10/27 Abe Cohen
12/15 Harild Perlman
12/28 Herman Rothman

1937
1/13   Chira Simons
1/28   Tilda Love
3/9   B. Cruz
4/25   Moses Axelrad
5/14   Harry Albert
6/3   Emma Stein
7/11   Davis Rosenthal
8/7   Hannah Krixtein
9/11   Mortimer Brown
10/17 Oscar Feldscher

1938
4/7   Abe Scheinberg
4/12   Sofia Scheinberg
4/14   Harry Simon
7/26   Minnie Hoffman
8/16   Abraham Pepper
9/1   Sara E. Greenhood (?]
12/2   Samuel Salmenson

1939
3/21   Mary Hecht
9/30   Celia Glaser
10/25 Abe Tannenbaum

1940
6/9   Frieda Tasem

1941
2/1   Bernard Medalie
2/20   Harry Rosen
3/25   Harris Appleman
4/18   George Israel Norman
6/23   Sam Weinger
7/12   Ida Block Nathan

1942
2/19   Sophia Cohen
2/26   Samuel Goldstein
4/15   Morris Weiss
6/25   Betty Marovitz

1943
1/2   Libby Bonstik
1/9   Mose Norman
1/22   Lula Klein
1/27   Morris Simon

4/23	Pauline Milkoff
9/1	Hyman Werber
9/16	Jessie Gilbert
11/4	Fred Pepper
11/14	Sam L. Gillis

1944

1/23	Joe Beckman
2/13	Morris Altman
3/5	Henry Weyl
8/24	Abe Rosen Wise
10/12	Annie Matz
11/20	Rosie Paver Mednick
11/22	Joseph Guss

1945

3/15	Rose Mastrow
3/28	Robert F. Miller
9/29	Morris Axelrad

1946

2/16	Nathan Rosenblatt
8/24	Hattie B. Axelrad
9/14	Edith Cohn
10/30	Eva Cohn
11/8	Helen Appleman
12/30	Robert A. Shurkisi

1947

2/12	Herman Schaztenberg
4/4	Benjamin Doctorman
7/26	Isadore Appleman
8/24	Joshua Shapiro
9/4	Frank Cohen
10/7	Eva L. Fox
10/23	Anna Simon
12/8	Moritz D. Davis

1948

1/21	Simon Rosenblatt
7/29	Ida Milkoff Bloom
9/12	Kate Oliner
12/20	Albert J. Hertz

1949

3/24	Infant Pollock
5/24	Herman Ottenheimer
8/2	Ignatz Tasern

10/13	Richard Kirshbaum
10/24	Nettie L. Marks
12/23	Harry Mednick

1950

6/22	Albert Ottenheimer
6/30	Clara Shapiro
7/16	Wolf Fleisher
10/5	William Benowitz
10/20	Henry Klein

1951

8/30	Celia Jacobson Peper
10/25	Isaac Simons

1952

3/9	Bery D. Cohen
3/14	Mollie Benowitz
6/14	Barry S. Reigelhaupt
9/12	Joseph Katz
9/26	Ernestene L. Budofzen
10/5	Harvey J. Menlove
10/10	Frieda B. Conley
12/29	Fannie Alder

1953

3/4	Cecelia Werber
5/3	Michael H. Sher
9/2	Alfred Hertz
9/18	Sarah Claschko
10/11	Lewis Levetan
10/13	Philip P. Evdasin
12/13	Moses Nathan

1954

1/9	Hannah Lutzke
4/25	Aaron F. Rosenthal
6/17	Isadore Susman
6/20	Charles Gallenson
6/22	Sarah Guss
7/28	Annie Weiss
8/21	Abraham Loe Rose
9/16	Allen Mednick
10/6	Julius Dreyfuss
12/12	Benjamin Davis
12/26	Sophy Albert

INDEX